The Moral Foundations of Canadian Federalism
Paradoxes, Achievements, and Tragedies of Nationhood

D0219920

Focusing on key events in Canadian political history, Samuel LaSelva examines the moral foundations of the Canadian federal system of government and their implications. He explores the ideals, arguments, and rhetoric invoked by the debates surrounding crucial events in Canadian federalism – Confederation, patriation of the constitution, Meech Lake, and the Charlottetown accord – and situates them within the context of moral and political philosophy.

LaSelva argues that Canadian federalism is founded on a vision of a nation in which multiple identities and multiple loyalties can flourish within a framework of common political nationality. He contends that this dualistic belief affects not only our understanding of Canadian identity but also a host of fundamental concepts, including fraternity, justice, democracy, and federalism itself. LaSelva offers a compelling reconsideration of Confederation and of the pivotal role of George-Étienne Cartier, one of the Fathers of Confederation, in both the achievement of confederation and the creation of a distinctively Canadian federalist theory.

Given the current debates about Quebec sovereignty and Aboriginal self-government, the future of the Canadian federation is uncertain. *The Moral Foundations of Canadian Federalism* provides a timely and novel perspective in support of Canadian federalism.

SAMUEL V. LASELVA is associate professor of political science, University of British Columbia.

The Moral Foundations of Canadian Federalism

Paradoxes, Achievements, and Tragedies of Nationhood

SAMUEL V. LASELVA

McGill-Queen's University Press
Montreal & Kingston • London • Buffalo

® McGill-Queen's University Press 1996
ISBN 0-7735-1405-8 (cloth)
ISBN 0-7735-1422-8 (paper)

Legal deposit second quarter 1996
Bibliothèque nationale du Québec
Printed in Canada on acid-free paper

This book has been published with the help
of a grant from the Social Science Federation
of Canada, using funds provided by the
Social Sciences and Humanities Research
Council of Canada.

McGill-Queen's University Press is grateful
to the Canada Council for support of its
publishing program.

Canadian Cataloguing in Publication Data

LaSelva, Samuel V. (Samuel Victor), 1952–
The moral foundations of Canadian
federalism: paradoxes, achievements, and
tragedies of nationhood
Includes bibliographical references and index.
ISBN 0-7735-1405-8 (bound)
ISBN 0-7735-1422-8 (pbk.)
1. Federal government – Canada – History.
2. Canada – Constitutional history.
3. Canada – Politics and government. I. Title
JL65 1996 L38 1996   320.471'049
c95-920895-x

Typeset in New Baskerville 10/13
by Chris McDonell, Hawkline Graphics

To my parents
Clara and Angelo LaSelva

Contents

Preface

This study attempts to contribute to our understanding of Canadian federalism by focusing on the moral dimensions that underpin it. Students of Canadian federalism normally prefer to focus on the legal, historical, political, and institutional dimensions. It is my belief that a sustained examination of the moral dimensions of Canadian federalism can provide new answers to old questions, as well as entirely new questions. The focus that I have adopted connects the exploration of Canadian federalism to the study of political philosophy as it has been traditionally understood. For Socrates, the acknowledged founder of political philosophy, the most important question was how we should live. Canadian federalism provides a partial answer to his question, even if the answer is difficult to discern and even more difficult to realize. Ultimately, the answer rests on the belief that Canadians, who live in different provinces and possess diverse cultural identities, can and should have both a common way of life and different ways of life. So stated, this belief seems simple enough, yet its implications are enormous: it not only affects our understanding of the Canadian identity, but also compels us to reconsider a host of topics, including fraternity, justice, constitutional amendment, democracy, and federalism itself. What emerges is an unorthodox understanding of Canadian federalism and a distinctively Canadian understanding of nationhood.

Some Canadians do not believe that it is possible for a country to sustain both a common way of life and different ways of life; among them are Québécois separatists, Aboriginal sovereignists, and Canadian nationalists. All of them embrace visions of a future that are uncongenial to Canadian federalism and dispute its moral foundations.

In coming to terms with the moral foundations of Canadian federalism, I have found the writings of the critics as important as those of individuals who work to sustain their country because the critics challenge complacencies, expose inconsistencies, and compel a critical rearticulation of moral principles and political commitments.

Equally important are a number of issues that appear to fall outside the conceptual boundaries of my study. Two such issues are the legal basis of Canadian federalism and the historical significance of Confederation. The former appears to belong exclusively to law; the latter, solely to history. However, both issues have enormous significance for an understanding of moral foundations. Confederation is important because it is frequently interpreted as a political scheme that was forced on unwilling partners and that continues to work against them. The question of the legal basis of Canadian federalism is also difficult to avoid because influential scholars and judges have asserted that the Canadian constitution is not federal at all, but at most quasi-federal. Moreover, quasi-federalism, which holds that Canada is virtually a unitary state, structured the Supreme Court decision on patriation and was used to justify the most significant constitutional changes since Confederation; those changes, in turn, engendered the constitutional struggles of the failed Meech Lake and Charlottetown constitutional accords, as well as the malaise that has resulted. In such circumstances, a discussion of the moral foundations of Canadian federalism that ignored questions about its historical and legal basis would become a formal exercise devoid of practical importance and unconnected to the living constitution. Symmetry and conceptualism need not be valued more highly than relevance and understanding. Consequently, I have not hesitated to discuss legal and historical issues when appropriate, and my willingness to do so has necessitated the adoption of methodologies appropriate to them. But even in such cases, my objective has been to facilitate a deeper comprehension of the moral foundations of Canadian federalism and to discuss those foundations from within the tradition of political philosophy.

Political philosophy is not monolithic. In the English-speaking world, perhaps the still-dominant approach to political philosophy models itself on analytical philosophy, with which it shares a concern for formal definition and rigorous systematization. When it is so understood, its contemporary exemplar is undoubtedly John Rawls's *A Theory of Justice.* Canadian federalism awaits its Rawls. No one has yet produced a treatise on Canadian federalism that strips it of particularity and reconstructs it in accordance with elementary principles which would be accepted by rational, self-interested individuals devoid of knowledge of their own lives. But there is also a tradition of political philosophy that attaches enormous, although by no means exclusive, importance to particularity. Its historical exemplars include Vico and Herder; among its contemporary practitioners are Isaiah Berlin and Charles Taylor. Within this tradition, the concern is not with definition and systematization so much as with interpretation, understanding, and imagination. An important example is Taylor's *The Malaise of Modernity*, a work that seeks not to reconstruct the modern world according to a few rational principles, but to understand its enormous complexity and to discover ways of eliminating its most pernicious aspects. Taylor has also written illuminating essays on Canadian federalism, published as *Reconciling the Solitudes*. The methodological orientation that I have adopted is similar to his, although my conclusions about the moral foundations of Canadian federalism differ from those he has brilliantly defended.

My conclusions also differ from a number of other recent works on Canadian federalism that, as Jeremy Webber suggests, are "reimagining Canada." Together with the books by Taylor and Webber, there are significant works by, among others, Guy Laforest, Reg Whitaker, Will Kymlicka, and Wayne Norman, as well as the stimulating book co-authored by Donald G. Lenihan, Gordon Robertson, and Roger Tassé. One of the most significant differences between my work and theirs is the importance I attach to George-Étienne Cartier, who was the coequal of John A. Macdonald. In recent years, Cartier has been virtually forgotten, partly because of the labours of Donald Creighton, who allocated to Macdonald the central role both in the achievement of Confederation and in its subsequent success. Moreover, Confederation has itself become something of an antiquarian subject, largely because many scholars, politicians, and citizens appear to believe that Canada no longer possesses a living constitution and faces a future unconnected to its past. What I attempt to show is that such an estimate of the future radically misunderstands the past, distorts the kind of settlement achieved by Confederation, and ignores the key role of Cartier both in the achievement of Confederation and in the creation of a distinctively Canadian federalist theory.

Cartier distrusted abstraction, yet he produced a federalist theory that rivals James Madison's and accomplishes for Canada what number ten of *The Federalist* does for the United States. In the United States, the key problem for federalist theory has been the issue of republican liberty, which Madison attempted to solve by his famous theory of the compound republic. Put differently, the issue was how to create a large country without destroying individual liberty and local initiative. In Canada, the problem was different, largely because the existence of a Canadian nation could not be taken for granted. Madison's theory, in other words, presupposes the nation and simply addresses the issue of the kind of government it should have. In contrast, Cartier had to demonstrate not only that federalism was desirable, but also that a Canadian nation could exist. Moreover, he had to confront such issues amid reminders of the war of races, a problem unknown to Madison. Cartier's solution was to articulate a federalist theory based mainly on the twin ideas of multiple identities and political nationality. In his understanding, Canada was to be a nation in which multiple identities and multiple loyalties could flourish within the framework of a common political nationality. Far from presupposing the nation, federalism created it.

The historical significance of Cartier is that he discovered a middle ground between Macdonald and his opponents without which Confederation would have remained a political dream. His significance for the moral foundations of Canadian federalism is that he articulated values – sometimes implicitly, at other times explicitly – which express many of its leading principles. In his now-famous speech in support of Confederation, delivered in 1865, Cartier spoke of justice and injustice, of pluralism and homogeneity, of racial harmony and the war of races, of political nationality and the greatness of Canada. He said, against Lord Durham, that a project of racial unification was not only utopian; it was impossible. Cartier believed that racial diversity was a benefit because different races existed to promote the general welfare, rather than to war one with the other. Implicit in his belief was an understanding of federalism as an exercise in the difficult art of separation, together with a supposition that Canada would be held together by an intricate and novel form of fraternity.

The irony and tragedy of Cartier is that he was the pivotal figure in the creation of Canada and yet his understanding of Canadian federalism has been almost forgotten. The same cannot be said of Macdonald; his views were intensively studied for more than a century after Confederation. In recent years, the focus of attention has shifted to Pierre Trudeau, who, as Guy Laforest has aptly noted, straddles contemporary Canadian history like a colossus. Largely as a response to

Quebec separatism, he attempted to provide a new foundation for Canadian nationhood, primarily through the adoption of a charter of rights. The Canadian Charter of Rights and Freedoms contains a large number of moral and political values, yet it has not provided the new beginning envisaged by Trudeau. Far from uniting Canadians, the Charter has driven them further apart. What requires re-examination, however, is not simply the Charter of Rights, but the basis of Canadian nationhood, including the original values of Confederation and their capacity to address contemporary issues such as Aboriginal self-government and the special nature of Canadian democracy. The aim of this study is to contribute to the debate about Canadian nationhood, partly by examining key issues on their own terms and partly by attempting to demonstrate the continuing relevance of Cartier. No one can hope to tell the whole story of Canadian nationhood, but there are defining moments, political crises, and even dominant intellectual traditions that can be discussed.

Although I have not attempted to offer a formal reconstruction of the moral foundations of Canadian federalism à la Rawls, the beginnings of such a project are embedded in what I have written. Stated conceptually, the outlines of my argument are that Canadian nationhood presupposes Canadian federalism, which in turn rests on a complex form of fraternity that can promote a just society characterized by a humanistic liberalism and a democratic dialogue. By contrast, Canadian nationhood is not sustained, and Canada's constitutional dilemmas are not solved, by appealing to communitarianism, Lockean majoritarianism, ethnic nationalism, consociationalism, or decolonization. A study of Canadian nationhood modelled on Rawls would rigorously define each of the above terms and explore the logical connections between them in an effort to make its conclusions acceptable to a representative Canadian. Such a study of Canada is unquestionably worth doing, but it would not eliminate the need for other approaches, if only because there are important dimensions of Canadian nationhood that elude a Rawlsian reconstruction.

What a Rawlsian approach does not capture adequately is aptly conveyed by two well-known insights, one by Lord Sankey, the other by Ernest Renan. In a famous opinion that rejected legal formalism and recognized women as persons capable of holding office in the Senate, Lord Sankey said that the Canadian constitution was a living tree capable of growth and expansion within its natural limits. Renan's insight comes from his classic lecture on the definition of a nation.

Essential for the formation of a nation, he said, was the memory of its citizens, especially their ability to remember some things and to forget others. Citizens should recall glorious events and celebrate national heroes; they should forget the conflicts they experienced before becoming a nation. Unquestionably, Canadians have lived under a constitution capable of growth, but they have not always used their memories to sustain their country. The result is that the Canadian constitution has grown: yet it has not always grown in ways that strengthen the foundational principles of Canadian nationhood. Sometimes Canadians have forgotten, with near-disastrous results, that their country rests on such principles and even that it is a federal polity. A study of moral foundations faithful to the insights of Lord Sankey and Ernest Renan will necessarily lack the symmetry, conceptualism, and systematization characteristic of Rawlsian political theory. What such a study embodies is a different tradition of political philosophy; what it attempts to glimpse are some of the paradoxes, some of the achievements, and some of the tragedies of Canadian nationhood. So understood, nationhood is an achievement far removed from the harmonious understanding of Rawls and the tradition to which he belongs; it is much closer to the tradition that includes the fragmentary moral vision of Pascal, a vision that simultaneously grasps both the grandeur of human existence and its misery. To use a now-famous metaphor, Canada can be compared to a mosaic, but as portrayed in this study, it is neither a vertical mosaic nor a cultural one. Rather, it is a moral mosaic embedded in a Pascalian universe.

It is a pleasure to acknowledge the obligations that I have acquired to friends and colleagues who have helped me to clarify my ideas. They include Kathy Brock, David Elkins, Roger Gibbins, Jean Laponce, Geoffrey Marshall, Ted Morton, Max Nemni, Sid Noel, Daniel Salée, Bob Sansom, the late Donald Smiley, Jennifer Smith, and Richard Vernon. As Cecil and Ida Green Lecturer at the University of British Columbia, Charles Taylor provided an early and important stimulus to my own thinking about the philosophical dimensions of federalism. My greatest debt, however, is to Alan Cairns; he read the entire manuscript, provided valuable suggestions and criticisms, and has continued to illuminate through his written works many of the key problems of federalism. The anonymous reviewers performed an important role in the last stage, and I am very grateful to them. Needless to say, I alone am responsible for any misunderstandings that may remain.

Chapters 1, 3, and 6 appeared in the *Canadian Journal of Political Science* (1993, 1983, 1993). Each of the articles has been revised, although the most substantial changes have been to chapter 3. Chapter 4 appeared in the *Windsor Yearbook of Access to Justice* (1988); it has been reworked to take account of developments since then. I am grateful to the Social Sciences and Humanities Research Council of Canada for providing three research grants through funds allocated to the University of British Columbia, initially for the purpose of investigating group rights and subsequently in order to explore the broader question of moral foundations.

The Moral Foundations of Canadian Federalism

Tragedy, Justice, and Community
as Elements of Canadian Federalism

Canada is a difficult country to understand, and Canadians tell more than one story about Canadian nationhood. English-Canadian nationalists do not tell the same story as Québécois separatists, and both disagree significantly with Aboriginal nationalists. There are also immigrants and other groups who have their own histories. For some, the very existence of different stories is indicative of a kind of mosaic madness or a sign that Canada should be divided into two or more nations. Of course, there are also Canadians who celebrate this plurality on the ground that pluralism is a prerequisite of the tolerance and political compromise characteristic of their country. A third possibility is that the different stories implicitly reveal a single, but complex understanding of Canadian nationhood. Canadians, that is to say, have both different stories and the same story precisely because Canadian nationhood presupposes Canadian federalism. Moreover, Canadian federalism recognizes that citizens have both a common identity and different identities. When nationhood and federalism are connected, a new theme emerges – the presence of justice and community among Canadians, intermixed with tragic relationships and events. Narratives characterized by a particularistic point of view are replaced by a common tale filled with ironies, dilemmas, and paradoxes. The story of Canada becomes one of great achievements, but also of great tragedies.

In some of its dimensions, the chronicle is unquestionably one of tragedy. "The story of Canada in a sense is a tragic story," A.R.M. Lower intimated. "There's tragedy there, if people can be made to see it."[1] André Siegfried glimpsed part of the tragedy when he called Canada a precarious creation. For him, it was a country characterized not by unity of purpose, but by "impassioned rivalries" and by an "im-memorial struggle." A tragic contest existed between French and English, who were "like brothers that hate each other ... [and] have to dwell under one roof."[2] There is also tragedy in the suffering of Canada's Aboriginal population. Much of their suffering is neither gratuitous nor accidental, but is inflicted by Canadians who possess, paradoxically, benevolence towards them. The white man, observed Harold Cardinal, "believes in freedom," but he also believes that "he should be his brother's keeper," and the conflict between the two ideals has produced enormous difficulties for Canadian Indians.[3] The tragedy of Canada's Aboriginal population had its beginnings in the triumph of benevolence over liberty and in the corresponding failure of Aboriginals to vindicate the justice of their claim to a measured in-dependence. The result has been enormous destitution for Canadian Aboriginals and a profound sense of guilt among other Canadians, who seem unable to understand why benevolence should have such disastrous effects.

The tragedy of Canada is compounded and complicated by the pres-ence of minorities of various kinds. Among them are "third force" Canadians, recent immigrants who belong to neither the French nor English majorities and who regard their membership in Canadian so-ciety as precarious.[4] Their fear – which is shared by women, gays, and other groups – is that they will be relegated to second-class citizenship and suffer the disabilities and indignities that accompany it. As a re-sult, these divergent groups often join together in demanding the cre-ation of "one Canada," which they associate with undifferentiated citizenship for all Canadians. Together with Aboriginals, they opposed the (failed) Meech Lake Constitutional Accord of 1987 because they believed that the recognition of Quebec as a distinct society under-mined the rights and dignity of their group.[5] Québécois have re-sponded, in turn, by threatening to dissolve Canada on the ground that their status within Confederation is more precarious than ever before. What has emerged – especially with the failure of yet another constitutional accord in 1992 – is a country composed of groups that, at least in the short run, appear to be on a "collision course."[6]

Some believe that the collision is to be welcomed rather than re-gretted. For them, the disappearance of Canada (as it has existed) would not be a tragedy because healthy nations would emerge from the constitutional ruins. These Canadians regard the existence of Canada as an accident of history with roots no stronger than the

Conquest of 1760; they believe that the disappearance of Canada would expiate both the original Conquest and the tragedies that have flowed from it. Such a belief is most often voiced by Québécois separatists, although a number of other Canadians also subscribe to it. "The departure of Quebec," David Bercuson and Barry Cooper have written, "would provide a magnificent opportunity for Canadians to undertake a genuine restructuring of the political order in which they live." Indeed, Canada without Quebec, Bercuson and Cooper go on to say, "is the necessary condition for serious thinking about Canada's future."[7] Many Canadians, however, have difficulty accepting such a view. For them, the disappearance of Canada would be a tragic event, a genuine catastrophe in which virtually all parties would experience ultimate defeat. A fragmented Canada, it is often suggested, would simply be swallowed by the United States and gradually assimilated into the American melting-pot.[8] If such a result occurred, it would represent not only the loss of political independence, but also the disappearance of distinctive identities and admired ways of life. Those who initially favoured the disappearance of Canada might experience short-term success, yet they too would suffer ultimate defeat.

Such, in outline, is the story of Canada told as one story of tragedy. The essence of all tragedy, according to A.C. Bradley's famous Hegelian interpretation, is "the self-division and intestinal warfare of the ethical substance, not so much the war of good with evil as the war of good with good." Powers good in themselves face each other and make incompatible demands. Their claims are rightful and equally justified, but the right of each is pushed into a wrong "because it ignores the right of the other, and demands that absolute sway which belongs to neither alone, but to the whole of which each is a part." Similarly, the nature of the tragic hero, at once his greatness and his doom, is that "he knows no shrinking or half-heartedness, but identifies himself wholly with the power that moves him, and will admit the justification of no other power." The tragic conflict comes to an end when exclusive claims are moderated so as to allow each claim its rightful place or when the quarrel is pressed to extremes and a catastrophe occurs. However resolved, a tragedy depicts "a self-division and a self-waste of spirit, or a division of spirit involving waste and conflict."[9]

The paradox of Canada is that its divisions have had tragic results and yet they have also provided a foundation for a distinctive and enduring nationhood. This is another way of saying that the story of Canada can also be told without tragedy, as the chronicle of a country that accepts division and difference as part of a conception of the good. Behind this story is the recognition that the elimination of division can itself produce unacceptable consequences, among them the destruction of admired ways of life and the imposition of alien values on unwilling people. When the story of Canada is told in this way, its landmark events include the repudiation of Lord Durham's assimilation proposals and the rejection of the Statement on Indian Policy (1969), in favour of structures and programs that recognize diversity and accept division.[10] The Confederation settlement of 1867 is part of the same story because it instituted a federal state and thereby used the divisions of federalism to create a Canadian citizenship that could be shared by French and English. Cartier, who had the pivotal role in the achievement of Confederation and articulated a distinctively Canadian federal theory, eulogized this story of Canada when he insisted that French and English were forming a new country, "not for the purpose of warring against each other, but in order to compete and emulate for the general welfare."[11] Others praise the cultural pluralism of Canada and contrast it with the uniformity of the American melting-pot, which they abhor. In this story of Canada, there is solitary peace or harmonious cooperation between the members of Canadian society, rather than tragic collision.

Canada is an intriguing country because both stories are true, or at least partly true. It would be difficult to deny the existence of tragic events throughout Canadian history, but it would be equally mistaken to overlook the constructive dimensions. "Some of the Great Goods," Isaiah Berlin has suggested, "cannot live together." Not only are we "doomed to choose," but choice may entail "an irreparable loss." Canadian history supports such a judgment. But it also supports Berlin's other beliefs, that "we must not dramatise the incompatibility of values [because] there is a great deal of broad agreement." And when collisions cannot be avoided, they often can be softened. "Claims can be balanced, compromise can be reached, ... priorities, never final and absolute, must be established." For Berlin, such responses are justified because there is "no final solution," no "perfect whole."[12] Others, such as John Rawls, arrive at similar conclusions by appealing to the cooperative virtues, which are "*very great* virtues"; they include "the virtues of tolerance, and being ready to meet others halfway, and the virtues of reasonableness and the sense of fairness."[13] Historically, Canadians have been profoundly shaped by the cooperative virtues, even though they have also experienced tragic conflicts.

Tragic conflicts, it has been observed, come to an end either when catastrophe occurs or when justice is established. Appearing as a divine being, wrote A.C. Bradley, the spiritual unity reconciles by mutual adjustments the contending powers, or at its bidding one of them softens its demands, so that supreme justice is established.[14] Partly because their situation contains tragic elements that can end in catastrophe, Canadians as a people constantly address and readdress issues of justice and injustice. Justice for minorities – including the French-speaking minority within Canada and the English-speaking minority within Quebec – was a key issue of Confederation, was canvassed in the debates of 1865, and provided a foundation for the development of a distinctively Canadian federalist theory. Others have spoken of the need to secure justice for the regions that compose Canada, for the two nationalities, and for the individual. The Canadian state, W.L. Morton suggested, cannot be devoted to absolute nationalism because "the two nationalities and the four sections of Canada forbid it." Rather, the state in Canada "must promote liberty of persons and communities, and justice, which is the essence of liberty."[15] Not only is the demand for justice a constant theme of Canadian history, but it also sustains an ideal of national greatness. Some nations associate greatness with cultural homogeneity and military aggrandizement, but in Canada it is more often identified with the acceptance of difference and with the creation of a more just society.[16] Failures do of course occur, but they are regarded as injustices and call for rectification.

Moreover, justice has a special role in sustaining Canada's existence as a nation. Pierre Trudeau understood as much, even though his attempt to create a more just society by means of a charter of rights has turned out to be more controversial than he anticipated. He understood justice largely in terms of individual rights; he also supposed that the protection of individual rights would enable citizens to identify with the national political community, thereby counteracting Québécois separatism and other disintegrating forces. But many French-speaking Quebeckers believe that the Charter provides less than just treatment of their language, especially within their own province. Many Aboriginals believe that justice for themselves can be achieved only through a significant measure of self-government, which the Charter does not recognize explicitly. Such criticisms sustain the complaint that the Charter has failed to provide justice for all Canadians, yet they also reinforce the belief that the attempt to achieve justice is a requirement of Canadian nationhood.

In Canada, justice sustains nationhood partly because it prevents tragic collisions and partly because it provides a basis for the creation of a national community. Justice prevents tragic collisions because (as Bradley said) it restrains the right of each from being pressed too far, and it thereby protects the right of the other. Canadians sometimes express much the same idea by saying that Canada is a tolerant society, or a society based on mutual accommodation, or a society that allows different ways of life to flourish. The other side of justice is the contribution it makes to the creation of a national community. In Canada such a community presupposes the rejection of a comprehensive cultural nationalism, coupled with the creation of a Canadian political nationality. As Donald Smiley observed, "the concept of a Canadian political community – or nationality – means that Canadians as such have reciprocal moral and legal claims upon one another."[17] Put in another way, justice dictates reciprocity among Canadians and contributes to their sense of belonging to the same nation and of sharing a common identity. The reciprocal moral and legal claims of Canadians have been held to include regional equalization schemes and the welfare state on the ground that such programs express a "commitment to promoting greater social justice" and contribute to a "sense ... of shared national community."[18] Not only does justice sustain community, but it has also been associated with a type of fraternity that accepts and even celebrates diversity, at least in Canada. French and English, wrote Henri Bourassa, are divided by language and religion, but "united in a sense of brotherhood."[19]

Community and fraternity move Canada beyond tragedy and provide it with an identity as a nation. Normally, a nation is associated with the existence of a monolithic community, and a country that lacks such a community is regarded as much less than a nation.[20] Such a country, it is often suggested, is better understood as a plural society, or as a multinational state, or as a contractual association, or as a consociational democracy, rather than as a nation. In the case of Canada, however, such analytical constructs fail to illuminate either the Canadian identity or the complex sense of community that exists. The Canadian sense of community is expressed partly through Canadian federalism, which has been described as "a device designed to cope with the problem of how distinct communities can live a common life together without ceasing to be distinct communities."[21] Differently stated, Canadian federalism multiplies community so that citizens can be members both of a common community and of distinct local communities; they can share a common life with those who are different from themselves without renouncing particularistic identities and particularistic affiliations. Consequently, Canada is unlike countries that presuppose the existence of a monolithic community or which are mere aggregations of disparate or incompatible communities. If Canada is a country with an identity, it is because the historic unwillingness to choose either "the one" or "the many" has produced a complex sense of community and has facilitated the realization of values that require the multiplication (rather than the unification) of community. It is the existence of a complex sense of community that provides Canada with its moral foundations.

However, Canada is a fragile nation, and the prospect of tragedy is never completely absent. Canadians sometimes express this idea by saying that Canada is a difficult country to govern. But the problem goes deeper. According to Alan Cairns, "even if we leave the Québécois nationalist pressures aside, ... the grounds for optimism [in contemporary Canada] are slim." Part of the difficulty is that Canadians usually regard federalism as a solution to their difficulties, yet the instrumentalities of federalism are as often a source of the strains that afflict their country. What contemporary federalism has produced, Cairns suggests, is big governments that vie with each other for jurisdiction and resources without regard to the destructive long-term consequences on Canada's existence as a nation. The upshot is that "we are in imminent danger of being victimized by our own creations."[22] A tragic situation, if any is.

Federalism contains within it both a powerful vision of community and the ingredients for tragedy. Both aspects are magnified in Canada, partly because of the complexities of the Confederation settlement of 1867. According to Donald Creighton, "the acceptance of the 'federal principle,' against their own political traditions and wishes, was the great concession that the English-speaking delegates at Quebec were prepared to make to French Canada."[23] By joining in Confederation, wrote A.R.M. Lower, "the two races surely tacitly agreed to bury the hatchet and to try to live amicably together."[24] But Confederation also created a highly centralized federation, so as to avoid difficulties that had plagued other federations. K.C. Wheare described the Canadian Confederation as merely quasi-federal, because of its unitary features. Confederation was an expression of federal comity, but it also created a centralized state, and it left potentially tragic choices to future generations. One such choice was the explosive issue of constitutional amendment, which the Fathers did not resolve explicitly. Canadians eventually settled the question of constitutional amendment, although it required two Supreme Court decisions. Both decisions contain tragic elements, in that the court failed to grant to French Canadians the federal comity that underlies Confederation and that structures the only provision dealing with amendments to the division of powers found in the original constitution of 1867.

The Fathers also left to future generations the difficult issue of democracy. For them, the key problems of Confederation were those of federalism, and the kind of failures that most concerned them were federal failures. They attempted to solve those problems by creating a Canadian federalist theory. But Canada is now a democracy, and the failures that increasingly concern Canadians are democratic ones.[25] In a famous study of democracy in America, Alexis de Tocqueville attempted to reveal not only the image of democracy itself, but also the dangers faced by it. For him, the great danger was democratic despotism, which created a servile equality and destroyed individual liberty. In such a state of society, a people "is reduced to nothing better than a flock of timid and industrious animals, of which the government is the shepherd."[26] Canadian democracy is different because it struggles with cultural, ethnic, and local particularisms. The great danger faced by democracy in Canada is that French and English will deny each other mutual recognition, treat one another as strangers, and destroy the country. For Tocqueville, the difficulty to be resolved was "how to make liberty proceed out of that democratic state of society in which God has placed us." In Canada the difficulty to be resolved is how to infuse into democratic institutions the kind of kinship that the Fathers of Confederation attempted to instill into federal institutions.

The difficulty is exacerbated, and its resolution is made more urgent, by the demand for Aboriginal self-government. Behind this demand are the dismal statistics of Aboriginal poverty, the inadequacies of Aboriginal education, and an Aboriginal suicide rate far in excess of the Canadian average. As a result, Aboriginals not only criticize the democratic credentials of a society that has failed them; they also demand more democracy for themselves. They demand self-government so as to restore their dignity and to revitalize their communities.[27] But the right to Aboriginal self-government also has the capacity to dissolve moral and political ties between Aboriginals and other citizens, a result that disadvantages all Canadians. The potential for tragedy is compounded by the fact that self-government can twice marginalize those Aboriginals who live off a suitable land base. If such consequences are to be avoided, it is necessary to come to terms with the paradox of Aboriginal self-government. This paradox is that the right to self-government is the strongest claim to independence possessed by Aboriginal peoples, yet the realization of self-government presupposes the continuing moral and political interdependence of Aboriginals and other Canadians. If the paradox is accepted, Aboriginal self-government becomes part of a way of life that expresses the multiple dimensions of Aboriginal existence and that contributes to a dialogue of democracy within Canada.

A different solution is to regard Aboriginals as forming a distinct and incommensurable solitude within Canada, entitled to govern itself without regard to its membership in Canadian society.[28] Moreover, Canada can itself be conceptualized as a country of solitudes, such that the Aboriginal solitude joins the French and English solitudes. When Canada is so understood, it becomes a fragmented country, held together either by élite accommodation or by passive tolerance. Such conceptualizations are not free of difficulty, however. Not only does a country of solitudes lack a sense of common identity, but its members do not experience a feeling of common interest.[29] The danger is that the solitudes will become mutually intolerant and that the process of fragmentation will extend to other groups in society. Women, gays, and ethnic minorities can also regard themselves as forming solitudes, with interests and identities that isolate them from other members of society and bring them into conflict with rival solitudes. There are those who believe that contemporary Canada is in danger of becoming such a country, if it is not so already. They describe the emergence of a group pluralism characterized by competition for status and power without regard to long-term consequences.[30] In a somewhat similar vein, Charles Taylor has warned of the danger of breakup, rooted in the increasing failure of French and English and other groups to grant each other mutual recognition.[31]

The new pluralism has so eroded the Confederation settlement of 1867 that many Canadians have begun to imagine a future that bears little relation to the past. But the Confederation settlement – and especially George-Étienne Cartier's understanding of it – is not irrelevant, even if many of its institutions have fallen into disuse or have lost their meaning. Confederation accepted that Canada was to be a country made up of peoples with different ways of life. It also assumed that

Canadians could become a great nation, provided that they made adequate provision for their differences while recognizing their mutual obligations and their common commitments. Confederation both recognized deep diversities and attempted to sustain a Canadian political nationality. In this way, the Fathers created a nation that differed from the American model and avoided the complex tragedy implicitly described by Lord Durham. For Durham, Canada was a country composed of "two nations warring in the bosom of a single state."[32] Moreover, he assumed that the only solution to the difficulty was assimilation. The Fathers made different assumptions, partly because they regarded assimilation as an untenable option, partly because they were able to appeal to the cooperative virtues. They accepted a fundamental Canadian paradox, that the recognition of deep diversities within Canada necessitates the acknowledgment of the interdependency of Canadians if tragedy is to to be avoided.

Recognition of the paradox has become more urgent in contemporary Canada because Canadians are witnessing a virtual explosion of group identities and are in danger of neglecting the complex political nationality that sustains them. Of course, Canada is not eternal. Other nations have disappeared, and the Canadian constitutional odyssey (to borrow Peter Russell's telling phrase) may face a similar destiny.[33] Reflecting on such a prospect, Pierre Trudeau has said that if Canada "is going to go, let it go with a bang rather than a whimper."[34] Much the same idea can be expressed by saying that the disappearance of Canada may not occur easily or without tragedy.

Such a conclusion implicitly challenges what has long been the most influential interpretation of Canada's destiny. In an important and controversial book, George Grant announced that Canada was a country without a future, because Canadians had accepted modernity. Modernity, with its belief in progress and its faith in technology, was destructive of distinct national identities and promoted the creation of a homogeneous, universal state. What awaited Canada was absorption into the United States, a fate that Canadians might lament, but were virtually powerless to resist. "Canada," wrote Grant, "has ceased to be a nation, but its formal political existence will not end quickly."[35] However, modernity may not have the consequences that he attributed to it. Not only has it produced a contemporary malaise that challenges the belief in progress and the faith in technology, but the real dangers that are to be avoided, according to Charles Taylor, are the slide into subjectivism and the adoption of atomistic or fragmenting forms of existence.[36] Others, including Michael Ignatieff, focus on the collapse of communism in the former Soviet Union and the emergence of a new ethnic nationalism that is transforming many nations, destroying old empires, and threatening long-established federations such as Canada. "Other people besides Canadians," Ignatieff writes, "should be concerned if Canada dies. If federalism can't work in my Canada, it probably can't work anywhere."[37] His implicit assumption, which is not his alone, is that Canada is still a nation. If Canadians fail to solve the problems of fragmentation rooted in their history and exacerbated by modernity, then the demise of Canada may not come (as Grant predicted) slowly and inexorably but suddenly and tragically, sparked by a referendum or fuelled by a failure of constitutional negotiations.

The failure of Canada, if such a failure occurs, may also turn out to be a significant intellectual tragedy. According to Jeremy Webber, Canadians have fashioned, through their constitutional practice, workable structures for accommodating difference, yet they do not have a constitutional theory that enables them to understand why those structures are good or how to work together to make a country. "That," Webber writes, "is the tragedy of our current constitutional debate."[38] His solution to the difficulty requires "reimagining Canada," in part by embracing the idea of a pluralist federalism that includes an asymmetrical constitution and refocuses attention on the participatory dimensions of democracy. A concern about the absence of an adequate theoretical understanding of Canada is also shared by a number of other scholars. For some of them, such as Guy Laforest, the problem is not that Canadians have no theory, but that they subscribe to the wrong theory. In particular, Laforest believes that, by embracing Pierre Trudeau's vision of federalism and rejecting the dualistic conception of Canada embedded in the the Meech Lake Constitutional Accord, Canadians have unwittingly undermined the basis of their country. The constitutional innovations introduced by Trudeau, he warns, will not "withstand the test of time," partly because they are based on "negative aims" and partly because they rest on a liberal philosophy unsympathetic to the rights of the people of Quebec.[39] The implication of such an analysis is that Canadians must rethink their theoretical commitments if disastrous political consequences are to be avoided.

In the history of political thought, the most profound and original philosophies have often been produced during great crises. Viewed in these terms, the constitutional struggles of contemporary Canada provide an almost unique intellectual opportunity which, if anything, is enhanced by the transformations in international society. For Canadians concerned with federalism, one of the most intriguing intellectual developments is what Yael Tamir has aptly called "liberal nationalism." According to Tamir, there is a form of nationalism that is not antithetical to liberal values but, on the contrary, sustains them. Behind her liberal nationalism is the pluralism of Isaiah Berlin and, in turn, the cultural nationalism celebrated by Herder. Not only is liberal nationalism the antithesis of racism, but it is equally critical of liberal neutrality as a panacea for dealing with ethnic, national, and other differences.[40] It contains no blueprint for the future, although the European Economic Community is regarded as an important experiment in a new form of political association. A parallel insight is articulated by James Tully, who suggests that "the prevailing normative vocabulary and institutions of the modern state and federalism [require revision] to accommodate deep diversity."[41] He begins the task of revision, in part by rejecting assimilationist nationalism in favour of pluralism and by revising legal sovereignty to include negotiated settlements among a culturally diverse people. The task ahead, Tully concludes, is "neither hopelessly complex nor a threat to liberal democratic constitutionalism."[42]

Canadian intellectuals have accepted the need for substantive change and conceptual revision. Some, such as Will Kymlicka, have challenged what they take to be Pierre Trudeau's assimilationist liberalism and have articulated a theory of liberalism that seeks to accommodate group identities, including the right to self-government asserted by Aboriginal Canadians.[43] Others, including Ovide Mercredi and Mary Ellen Turpel, have used concepts and metaphors drawn from Aboriginal history to articulate new understandings of Canada.[44] Some, among them Wayne Norman, have suggested that Rawls's idea of an overlapping consensus can provide the basis for a deep and comprehensive philosophy of Canadian federalism.[45] Others, such as Lenihan, Robertson, and Tassé, believe that Canadians already have available to them a meta-vision that dissolves their constitutional malaise. The core of the meta-vision is a form of federal pluralism that attempts to accommodate both liberalism and community within a distinctively Canadian context.[46] There are also those who, like Reg Whitaker and Jean Laponce, believe that Canadians can benefit by considering the experiences of other federal nations or the thinkers identified with them. Whitaker focuses on John C. Calhoun, especially his analysis of American federalism in terms of a concurrent majority; Laponce believes that the language laws of Canadian federalism should conform more closely to the Swiss policy of territorial unilingualism.[47] All of them are rethinking federalism, and their work is part of what one author has aptly called "reconfigurations."[48]

Reconfiguration is not the same as recovery, and the the difference is crucial for the moral foundations of Canadian federalism. Canadian federalism does not require moral foundations borrowed from the history of political thought or imported from other countries. The foundations already exist; for the most part, they need to be recovered, restored, and reapplied. The process of recovery dictates an imaginative leap into the Confederation settlement of 1867, in order to understand the kind of moral foundations that underpin Canadian federalism. At that time, a great debate occurred that raised vital questions about the kind of country Canada should become. The debate was imbued with pragmatism, yet moral values were also vigorously debated. What finally emerged was a unique type of federation resting on moral foundations that found their most forceful defender in George-Étienne Cartier. Canada cannot return to the lost world of 1867. But if Canadian federalism rests on moral foundations, it is problematic to neglect those foundations or to engage in significant constitutional innovation without understanding them. Moreover, the story of Canada, when told as one of tragedy, acquires even greater pathos as a result of the apparent loss of historical memory about the meaning of Confederation. As depicted by poets, tragedy often results because crucial facts and events are misunderstood or forgotten when they need to be comprehended or acted upon. In Canada there is irony as well as pathos because Canadians are forgetting their achievements at a time when Aboriginal and Québécois nationalists are recalling theirs. Those Canadians intent on dispelling the contemporary constitutional malaise may need to reflect on the past as well as the future, and to ponder Ernest Renan's insight that a nation can disintegrate if its memory is not strong enough to sustain it. For Canadians, the past contains a story of tragedy, but there is also a Canadian past that reveals a story about justice and community.

This prologue has attempted to provide a thematic guide to the complex story of Canada that comprises the substance of the book. Issues have been simplified and partly decontextualized in order to allow the broad contours of the story to receive greater prominence.

The following chapters restore the balance by adding analytical complexities and contextual features. What the chapters do not attempt to provide is a story of Canada told as sequential unfolding of events or as a schematic arrangement of principles. Instead, each chapter discusses a significant problem, in an effort to reveal a moral dimension of Canadian federalism and thus to tell a somewhat neglected story. If there is a story of Canada, its meaning is found as much in the parts as in the whole, and more in the dilemmas and difficulties that confront Canadians than in historical generalities or intellectual abstractions.

Taken together, the chapters tell a story of Canada that defies a simple summary; yet the main point of each chapter can be briefly stated. Chapter 1 begins the story by considering the crisis of Canadian federalism occasioned by the adoption of the Charter of Rights and the failure of two constitutional accords. Not only does the crisis raise novel questions, but it compels a reconsideration of Confederation. Chapter 2 discusses Confederation and examines its distinctive moral foundations, as well as the pivotal role of Cartier in its achievement and in articulating a Canadian federalist theory. The Supreme Court decision on patriation is the subject of chapter 3; the objective is to show that, by neglecting a key provision of the Confederation settlement, the court misunderstood the Canadian constitution and significantly eroded the legal, as well as the moral, foundations of Canadian federalism. Chapters 4 through 6 consider some of the changes that accompanied patriation, devoting special attention to the constitutional vision of Pierre Trudeau. Despite its many insights, his vision of Canada is flawed because it fails to recognize adequately the divergent ways of life that are constitutive of Canadian federalism. Democracy in its relation to federalism is the focus of chapters 7 and 8. Not only does Canadian federalism require a distinctive understanding of democracy, but the demand for self-government voiced by Aboriginal Canadians is crucial to how Canadian federalism and Canadian democracy should be understood. Chapter 9 considers the Canadian political nationality, a phrase made famous by Cartier and used by him to explore the moral complexities of Canadian nationhood. What he knew, Canadians are in danger of forgetting. Chapter 10 concludes the argument by attempting to show that the moral foundations of Canadian federalism have been neglected by politicians as well as intellectuals; they need to be recovered.

CHAPTER ONE

Federalism as a Way of Life:
The Canadian Experiment

"Canadian federalism," Pierre Trudeau told the United States Congress, was "a brilliant prototype for the moulding of tomorrow's civilization."[1] Canada was the kind of society in which different nations could live within the same state, and such a combination was "as necessary a condition of civilized life as the combination of men in society."[2] A society is made up not simply of individuals, as the great social-contract theorists of the seventeenth century had imagined. An obvious fact about many societies is that they also consist of groups with distinctive ways of life. The Canadian constitutional settlement of 1867 had responded to this fact, and the Canadian Charter of Rights and Freedoms appears to acknowledge that group rights are no less important than the rights of individuals. In these ways, the Canadian constitution not only rejects the atomizing individualism of the American constitution, but also attempts to respond to a different type of society.

There are, however, unresolved difficulties in the Canadian constitutional experiment, and in any case, virtually the whole of Western political tradition appears to be against it. Reflecting on the cultural diversity of humankind, Kenneth McRae has noted that Western political thought has shown little respect for such diversity, preferring instead to adopt universalistic, integrationist, or assimilationist principles.[3] Nationalist thinkers did, of course, challenge the belief in universalism, but even they denied that the state could embrace more than one way of life. For them, the only legitimate states were nation states. In the history of political thought, the Canadian constitutional experiment appears to be caught between universalism and particularism. Even in Canada itself, many scholars either envisage the evolution of Canadian federalism into a unitary state, or predict its disintegration in response to particularistic demands for local autonomy.

Canadians have available to them, however, an understanding of federalism that mediates the destructive demands of universalism and particularism. To recapture that understanding of Canadian federalism, it is necessary to explore its moral foundations and to think of federalism as a way of life. When federalism is understood in this way, it ceases to be a political or economic expedient and becomes a fundamental moral value. The value that federalism as a way of life is most intimately connected with is not freedom or diversity but fraternity. Federalism as fraternity responds to universalism and particularism by incorporating and transcending the very forces that are set against it. By so doing, it supplies a moral foundation for the Canadian experiment, identifies crucial inadequacies in the Charter of Rights, and provides an alternative to the theory and practice of consociational federalism. Moreover, the basis of federalism as fraternity is Confederation itself – provided that Confederation is understood as it was perceived by its most unequivocal supporter, George-Étienne Cartier.

THE CRISIS OF CANADIAN FEDERALISM

Federalism is almost never equated with fraternity or described as a way of life. It is more commonly depicted, in Canada and elsewhere, as a political expedient, or as a constitutional arrangement, or as a sociological characteristic of some societies.[4] In fact, Canadian federalism has even been described as an affair of governments, in which the most important issues are resolved by judicial, political, and bureaucratic élites. So long as it was understood in this way, it could be regarded as a form of political and constitutional pragmatism devoid of moral principle and preconception. However, with the adoption of the Charter of Rights in 1982 and the failure of the Meech Lake Constitutional Accord in 1990 and the Charlottetown Consensus Report on the Constitution in 1992, such an image of federalism has become increasingly unrealistic.

Canadian federalism, as Alan Cairns has observed, is no longer an affair of governments; it now includes citizens and groups who have acquired a new constitutional status through the Charter.[5] Not only do these new actors compete with politicians and judges to shape the constitutional order; they have also transformed the language of constitutional discourse. Canadian federalism is now discussed in terms of conflicting constitutional images and competing ways of life.[6]

Constitutional discourse has ceased to be a language of political expediency and political compromise and is increasingly becoming a branch of moral philosophy.

Virtually no one was able to predict that the Charter would effect such a radical transformation of the constitutional order. When it was adopted, some constitutional scholars even speculated that it would have no effect at all.[7] Others saw the Charter as an attack on the sovereignty of the legislators; their concern was that judges would displace legislators as policy-makers. Still others feared that the Charter was part of the increasing Americanization of Canadian society; they supposed that it would bring increased "bureaucratization, centralization and atomization."[8] Those who supported the Charter saw it both as a way of protecting the rights of the people and as a device for promoting national unity in the face of provincializing tendencies.[9]

What the Charter has not yet produced is greater national unity. Even as it was being adopted, some critics warned of its "limited capacities" for furthering national unity. Donald Smiley, for example, objected to the Charter because it was adopted without Quebec's consent and would therefore fuel Quebec nationalism; because it did nothing to satisfy the demands for intrastate federalism or to alleviate western alienation; because it spoke of rights as the common possession of Canadians, yet it encouraged individuals and groups to assert special claims and to defend particular interests.[10]

Smiley's last point might be stated differently. What the Charter has effected, according to Alan Cairns, is a transfer of sovereignty from government to the people. Moreover, the transfer has been real and not merely symbolic in the sense that the Charter has brought the citizenry into the constitutional order and has created a tension between citizens and governments.[11] Jealous of their rights, individuals and groups now compete with governments to control the constitution. Governments can no longer treat the constitution as their possession and modify it as they please. In a sense, the Charter represents a victory for Canadian democracy because governments are now more responsive to the people. What may be of even greater significance is that it has also brought about the demise of executive federalism, at least with respect to constitutional matters.

The Charter has produced a crisis of federalism partly because it has undermined the legitimacy of executive federalism. Executive federalism, or federalism by élites (judicial, political, and bureaucratic), is virtually the only kind of federalism that Canadians have known. Moreover, federalism by élites is more than a political arrangement; it also makes crucial moral assumptions. Not only does executive federalism require élites to practise accommodation and to be committed to national unity, but it supposes that Canada will continue to flourish only if the French and English subcultures are kept separate. "Consociational federalism," S.J.R. Noel has written, "works best when the 'two solitudes' are preserved." "'National' policies aimed at promoting bilingualism and biculturalism," he goes on to say, "may be misguided in the sense that they may increase friction between separate communities which previously had little direct contact with one another."[12] Because the Charter has undermined federalism by élites or consociational federalism, some scholars suppose that it has displaced federalism. They assume that Canadians must choose either the Charter or federalism.[13] But there may be more to federalism than élite accommodation and the two solitudes. The Charter may not be antagonistic to all forms of federalism, although it requires some rethinking of the moral dimensions of federalism and, in turn, a reconsideration of some of its own provisions.[14]

UNIVERSALISTS AND PARTICULARISTS

The current crisis of Canadian federalism is not simply a political and constitutional one. It is also a moral crisis. By undermining consociational federalism, the Charter has forced Canadians to seek alternative foundations for federalism. But such a task is enormously problematic because Canadians have frequently justified their existence as a nation by appealing to ideals that are ultimately uncongenial to federalism. Put differently, many Canadians have not been federalists.[15] Moral philosophers have not been federalists either. In fact, most moral philosophers have embraced either universalistic or particularistic principles, and such principles are ultimately antagonistic to the way of life that federalism presupposes.[16] "The sentiment which creates a federal state," wrote A.V. Dicey, "is the prevalence throughout the citizens of ... two feelings which are to a certain extent inconsistent." The citizens of a federal state must have both "the desire for national unity and the determination to maintain the independence of each man's separate State."[17] Many Canadians have possessed one or the other of these two feelings but not both. If Canadians are to rethink federalism, they will have to take Dicey's insight seriously and discard some of their most prized self-images, as well as a good deal of contemporary moral philosophy.

The problem that confronts Canadians begins with Confederation.

Confederation has failed Canadians in a crucial respect: it has not provided them either with a foundation myth or with a moral ideal that can sustain them during their times of trouble. It was once supposed that Confederation could not generate these things because it was the work of pragmatic politicians who avoided issues of principle in order to achieve political consensus. Sir John A. Macdonald, for example, has been described as someone who "did not attempt to plumb the depths of political theory or speculate on the rights of man." Rather, he is said to have been concerned "with the intricate details of concrete complexities" and to have believed that the politician should never aspire to the "alien role of prophet, philosopher or engineer."[18] Such an assessment of Macdonald and of Confederation captures only part of the truth. He may not have been a philosopher, but he did have a vision. And Confederation was much more than a series of pragmatic compromises. In fact, it was inspired by several conflicting visions, and most of them were incompatible with federalism.

That Macdonald was no federalist hardly needs emphasis.[19] He explicitly stated that his own preference was for a unitary state, so as to avoid the turmoils that had plagued American federalism. But there was more to his view of Canada than a strong central government. Macdonald was a believer in empire, of the commercial kind. He saw himself as the custodian of the idea of the St Lawrence empire, which, for him, implied that the provinces would have to recognize their subordinate role and give way to the supreme authority of the federal government. As a result, he attached great importance to devices such as the dual mandate, which habituated the provinces to their subordinate position while allowing them to participate in commercial development.[20] Moreover, the idea of empire appealed to others as well. "The big, unexpressed 'theory of Confederation,'" A.R.M. Lower wrote, "... was the one that lay behind all the arguments for the new union: build a new state, and BUILD! Build the state, shove out its boundaries as far as possible, build railways, build industries and cities!"[21] Many of those who supported Confederation, as Frank Scott said, had tired of "the pettiness of the politics and of public life in the individual provinces, the inefficiency of their local economies, the scant opportunity they offered to men of ability and ambition."[22] Such an understanding of the purpose of Confederation lends support to the French-Canadian complaint that it was engineered by men who cared relatively little about the local cultures and the local autonomy that form a crucial part of a federal state.[23]

Many French Canadians are not federalists either. They support the

Confederation settlement only to the extent that it enables them to flourish according to their own culture, to control their own destiny, and to create a society in their own image.[24] French Canadians have a "fatherland," and it is Quebec.[25] Their relationships with the rest of Canada are instrumental. This is why the economic benefits of unity are so often relied on to counter Quebec separatism and to re-establish a *modus vivendi* between Quebec and the rest of Canada. But even instrumental federalism can come at too high a price. "The two majorities," René Lévesque predicted, "will inevitably collide with one another ..., causing hurts that finally will be irreparable."[26] Moreover, federalism is regarded as a mistaken and dangerous ideal since it divides the self and requires an individual (both human and collective) to be two things at once. "To divide one's allegiance, affiliation, or identity," it has been said, "is to court disaster."[27]

Opposition to federalism is not uniquely Canadian. A recent study of Confederation has attempted to show that Sir John A. Macdonald's understanding of commercial empire was ultimately rooted in the Scottish Enlightenment and its economic ideology.[28] That ideology, it has been frequently suggested, is destructive of local cultures and looks ultimately to a homogeneous, universal state. This kind of state can enhance its appeal enormously by drawing on moral universalism, the belief that there must be a single scale of values for all people. Such a belief is the old theory of natural law in a new form. As opponents of universalism, Quebec separatists can draw on equally respectable and potent philosophical ideas. Behind the separatists are the nationalists and romantics who revolted against the Enlightenment. Few changes, Arthur Lovejoy observed, have been more profound or more momentous than that revolt. Those thinkers came to believe "that diversity itself was of the essence of excellence"; they coupled a strong antipathy to standardization with the cultivation of individual, national, and racial peculiarities.[29] The current crisis of Canadian federalism is, in one of its dimensions, little more than an instance of the crisis that has repeatedly plagued philosophical thought, a crisis that has occurred whenever universalism and particularism have dominated an epoch and set themselves against each other.

FEDERALISM AND FRATERNITY

The real challenge is to find a way of embracing both the universal and the particular. That challenge also forms a key problem of

Canadian federalism. In the context of Canadian federalism, however, the terms of discourse have changed, and the problem has become how citizens can have two identities and two sets of loyalties. Many Canadians, David Elkins and Richard Simeon have written, have strong ties to their local communities and equally strong ties to the national community. They want more freedom of action for their provincial communities as well as a centre that can speak for all of Canada. "The imaginative feat required," Elkins and Simeon go on to say, "is to find a way to reconcile and harmonize what may on the surface appear to be irreconcilable images."[30] The simplest answer is to say that federalism is predicated on the existence of multiple loyalties. There is also a more complex answer. Behind Canadian federalism is George-Étienne Cartier's intriguing idea of a Canadian political nationality, which has roots in the ideal of fraternity. Canadian federalism has moral foundations precisely because of its connection with this powerful ideal. Moreover, the concept of fraternity contains within it the very identities and loyalties that federalism presupposes.

The most vigorous defender of federalism in Canada was not John A. Macdonald but George-Étienne Cartier. Unlike Macdonald, who desired a unitary state and did what he could to secure it, Cartier was an unequivocal federalist. He was also the virtual equal of Macdonald in the accomplishment of Confederation. Yet his view of Confederation remains something of a mystery. His most recent biographers have attempted to dispel the mystery, but have arrived at conflicting conclusions. In one account, Cartier is presented as a leader who had the good sense to abandon the destructive French-Canadian nationalism of his youth and become in his mature years a liberal constitutionalist and a great Canadian nation-builder.[31] In the other account, he is viewed as a Montreal bourgeois who served the economic interests of his class and regarded Confederation as a means for the accomplishment of his bourgeois objectives.[32]

Despite their opposing assessments, Cartier's biographers are agreed that he was a man of action rather than a political thinker. In one of the few systematic studies of his political ideas, it is even suggested that "Cartier was not the man to whom abstractions appealed."[33] In fact, he liked to point out that a man could read twenty books on national policy and remain a political blunderer. But Cartier made at least one important exception to his own rule of political prudence. His great speech in support of Confederation, delivered at Quebec in 1865, contains the very abstractions that he claimed to abhor. In it, he addressed the vital issues of Confederation in a language more suited to the political theorist than to the practical politician. He spoke of justice and injustice, of democracy and mob rule, of national greatness, of assimilation and cultural pluralism.[34] Cartier's speech is not the work of an accomplished political thinker, yet students of Canadian federalism have turned to it as a crucial statement of the ideals and objectives of Confederation.

For no student of Canadian federalism has Cartier's speech had more significance than for Donald Smiley. In his last book, Smiley spoke of "Cartier's noble vision."[35] In an earlier work, he relied on Cartier to establish that Canada must be one political community rather than two, otherwise "it is not worth preserving."[36] He understood the core of Cartier's position to be the rejection of assimilationist nationalism, coupled with the belief that political allegiance should be uninfluenced by linguistic and cultural affiliation.[37] Put differently, Canada is sometimes said to be a country based on "limited identities"; it is a country based on political allegiance alone, or one that does not impose a single way of life on its citizens.[38] Canada may be the kind of country that Cartier wished it to become, but what still needs to be made explicit is the foundational value that unites Canadians. If they are so different among themselves, what moral value keeps them together?

Cartier himself provided no simple or direct answer to this question. Those who have come after him, however, have been more explicit. Pierre Trudeau once argued that Canadian federalism was incompatible with emotional appeals and should base itself on reason. For him, federalism rejected the emotionalism of separatists and nationalists and grounded itself on the rational consensus that held Canadians together.[39] W.L. Morton pinned his hopes on the Canadian belief in mutual accommodation and tolerance. And A.R.M. Lower would not allow himself to believe that "we [have] lived together for [so long] merely to see the Canadian experiment fail."[40] These answers may be satisfactory in themselves, but they are feeble responses to the kind of challenge that federalists must meet. Nationalists and separatists, after all, do not appeal solely to emotion. Their strongest appeal is to community. They insist that there is a common bond and natural identity among those who share a language or a culture. If Canadian federalism is to be regarded as more than a political or economic expedient, it must draw on a value that can rival the moral appeal of nationalism.

The value required appears to be implicit in Cartier's vision of Confederation and his corresponding idea of a Canadian political nationality. For Cartier, Confederation had three great objectives, one of which was shared by virtually all those who supported it. Confederation, he said, "was necessary for our commercial interests, prosperity and efficient defense."[41] But he was also devoted to the French nationality, and he believed that the union of French and English in a British North American confederation was the best assurance of the survival of the French race.[42] Having said that Confederation provided economic advantages as well as guarantees for the survival of the French race, Cartier might have concluded his speech. Yet he went on to say that it would bring into existence a new kind of nationality. Confederation would be unacceptable if French and English had come together merely to war with each other; it would be equally unacceptable if it created an all-inclusive Canadian nationalism.[43] If Confederation was to succeed, it had to create a new kind of nationality, which Cartier called a political nationality.

By advocating the creation of such a nationality, Cartier did not simply reject assimilationist nationalism; he also envisaged a new kind of relation between people with different languages and cultures. "We were of different races," he said, "not for the purpose of warring against each other, but in order to compete and emulate for the general welfare."[44] Cartier was not appealing merely to the economic advantages of cooperation. He did have a great vision of national development, but even that vision, as John Cooper observed, "had an importance beyond the strategic or the commercial." For Cartier, projects of national development presupposed a degree of cooperation that would join all British America "in the bond of common endeavour" and produce "a common, or national pride."[45] He also believed that French and English shared an identity. "We had," Cartier said, "the same sympathies and we all desired to live under the British Crown."[46] For him, Canada was to be a country in which different ways of life flourished, but whose peoples had come together to promote the good of all and were united by a political nationality with which "neither the national origin, nor the religion of any individual would interfere."[47]

By joining in Confederation, French and English agreed both to live apart and to live together. Canada would stand for a new kind of nationality and a new kind of fraternity. Cartier did not himself use the word "fraternity," yet his discussion of a Canadian political nationality appears to presuppose it, at least in some measure. Of course, the Canadian political nationality could be only a partial fraternity; it could not require intense emotional bonds between French and English or demand a complete identity of sentiments and interests. What the Canadian fraternity did suppose was that peoples with distinctive ways of life could possess goodwill towards each other, participate in common endeavours, develop and sustain common allegiances and common sentiments, and operate political institutions for the welfare of all. Cartier spoke of such things, but left them nameless. There is, however, a tradition of Canadian federalism – to which he appears to belong – that explicitly connects federalism and fraternity. "The fatherland, for us," wrote Henri Bourassa, "is the whole of Canada, that is a federation of distinct cultures and provinces." French and English are separated by language and religion, he added, "but united in a sense of brotherhood."[48]

If Cartier's political nationality and a tradition of Canadian federalist thought contain within them an appeal to fraternity, then federalists can respond to the separatist challenge by appealing to a value that nationalists themselves embrace.[49] When nationalists and separatists describe their country as their "fatherland," they imply that citizens should treat each other as brothers and sisters. The value that nationalists appeal to is fraternity. It is the imagining of fraternity, as Benedict Anderson has observed, that gives meaning to the nationalist's idea of the nation and motivates citizens willingly to die for it.[50] The fraternity of nationalism unites a strong emotional content with the sentiments of kinship, friendship, and love in the heightened atmosphere of something like religion.[51] Nationalists embrace a primordial idea of fraternity, attach it to the nation, and use it to characterize the type of relation that exists between those who share a culture or a language or a way of life. But the concept of fraternity is more complex than nationalists appear willing to allow. What they fail to notice is that the idea of fraternity looks two ways. It looks to those who share a way of life; it also looks to those who have adopted alternative ways of life. There is no greater fraternity than the brotherhood and sisterhood of all people.[52] Moreover, it may not be possible to confine fraternity in the way that the nationalist program presupposes. "If fellowship," it has been asked, "is morally compelling in part because it connotes respect and concern for others ..., is it not compromised when confined in expression to a particular group of people?"[53]

Nationalists want to confine fraternity; federalists want to expand it. Moreover, the fraternity of federalism does not necessarily exclude the fraternity that nationalists seek to realize, since federalism divides the identities and loyalties of citizens and assumes that each citizen will be a member of two communities. Henri Bourassa appealed to such an idea when he insisted that French-Canadian patriotism must include all Canadians. "Our duties," he wrote, extend not only "toward ourselves and our nationality" but also "toward Canada and our fellow citizens of a foreign origin."[54] Duties to other Canadians may sometimes conflict with those towards the French-Canadian nationality, but both can be duties of citizenship and fraternity. Ultimately, it is fraternity or some equivalent bond that sustains Canadian federalism because, as Wayne Norman has noted, "without some moral or quasi-moral bond ... one side or the other will quickly sour of the relationship when short- to medium-term considerations suggest that it could be doing better out of the federation." Failure to recognize the need for this moral bond, he goes on to say, has been "the great shortcoming of much of the theory and practice of federalism around the world."[55] Of course, fraternity is too important an ideal to be confined only to other Canadians. That is why federalists can envisage the disappearance of Canada.[56] They turn not to Aristotle but to Thucydides: Aristotle was unable to imagine a world without Athens; Thucydides could see a world in which Athens was no more.

FEDERALISM AS A WAY OF LIFE

Federalism is not simply a moral ideal. It is also a constitutional device that has crucial implications for the kind of life that citizens can lead. Politicians and ordinary Canadians understand as much. That is why some Canadians complain that the constitution is not federal enough, while others believe that federalism is inhospitable to their way of life. Canadian constitutional scholars, however, normally prefer to analyse federalism formally, with almost no regard to its substantive moral content. Not only does formal federalism leave the most important issues to the political process, but it transforms federalism into another form of politics. As such, federalism may fail to realize the way of life presupposed by it.

Even political theorists do not give sufficient attention to the moral dimensions of federalism. They almost always connect it with the *political* virtues. Federalism, it is often said, is a form of pluralism; and pluralism implies diversity and freedom.[57] The American Constitution is often considered the most famous example of such an understanding of federalism. Federalism has also been connected with civic humanism and the republican tradition, both in Europe and America.[58] In European political thought, it was Pierre-Joseph Proudhon who most closely linked federalism with democracy and civic humanism. For him, federalism was a device for enhancing citizen participation in atomized societies.[59] Others, such as Lord Acton, regard federalism as the solution to the problem of totalitarian nationalism; by dividing loyalties, federalism prevents the all-inclusive politics that such nationalism presupposes.[60]

When federalism is taken to be a political virtue, it is almost always connected with one of the dimensions of freedom and, as such, either neglects or diverts attention away from the moral aspects of community. As a political virtue, federalism appears to express no more than "agnosticism about community," and it recognizes at most that multiple community identities can coexist without exclusivism.[61] But it can also be a moral virtue. As a moral virtue, federalism moves beyond agnosticism and affirms the moral dimensions of community. Moreover, the moral virtue of federalism is such that it aims to realize the two types of fraternity, together with the communities they imply.[62] American and European federalists appear to give primacy to the political virtues, but Canadians can ground federalism in the moral value of fraternity.

The fraternity of Canadian federalism is expressed not only through regional equalization schemes, but also through the welfare state. These features of Canadian federalism, Pierre Trudeau has written, "give Canadians a sense of belonging to one nation."[63] National social and economic programs, Deborah Coyne has written, contribute "to our sense, however fragile, of shared national community." They express "our commitment to promoting greater social justice and a fairer, more compassionate society."[64] The Charter of Rights was directed at a similar objective. It aimed at creating a common identity and fellowship among all Canadians, even if some of its provisions have had virtually the opposite effect.[65] Canada, it is sometimes suggested, is superior to the United States because it is a more humane and fraternal society.[66] If Canada is such a society, the reason is that fraternity has been a concern not only of Canadian socialists, but also of Canadian federalists.

Unlike socialists, however, federalists value diversity. Moreover, the diversity that they value is itself a type of fraternity. There is a kind of fraternity that can be realized only in local and regional communities, or only by those who share a culture or a language. An individual who is deprived of her culture or local community cannot sustain herself. Outside my community or culture, Charles Taylor has written, "I wouldn't know who I was as a human subject ... I would be unable to function as a full human subject."[67] Federalists are not universalists precisely because they value local communities and local cultures. But they are not particularists either. The imaginative feat of federalism is that it uses the complex concept of fraternity to accommodate both the universal and the particular within the same state.

WHY FEDERALISM MATTERS

Academics spend endless amounts of time studying federalism, William Riker has complained, even though federalism makes "hardly any difference at all" in the way people are governed.[68] But he was writing as a political theorist and behavioural political scientist, rather than as a moral philosopher. Federalism can matter morally because it can seek to realize fraternity. Some Canadian students of federalism have understood as much, although they have not always expressed themselves adequately. They have said that Canada is a tolerant society, or is based on mutual accommodation, or allows many ways of life to coexist. But there is more to the Canadian experiment. Canada is a country in which many ways of life flourish, but it is also a country that has attempted to create a single way of life. Canadians have diverse ways of life and a common way of life precisely because they have sought to realize the complex, but powerful ideal of fraternity.

Fraternity, however, is a difficult ideal to realize. Not only has Canada sometimes failed to realize fraternal relations between French and English, but Aboriginal Canadians have not been treated fraternally at all. Their treatment has been paternalistic, and their demand for native self-government within Canada can be interpreted as a demand that the ideal of fraternity should apply to them as well. Federalism can facilitate the realization of such a demand because it enables each citizen to have more than one loyalty and more than one identity. As federal citizens, Aboriginal Canadians would retain their distinctive way of life and share in a way of life that is common to other Canadians. But there are limits to what federalism can accomplish. Its very divisions can also frustrate the realization of fraternity since they do not preclude conflict between the ways of life that are constitutive of Canada. When such a conflict occurs, it not only turns Canadians against each other, but often creates a tension within each citizen. To eliminate the conflict completely, it would be necessary to abandon federalism and embrace either particularism or universalism.[69] To do so, however, is to reject the Canadian experiment and to give up a way of life.

There are, of course, ways of thinking about federalism that do not give prominence to fraternity. Federalism can be regarded as a political and economic expedient with almost no moral content. When it is viewed in this way, it is an institutional arrangement that divides powers between national and local governments but makes no attempt to develop a common way of life among all citizens. Canadians are familiar with such an understanding of federalism and have come to know it as consociational federalism. A key assumption of consociational federalism, as Arend Lijphart has observed, is that social peace is possible in culturally heterogeneous societies only if the subcultures are kept separate. "Close contacts," he has written, "are likely to lead to strain and hostility."[70]

Canadians also have available to them an image of federalism that disputes Lijphart's assumption. The beginnings of the alternative image can be traced to Confederation and to Cartier's idea of a Canadian political nationality. Henri Bourassa contributed to the alternative image and, in some respects, so did Pierre Trudeau. Trudeau illuminated one dimension of the alternative image when he said that British Columbians could "go it alone" but had agreed to pay taxes to the federal government so that some of the money could be used "to help the less fortunate provinces." Regional economic inequities, he added, can lead to disunity "if we are not willing to consider that we are our brother's keeper in all of Canada."[71] The alternative image sees federalism as the means that enables different nationalities both to live together and to live apart. "Federalism," K.C. Wheare wrote, "has provided a device through which differing nationalities could unite, and while retaining their own distinctive national existence, attempt to create in addition a new sense of common nationality."[72] There is a tradition of Canadian federalist thought that shares K.C. Wheare's idea of federalism, links it to the two faces of fraternity, and makes moral demands on both citizens and governments.

CHAPTER TWO

Confederation and the Beginnings of Canadian Federalist Theory

Disagreements about federalism are not new in Canada. Canadians have almost always disagreed about it, and their disagreements were, if anything, even more intense in the years that immediately preceded Confederation. In 1867 Confederation had supporters as well as opponents, but few Canadians were unequivocal federalists. "The Fathers of Confederation," Donald Creighton wrote more than a century later, "recognized the inevitability of federalism, [but] they could not help regarding it as a suspect and sinister form of government."[1] It was suspect partly because federation was commonly believed to be an unstable form of government. In 1865 John A. Macdonald believed that the unitary features of the Constitution would save Canada from the common afflictions of federations; yet even he later admitted that the difficulties raised by federation could not be settled so simply. The divisive question of "States Rights," Macdonald complained in 1869, "has already made its appearance in Canada!"[2]

But states rights was an old question, and it did not emerge only after Confederation. In fact, the issue was raised repeatedly in the Confederation debates of 1865 and was frequently coupled with the even more explosive issue of nationality. Opponents of Confederation warned that Canada would suffer the common and unhappy fate of federations, of which the American Civil War was the immediate reminder. Even Switzerland, Henri Joly insisted, was no exception; it too had had a civil war.[3] Others believed that "the old aggression of race against race ... has not disappeared" and was destined to disrupt Confederation.[4] Those who supported Confederation did not evade such objections. In speeches delivered at the Quebec Conference and published in the Confederation debates of 1865, they insisted that

Canada could succeed, even if other federations had failed. Moreover, the debates contain at least two distinctive justifications for such a belief. One of them is contained in Macdonald's now-famous speech in support of Confederation; the other was given classic expression by George-Étienne Cartier.

The debates of 1865 provide an image of Confederation that is obscured by the orthodox accounts. Canadian Confederation is often fitted into a practical mould, devoid of philosophical interest; yet the Confederation debates raise vital questions of political and constitutional theory. Once the Fathers agreed that Canada was to be a federation, difficult issues of political and constitutional theory could no longer be avoided. Opponents of Confederation raised those issues in their discussions of federalism, and the Fathers responded to them. The Fathers had to justify their adoption of a federal form of government to those who believed that the aggressions of race had not disappeared and who regarded the American Civil War as symptomatic of federations. As a result, the debates of 1865 record an important Canadian discussion about federalism and the beginnings of a distinctively Canadian federalist theory. This chapter seeks to recover the original significance of Canadian federalist theory by focusing in large measure on the debates of 1865. Those debates not only record the ideological context from which Canadian federalist theory emerged, but they also provide evidence of the crucial role assumed by Cartier in its formulation, a role that is not adequately recognized. Like James Madison before him, Cartier provided middle ground between opposing positions, neither of which could prevail in the social and political conditions from which Canadian Confederation emerged. Madison had focused on American problems and had created an American federalist theory; Cartier addressed Canadian problems and provided the beginning of a Canadian federalist theory.

THE IDEOLOGICAL CONTEXT OF CONFEDERATION

In its accomplishment, Confederation was a practical achievement as well as the achievement of practical men. Macdonald has been described as a natural empiricist and Cartier as a man who avoided abstract ideas. As a consequence, Canadians are said to lack the kind of ideological debate that surrounded the adoption of the United States Constitution.[5] But such a view is unsatisfactory, partly because it neglects the ideological origins of the *idea of Confederation*. Proposals for the union of British North America, as a recent study has shown, not only preceded the accomplishment of Confederation by a century or so, but also took sides in the eighteenth-century debate between commercial wealth and classical republican virtue.[6] That debate continued into the nineteenth century, became a key component in the debate over Confederation, and gave Canadian Confederation commercial, as well as ideological, dimensions. The eighteenth-century debate between wealth and virtue also divided federalists and anti-federalists in the ideological debate over the United States Constitution. Not only did Canadian Confederation have ideological dimensions, but the earliest proposals for Confederation produced debates similar to those in the United States. In the case of Canada, however, the eighteenth-century debate between wealth and virtue was eventually linked to the nineteenth-century one about nation and nationality, with the result that Canadian Confederation also acquired ideological dimensions that were absent from the American debate.

There is, however, a traditional understanding of Canadian Confederation and of the American influence that owes much to Macdonald himself. In the debates of 1865, he described the United States Constitution as "one of the most skillful works which human intelligence ever created"; but he quickly added that it was "not the work of Omniscience." The United States Constitution "commenced ... at the wrong end" because it declared that "each state was a sovereignty in itself."[7] By contrast, the Canadian constitution, Macdonald said, would confer all the great powers of legislation, as well as the residuary power, on the general legislature, thereby avoiding the fatal defect in the United States Constitution that had resulted in civil war. "Canadian Confederation," Peter Waite has written, "was a native creation. There was no intention of imitating the United States."[8] Behind Waite's assessment is Macdonald's belief that the United States Constitution was not to be emulated so much as improved upon.

This belief – that Confederation corrected American errors – did not go unchallenged in the debates of 1865. Christopher Dunkin not only accused Macdonald of failing to respect the distinction between legislative and federal union, but also predicted the early demise of Confederation.[9] Others warned that the proposed Confederation would cause rebellion among French Canadians, who wanted "a real confederation, giving the largest powers to the local governments, and merely delegated authority to the General Government."[10] Such a union was similar to the kind that the United States Constitution was believed to have established, but which Macdonald rejected. According to Robert Vipond, it was the Reformers who, unlike Macdonald, "defended a constitutional position in 1865 that was in many ways similar to the Federalists' defense of the American Constitution some eighty years before." Moreover, the ideas of the Reformers, Vipond adds, acquired new importance in the years after Confederation by providing "a foundation" on which advocates of provincial rights could build a constitutional theory that treated "Macdonald's centralizing mechanisms as if they were impurities that had to be removed from the constitutional system."[11] What Reformers and other opponents of Canadian Confederation did not probe, however, were the political theories behind the United States Constitution. For the Reformers, as for Macdonald, it was the American Civil War, together with its implications for federalism, that required attention.

The Framers of the United States Constitution had not concerned themselves with the problem of civil war. Their attention was fixed on a different issue. For the American Framers, the crucial problem had been raised by Montesquieu, who believed that large countries turn into despotisms and destroy republican liberty.[12] So long as his problem remained unsolved, most Americans could see no alternative to the ineffectual Articles of Confederation, other than Alexander Hamilton's unacceptable proposals for consolidated government. A solution to Montesquieu's problem was eventually provided by James Madison in his classic discussion of republicanism. Smallness, said Madison, was fatal to republicanism because faction would be worse in small states; but consolidated government was equally unacceptable because it destroyed republican liberty. His famous middle ground was the idea of a compound or extended republic, whose constitution was both national and (con)federal in character.[13] A stable republican state required the compounding of various economic interests of a large territory with a federal system of semi-sovereign political units, and the adoption of a scheme of indirect elections that would refine the voice of the people at the national level.[14] The compound republic, so Madison believed, provided the commercial and military advantages of energetic union without sacrificing either republican government or the states.

The theory of the compound republic was not unchallenged. In the debates over the ratification of the Constitution, anti-federalists reasserted their belief in the small-republic theory and the virtues presupposed by it. They defended their belief in homogeneity, their contempt for extremes of wealth, their sympathy for Christian piety, and their conviction that republican government depended on the citizen's active participation in public affairs and his devotion to the public good. They argued that standing armies and commerce would undermine classical republican virtues and lead to a decline of morals.[15] Although anti-federalists were unsuccessful in their campaign, their protests were instrumental in securing the adoption of the the original Bill of Rights and have become a recurring theme of American political thought. But there was at least one crucial assumption that anti-federalists did not dispute in 1789. Everyone agreed, including the anti-federalists, that the United States was one nation; their disagreement, as Herbert Storing said, was about the kind of government it should have.[16]

Such an assumption was precisely what Canadians could not take for granted in 1867. In his famous report of 1839, Lord Durham had found in Canada "a struggle not of principle, but of races": "two nations warring in the bosom of a single state."[17] The debates of 1865 constantly returned to Durham's theme. Henri Joly, for example, spoke of the "great difference of nationality, which is certainly fated to play an important part in the destinies of the future Confederation."[18] Joseph Perrault admitted that times had changed, but denied that racial hatred had disappeared. French and English had come to the New World, he said, but had brought their old national hatreds with them.[19] And Christopher Dunkin surmised that "the two differences of language and faith ... [were] the real reasons" for the supposed federal union, whose purpose it was to meet a "probable clashing of races and creeds."[20] Students of American federalism have frequently noted the great difference that exists between their federalism and that of Canada. "Canadians ...," wrote Carl Friedrich, "had a very special problem to deal with which found no parallel in the American experience: that was how to arrange a federal system that would satisfy their French-speaking citizens."[21]

Because Canadians had special problems, Confederation had a distinctive ideological context. But they also had problems and objectives similar to those that shaped the United States Constitution. "The American Union and the Canadian Federation," wrote W.B. Munro, "were the outcome of essentially similar conditions. Both arose in part from a desire to promote the common defense, and in part from the hope that commercial prosperity would be attained through union."[22] In Canada, commercial prosperity was frequently connected to Tory ideas of union. In 1854 a Halifax newspaper called for the union of the British North American colonies and insisted that "the union should be perfect, unqualified and absolute."[23] In pre-Confederation Canada, it was the Tories who most favoured union, and their proposals for union were for highly centralized and supported executive power. They tended to associate the provinces with local prejudices, regarded democracy as a faction-ridden system of government based on the will of uneducated and uncultivated people, and looked to commercial empire in order to provide opportunities for ambitious men. Tories, it has been said, wanted the kind of imperial or consolidated government that Alexander Hamilton had failed to obtain.[24]

The leading proponent of the Tory vision of Canada was Macdonald himself. His preference, as he revealed in the debates of 1865, was for a legislative union because such a union was "the best, the cheapest, the most vigorous, and the strongest system of government we could adopt." Moreover, Macdonald urged the provinces of British North America not only to establish a commercial union, but also to become "a great nationality, commanding the respect of the world, able to hold our own against all opponents."[25] "The Nation," Donald Creighton wrote in his account of Macdonald's idea of union, "transcends the group, the class, or section."[26] Macdonald admitted, however, that the Tory idea of legislative union was "impracticable," not only because Lower Canada refused to accept it, but also because the Maritime provinces rejected it. A federal union was the only "practicable" solution. Yet Macdonald seemed to imply that the Canadian union would still be a Tory union because only minimal concessions were made to the federal principle.[27]

The concessions were limited, but powerful social and political forces had made them necessary in the first place. Behind the concessions was Lower Canada and the issue of French-Canadian nationality. Moreover, the idea of a distinct local identity and a distinct provincial destiny also had wide support in the Maritimes. Such local identities and provincial destinies had received recognition from the British colonial practice, beginning in 1791, of granting popular representation in local legislatures. "The democratic element in Canadian politics," wrote W.L. Morton, "was always stronger than any other, including allegiance to the Crown."[28] Tory ideas of imperial government were also challenged by Reformers in Upper and Lower Canada in the decades before Confederation. Mackenzie and Papineau had defended local democracy and civic virtue against élite control and centralized government, and Canadians had witnessed the articulation of political ideas not unlike those of anti-federalists in 1789.[29] Opposition to Tory union came from a variety of ideological sources and represented powerful social and political forces.

Federation was offered as the compromise solution, even though federalism was widely regarded as a sinister doctrine. Not surprisingly, Macdonald provided a pragmatic account of Confederation and assured Canadians that they would avoid the maladies of American federalism. Confederation, he said, improved on the American union. But the story of Confederation is more complicated than Macdonald made it appear. Confederation was a practical achievement, but the idea had ideological origins, as well as a complex ideological context, from which it finally emerged. As a proponent of Tory union, Macdonald wanted a legislative union; he settled for a federal one. The difficult problems of Canadian federalism did not emerge only after Confederation; many of them already existed before 1867 and were canvassed in the debates of 1865. In the years after 1867, Canadian federalism avoided the malady of civil war that had disrupted the United States, but it continued to confront the Canadian problems that had compelled the adoption of federation in the first place. Macdonald had little enthusiasm for such a prospect. "It is generally believed," wrote Alfred DeCelles, that while the British North America Act was before the British parliament, "Macdonald desired ... to have it modified so that a legislative union should be substituted for the proposed federation."[30] Apparently, Cartier's intervention rescued the federation idea.

THE BEGINNINGS OF CANADIAN FEDERALIST THEORY

So long as federalism was understood as the American error, Macdonald occupied pride of place. But it was also intended as a solution to Canadian problems. In the debates of 1865, it was Cartier who most directly addressed the kinds of problems that distinguished Canada from the United States. Macdonald regarded federalism as a suspect idea; Cartier was an unequivocal federalist. "If Macdonald is entitled to be called the 'Father of the Canadian Constitution,' " wrote W.B. Munro, "... Alexander Hamilton has some claim to be designated as its grandfather."[31] But neither Alexander Hamilton nor

John A. Macdonald obtained the kind of constitution he preferred; both were compelled to concede more than they wished to federalism. In the case of Canada, it was Cartier who was instrumental in obtaining crucial concessions. His demands could not be ignored if Confederation was to include French Canada. Cartier, it has been said, was the Jefferson of Confederation.[32] But he did not share Jefferson's democratic sympathies, and in any case, his role was more like Madison's. He broke the deadlock that had developed between those who favoured the Tory idea of legislative union and those who either could see no alternative to the status quo or looked to a weak confederacy. In so doing, Cartier also provided the beginnings of Canadian federalist theory.[33]

In the United States, federalist theory frequently returns to its beginnings in the debate between classical republicanism and the compound republic. That debate creates a tension in American federalist theory and gives it richness. But the tension, it has been said, is comparable to "differences within the family."[34] The differences are far from negligible, but they are normally differences about the best means for the realization of republican liberty. Canadian federalist theory also contains a tension. The Canadian tension relates not to liberty but to identity and to the relation (or clash) between local identities and national identity.[35] Moreover, the Canadian debate about identity often takes place between those who dispute "family" membership. Put differently, American federalist theory has focused on the kind of government the nation should have; Canadian federalist theory has concerned itself with whether there is a nation at all.

Questions of identity and nationhood were prominent in discussions of Confederation. In 1867 the Toronto *Globe* hailed the "birthday of a new nationality. A united British North America ... takes its place among the nations of the world."[36] But the issue of nationality was far more controversial than the *Globe* made it appear. Not only was nationality the single most divisive issue of Confederation, but almost all the important questions of Confederation were somehow connected to it. The debates of 1865 record its significance and its contentiousness. Some speakers, such as Macdonald, urged that the happy opportunity of founding a great nation should not be allowed to pass. Others, including Joseph Perrault, complained that the real object of Confederation was not merely the creation of a new nationality and a vast empire, but the obliteration of the French-Canadian nationality. Christopher Dunkin, on the other hand, believed that there was no common nationality to which Confederation could appeal. "Have we any class of people," he asked, "... whose feelings are going to be directed to ... Ottawa, the centre of the new nationality that is to be created?"[37]

In the years after Confederation, Dunkin's question retained its importance. In fact, the apparent failure of the Macdonaldian constitution, as demonstrated by the genesis of provincial rights, has been traced to the lack of attachment to Ottawa that he foresaw. The weakness of Macdonald's constitutional program, Norman McL. Rogers wrote, "lay in the fact that it presupposed a general sentiment in the country which would support the dominion government in a dispute with a province." This assumption, Rogers added, "was not correct," partly because Ottawa was "a new and untried entity," whereas the provinces "were old and familiar friends."[38] In the debates of 1865, however, the task of meeting Dunkin's objection fell as much to Cartier as to Macdonald. Macdonald's general response was that the proposed Confederation had disposed of the problem of provincial rights because it created a centralized federation and radically diminished the authority of the provinces. Cartier's response was the idea that Confederation would bring into existence a new kind of nationality, which he called a political nationality.[39]

Connected to Cartier's idea of a Canadian political nationality was his philosophy of federalism. This philosophy distinguished him not only from Macdonald, who favoured Tory union, but also from early American federalists who assumed the existence of a single nation. As a federalist, Cartier's focus was multiple identities and their implications for Canadian nationhood. In the debates of 1865, he noted that opponents of Canadian federation either lamented the existence of racial and local diversities, and thus called for their elimination through a legislative union, *or* appealed to such diversities and particularities in their attempt to discredit any scheme of union, other than a weak confederacy, a defence league, or a free trade area. The implicit issue was homogeneity, and the belief that a nation either presupposed homogeneity or was compelled to create it. Not only had Lord Durham arrived at such a conclusion, but his assumption reappeared in the debates of 1865 and became an obstacle to Canadian Confederation. Cartier's response was to dismiss projects such as Durham's as "utopian." "The idea of unity of races," he said, "was ... impossible."[40]

At the core of his dismissal of Durham was his philosophical affirmation of diversity and his distinctive conception of Canadian nationhood. Against Durham, Cartier insisted that diversity of race would always exist because "dissimilarity ... appeared to be the order of the physical world and of the moral world, as well as in the political world."[41] The project of racial unity was not only utopian but impossible. Cartier also objected to those who used Durham to argue that the Confederation project of creating a great nation was misconceived because Upper Canada was British and Protestant, whereas Lower Canada was French and Catholic. Such an objection seemed to suppose not only that racial hatreds existed, but that they were irreducible. Cartier responded by insisting, in part, that racial diversity should be regarded as "a benefit rather than otherwise." The British empire, he said, had diversity of race, and each race contributed to the greatness of the empire. "We were of different races," he observed, "not for the purpose of warring against each other, but in order to emulate for the general welfare."[42]

At one level, Cartier provided an exhortation on racial harmony. But he coupled his exhortation with a defence of federalism. He had come to the conclusion "that federation was desirable and necessary" because it was the most practical means of bringing the colonies together, "so that particular rights and interests should be properly guarded."[43] Those who supposed that federation would not work, on account of the differences of race and religion, "were in error." On the contrary, it was on account of the variety of races and local interests that "the Federation system ought to be resorted to, and would be found to work well."[44] As Cartier understood it, federalism was an exercise in the art of separation. The general interest was to be separated from local interests, and questions of race and religion were assigned to their proper place. As an exercise in the art of separation, Canadian federalism, in his understanding of it, did not presuppose the nation so much as create it.

Canadian federalism did not create the Canadian nation out of nothing. Cartier supposed that the provinces of British North America had common "sympathies and interests" and "desired to live under the British Crown."[45] Canadian federalism separated common interests and sympathies from the local interests and racial particularities that were distinctive to the provinces. In so doing, it brought into existence a Canadian nation that was an "agglomeration of communities" having "kindred interests and sympathies," as well as a common political nationality.[46] Moreover, the Canadian political nationality was a new nationality, in the sense that it did not displace the French-

Canadian nationality or existing allegiances to the provinces. In a classic discussion of federalism, A.V. Dicey expressed a similar idea. For him, federalism presupposed a peculiar kind of sentiment because it required citizens to possess both a desire for national unity and the determination to maintain a separate political existence.[47] In the debates of 1865, Cartier appealed to such a sentiment not only to justify Canadian federalism, but also to legitimate the creation of the Canadian nation.

Canada was to be a nation in which multiple loyalties and multiple identities flourished. But Canada, in Cartier's understanding of it, also presupposed strong institutions at the national level, as well as the continued existence of English and French minorities within the provinces. Both beliefs were criticized in the debates of 1865. French Canadians, it was said, would be outnumbered in the federal parliament and their interests ignored. Others complained that the rights of the English minority would be trampled on in Quebec. In the case of the federal parliament, Cartier admitted that he had once opposed representation by population as being adverse to the interests of French Canadians, who were the weaker party. However, he was now willing to allow such representation in the House of Commons because he realized that it "would not involve the same objection if other partners were drawn in by a federation." "If three parties were concerned," he added, "the stronger would not have the same advantage."[48] In the case of minorities, Cartier appealed to considerations of fairness as well as to legal and constitutional remedies. "Any attempt to deprive the minority of their rights," he said, "would be at once thwarted." If unfairness occurred, he added, "it would be censured everywhere."[49] In Cartier's understanding of it, the Canadian nation presupposed the existence of multiple identities and allegiances, the solution of complex institutional problems, and a sense of fairness throughout the country.

In the debates of 1865, Cartier also addressed the issue of the American Civil War. The American union, he said, had fallen into civil war because it was a democracy, and "purely democratic institutions could not be conducive to the peace and prosperity of nations." But the Canadian union would form "a Federation with a view of perpetuating the monarchical element."[50] Cartier associated pure democracy with mob rule and political instability, and monarchy with national dignity and respect for principle. French Canadians, he said, supported constitutional monarchy because "their adherence to the

British Crown" had secured for them "their institutions, their languages, and their religions intact to-day."[51] They also knew that their own nationality would enjoy no such guarantees in the American democracy. "There was the instinctive feeling ... in French Canada," W.L. Morton wrote, "that monarchical allegiance allowed a diversity of customs and rights under law in a way that the rational scheme and abstract principles of republican democracy did not."[52] The Crown, in Cartier's understanding of it, typified a type of federal union that differed not only from the American union but also from Tory union. Its symbols were permanence, order, and unity; its practice was the difficult art of separation, which was crucial for the creation of the Canadian nation.

AFTER CONFEDERATION

Cartier died in 1873. Macdonald lived until 1891 and presided in large measure over the consolidation of the Canadian Confederation. But the Macdonaldian constitution was already faltering by the 1870s, and by the 1890s the Canadian constitution had moved decisively away from Macdonald's centralism and towards provincial rights. What eventually emerged was described in 1947 as "two streams of constitutional thought in violent opposition, represented by the supporters of federal authority ... and the advocates of the 'compact theory.' "[53] By the 1970s, Canada's constitutional crisis had acquired new dimensions. The governments of Canadian federalism, it was suggested in an influential study, were bent on increasing their own jurisdictions without regard to the self-defeating competition engendered by such policies. The new crisis was described as a crisis of big governments, which had turned the Canadian constitution into "a lame-duck constitution" and called into question even the limited goal of keeping Quebec in Confederation.[54] Behind the new crisis, however, was Macdonald's failure to settle the issue of provincial rights. Moreover, his vision of Canada – a vision that privileged imperial government and regarded federalism with suspicion – was as likely to fuel doctrines of provincial rights as to eliminate them.

In the years after Confederation, advocates of provincial rights challenged Macdonald's centralism by developing alternative constitutional visions. In some cases, the alternative vision presupposed Canadian nationhood and offered a new understanding of it. Oliver Mowat was the leader of the provincial rights movement in Ontario, but he also professed devotion to the success of Confederation. Unlike Macdonald, Mowat believed that the success of Confederation was to be obtained through the autonomy of the provinces and not through central power.[55] Confederation was itself described as a compact of provinces. In other cases, the affirmation of Canadian nationhood was less manifest, if not altogether absent. Some French Canadians focused on culture and race, and believed that Confederation rested on a compact between two races, in which each affirmed the right of the other to live according to its own culture. Confederation was understood as a racial *modus vivendi*, and Canada was taken to be a country that allowed two cultures or two nations to exist side by side.[56] In both cases, central authority was eroded and the idea of a common Canadian nationality diminished.

There were also provincialists, such as David Mills of Ontario, who associated the protection of provincial rights and the vitality of provincial communities with liberal principles that included respect for the rule of law, as well as a strong commitment to individual rights. "The provincialists," Robert Vipond has suggested, "strongly defended the autonomy and integrity of community, but they were also the carriers of a genuinely liberal strain in Canadian political culture that those like Charles Taylor would say threatens community."[57] For them, the Macdonaldian constitution represented not only centralism and paternalism, but also arbitrary power and corrupt government. Ultimately, provincialists such as Mills "could find no logically necessary and empirically rigorous connection between provincialism and liberalism."[58] But in their own minds at least, there was a deep association between provincial rights and liberal values, and their critique of centralized power in some respects laid a foundation for the eventual adoption of a charter of rights.

For Macdonald, however, provincial rights and the compact theory represented the refusal of the provinces to accept the subordinate status that Confederation conferred on them. "It is difficult to make the local Legislatures understand," he complained, "that their powers are not so great as they were before the Union."[59] The enhancement of provincial power also reminded Macdonald of the American Civil War, which he attributed to the weakness of central power and to the strength of states rights. But the expansion of provincial power did not simply diminish central authority; it also eroded minority rights. A survey of the growth of provincial jurisdiction in the decades after Confederation, undertaken by Frank Scott, dismissed as a "popular myth" belief in the protection of minority rights by the Judicial Committee of the Privy Council. The decisions of the Privy Council had reduced the jurisdiction of the central government, expanded the powers of the provinces, and upheld provincial jurisdiction at the expense of minority rights. Given the apparent hostility of provincial governments to minority rights, wrote Scott, "it is little comfort for the French-Canadian minorities [throughout Canada] ... to realize that the provincial governments on which they depend for their educational privileges and civil rights have had their powers enlarged."[60] Macdonald was more concerned about the reduction of central power, but the erosion of minority rights also raised questions about Confederation.

One of the most controversial cases of minority rights arose in 1871 as a result of the New Brunswick School Act. This act established a system of tax-supported, non-sectarian free schools, thereby abolishing the state-supported denominational schools that had existed before Confederation. Roman Catholics appealed to Macdonald to disallow the act under the powers given to the central government by the British North America Act; but he refused on the ground that the Roman Catholics had lost no *legal* rights, since their denominational schools had only the sanction of practice. Macdonald's opinion was eventually upheld by the Judicial Committee of the Privy Council; it was supported at the time by Cartier, among others. Strict law aside, the School Act not only disturbed New Brunswick politics, but also raised questions about the spirit of Confederation. Some of those opposed to the act believed that the spirit of Confederation was to maintain all minority rights enjoyed at the time of union, whether embodied in law or not.[61]

The New Brunswick School Act also raised questions about Canadian federalist theory because it opened old issues about the war of races, nationalities, and religions that Confederation was to have settled. In the debates of 1865, Étienne Taché had addressed the war of races and dismissed it. "Much had been said on the war of races," he noted, "but that war was extinguished on the day the British Government granted Canada Responsible Government."[62] The Fathers of Confederation settled on a more complex response that included both federalism and minority rights. Moreover, minority rights were to enjoy the protection, in Cartier's understanding of them, not only of the law courts and the power of disallowance, but also of the sense of fairness that pervaded the country. Taché also spoke of fairness in

1865. French Canadians, he said, had taken pains "to give our fellow subjects of English origin the whole of their rights and fair play in every respect."[63] In the Confederation debates, fairness for minorities was a critical issue, so much so that Cartier made it part of Canadian federalist theory.

In the United States, questions of fairness acquired critical importance in the decades before the war and produced new understandings of American federalism. Behind the Civil War was the issue of slavery, as well as difficult questions of economic policy and territorial expansion. Those questions also provided the background to John Calhoun's *Disquisition on Government*. As he understood the issue, the northern states, which formed a majority and opposed slavery, had used the central government to enact policies detrimental to the interests of the southern states, which formed a minority and favoured the continuation of slavery. Calhoun offered a complex solution to the problem, which included his famous idea of a concurrent majority. The will of the people, he said, could not be correctly ascertained merely by consulting the numerical majority. In a country such as the United States, which was composed of different interests and sections, it was also essential to obtain special consent for central government action by way of a concurrent majority of interests and sections.[64] The requirement of special consent also implied that interests and sections possessed a veto on central government action. Calhoun's proposal for a plural executive was a practical device for the achievement of a concurrent majority. The Framers of the United States Constitution had created a single chief magistrate; Calhoun regarded their creation as "a great mistake" and believed that a plural presidency would create harmony in the country since one section would not be able to oppress the other.[65]

Calhoun's ideas did not attract the attention of the Fathers of Confederation. There is, however, an indirect connection between him and Canadian Confederation that comes through Lord Acton. In twentieth-century discussions of Canadian federalism, Acton's essay on "Nationality" occupies a distinguished place. Pierre Trudeau, for example, frequently cited Acton in his own studies on Canadian federalism. Citation of Acton began at least as early as 1921, with W.P.M. Kennedy's critique of nationalist doctrines.[66] Since then Acton has been cited by scholars and statesmen to justify the kind of state that the Fathers of Confederation are thought to have created. "Not Mill and Durham," it has been said, "but Lord Acton was the thinker who provided the intellectual foundation which British North America ... was already destined to take."[67] It was Acton who said that "the coexistence of several nations under the same State is the test ... of its freedom [as well as] one of the chief instruments of civilization."[68] He said more about federalism in his 1861 essay on the United States Constitution, where Calhoun's ideas are described as "profound" and as "applicable to the politics of the present day."[69]

What Acton found attractive about Calhoun's theory was its rejection of absolutist politics. In the United States, such politics operated through Jeffersonian democracy, which Acton likened to "the spurious democracy of the French Revolution."[70] As he understood it, the French Revolution began by proclaiming a democratic republic and ended by creating a new theory of nationality, in which the nation was regarded as an indivisible whole and the diverse interests of the people were absorbed in a fictitious and tyrannous unity. The alternative was the spirit of English liberty, which substituted diversity for uniformity and harmony for unity. In the case of the United States, the spirit of English liberty produced the original constitution as a compromise based on "mutual concessions ... between opposite principles, neither of which could prevail."[71] Such mutual concessions, Acton said, were also the basis of Calhoun's concurrent majority. In other situations, the spirit of English liberty enabled several nations or races to coexist under the same state, thereby reviving exhausted nations and giving to every people "an interest in its neighbour." So understood, English liberty was antithetical to the nationalist state, under which "all other nationalities that may be within the boundary ... are exterminated or reduced to servitude."[72] For Acton, the spirit of English liberty produced an understanding of federalism that rejected extremist politics, whether based on principle or on nationality.

Canadian Confederation also relied on English liberty and the spirit of compromise. Despite such similarities, Actonian federalism has limited relevance for the critical issues of Confederation. In the case of Canada, it produces a critique of the nationalist state and a justification of the multinational state. Confederation shared such objectives, but it also attempted to create a single nation. Put differently, federalism, in the sense presupposed by Canadian Confederation, "is a device designed to cope with the problem of how distinct communities can live a common life together without ceasing to be distinct communities."[73] The Fathers of Confederation did not merely believe that nationalities could coexist under the same state; they also sought to create a great and single nation, united by a strong central government and a common nationality. Moreover, the Fathers had to confront the problem of minorities within the provinces, a problem that Actonian federalism does not address. Acton's federalism is premised on the rejection of absolutist and extremist politics. The Fathers of Confederation also rejected extremist politics, but coupled this rejection with a conception of nationhood that was not confined to the boundaries set by Lord Acton.

In their effort to create a great nation, the Fathers of Confederation accepted federalism. The Framers of the United States Constitution also sought to create a great nation, but unlike the Canadian Fathers, they could take the nation for granted, provided they solved the problem of republican liberty. Madison's solution was the idea of a compound republic. Years later, Calhoun attempted to improve on his checks and balances by adding the idea of a concurrent majority. But American theories of federalism contained assumptions that the Fathers of Confederation implicitly rejected. "The last thing the Canadian delegates wanted," Jennifer Smith has written, "was the petty and paralyzing intrusion of local concerns in their proposed new national forum."[74] Under the proposed Confederation, the federal principle would help to ensure that local and particular concerns were left at the local level. Madison and Calhoun made no such assumption. The Fathers of Confederation took pains to distinguish their federalism from the American form. For some of the Fathers, federalism, even in its Canadian version, represented an uneasy compromise. For others, such as George-Étienne Cartier, Confederation promised to create a nation that solved Canadian problems.

CONCLUSION

Canadian Confederation, it is often noted, was not a popular movement, but "the work of a few master-builders."[75] In the debates of 1865, Christopher Dunkin made a similar observation. The United States Constitution, he said, was adopted after a "successful war of independence," in which the men who framed it had gone "shoulder to shoulder" through a great trial, and "their entire communities ... had been united as one man." Moreover, Americans had tried "the system of mere confederation" and were ready "to build up a great nationality that should endure in the future." But Canadian Confederation, Dunkin observed, was "very different indeed" because it was preceded, not by a common struggle, but by a struggle that "pitted our public men one against another, and ... even our faiths and races against each other."[76] Such difficulties, coupled with the belief that federalism had contributed to the American Civil War, undermined the popularity of Canadian Confederation. Confederation, it has been said, "was imposed on British North America by ingenuity, luck, courage and sheer force."[77] But neither its opponents nor its supporters took its accomplishment for granted. At the Quebec Conference of 1864 and after, Canadians engaged in a full and famous debate. That debate contains a plurality of constitutional visions, in which ideas about imperial government were opposed to beliefs about popular sovereignty, and the war of races and nationalities was opposed to ethnic harmony and to the Canadian political nationality.

Macdonald initially favoured a unitary state; his opponents either favoured "state sovereignty" as embodied in a "real confederation" or defended the status quo. Cartier provided middle ground. Moreover, his middle ground differed in important respects from that provided by Madison some eighty years before. Madison had addressed the problem of republican liberty; Cartier confronted the issues of multiple identities, the war of races, and minority rights. In the debates of 1865, he not only addressed those problems, but he also believed that solutions were at hand. The years after Confederation demonstrated that Cartier's middle ground was politically and philosophically less secure than he seemed to suppose in 1865. Canadians continued to address issues that Confederation was to have settled, and they witnessed the articulation of new constitutional visions. Even if Cartier did not solve the problems of Canadian nationhood, he did provide a new beginning for federalist theory.

CHAPTER THREE

Patriation Revisited:
The Neglected Implications of Section 94

The Confederation debates of 1865 record a significant Canadian debate on federalism, yet they contain almost no discussion of the difficult issue of constitutional amendment. The Fathers of Confederation left to future generations a problem and a challenge. The problem was to settle the issue of constitutional amendment and thereby determine the location of sovereignty within the Canadian federation. The challenge was to fill the constitutional gap in a way that preserved the integrity of the settlement of 1867 and thus respected the intentions of the Fathers. No problem has been more difficult to solve and no challenge more difficult to meet. The constitutional gap was eventually filled, but only after repeated political failures culminated in a judicial determination. That determination provided a basis for a political compromise that, in turn, led to the adoption of the Constitution Act, 1982.[1] But the result has pleased almost no one.[2] Writing a decade after the patriation decision, Pierre Trudeau speculated that "Canada's future would have been more assured" if the Supreme Court had refused to intervene.[3] Peter Russell, among others, has expressed a similar concern about the country's future. "There was a profound sense," he writes, "in which the patriation round was inadequate as a resolution of Canada's constitutional debate." Patriation, he adds, "might make it more difficult than ever for Canadians to constitute themselves a sovereign people."[4]

The patriation decision, as Trudeau and others have suggested, is "arguably the most important decision [the Supreme Court] ever rendered or ever will render." What makes the decision so important is that it "went to the very roots of the Constitution, determining ... the nature of the constituent power for Canada."[5] That determination required the court to say a great deal about federalism and about Confederation itself. What a majority of the judges decided was that, although there were no legal limits on the power of the federal parliament to request of the British Crown amendments affecting provincial powers, constitutional convention required substantial provincial consent for such amendments. In a subsequent decision, the court elaborated its ruling, holding that Quebec possessed no right of veto and that substantial consent could be achieved even if Quebec dissented. Geoffrey Marshall, a British constitutional theorist, has glossed the patriation ruling as follows: "Canada's Federal system ... was legally speaking at the mercy of its central government and [the British] Parliament" because they could turn "Canada into a unitary state ... or any kind of state." There also existed a conventional rule of substantial provincial consent, Marshall goes on to say, the purpose of which was to protect the federal character of the Canadian constitutional order.[6]

What is remarkable about the patriation decision is that, by requiring only substantial consent, it provided Quebec and other provinces with much less protection than the only provision of the British North America Act dealing with the amendments to the division of powers. The irony and tragedy of the decision is that it fundamentally affected the future of Canada, yet it neglected a key constitutional provision and, arguably, subverted both the original intentions of the Fathers and the protection they had afforded to federalism. No less remarkable are the reasons for the court's neglect of a key constitutional provision. One reason is the misleading heading of the provision. Had it been headed "Transferring Constitutional Jurisdiction," rather than "Uniformity of Laws," its importance might have been more apparent.[7] There are also two deeper reasons. First, the majority of the court and many constitutional scholars assume that federalism is to be found only in the division of powers. As Noel Lyon has critically observed, "the Canadian Constitution is just the English constitution with a federal division of legislative power tacked on."[8] Second, lawyers and judges, in Canada and elsewhere, are ill-disposed to arguments based upon the structure of the constitution or its major provisions. As Charles Black has noted, they prefer "the method of ... exegesis of the particular textual passage ... as opposed to the method of inference from the structure and relationships created by the constitution."[9] Judges dominated by these assumptions are not likely to see federalism in section 94 of the BNA Act or to consider its implications for formal amendment. Justices Martland and Ritchie, however, rejected both assumptions, believing that "the dominant principle of Canadian constitutional law is federalism" and that "each level of government should not be permitted to encroach on the other, either directly or indirectly."[10] But by focusing on other constitutional provisions to the exclusion of section 94, they not only weakened their own arguments, but also missed an opportunity to challenge the centralist interpretation of Canadian federalism. As a result, an understanding of Canada prevailed and a future unfolded that were based on a misunderstanding of the legal and moral foundations of Confederation.

THE ORTHODOX UNDERSTANDING OF SECTION 94 AND ITS PUZZLES

Uniformity of Laws in Ontario, Nova Scotia and New Brunswick
Notwithstanding anything in this Act, the Parliament of Canada may make Provision for the Uniformity of all or any of the Laws relative to Property and Civil Rights in Ontario, Nova Scotia, and New Brunswick, and of the Procedure of all or any of the Courts in Those Three Provinces, and from and after the passing of any Act in that Behalf the Power of the Parliament of Canada to make Laws in relation to any Matter comprised in any such Act shall, notwithstanding anything in this Act, be unrestricted; but any Act of the Parliament of Canada making Provision for such Uniformity shall not have effect in any Province unless and until it is adopted and enacted as Law by the Legislature thereof.
British North America Act, 1867, section 94

It may at first seem paradoxical to suggest that Justices Martland and Ritchie might have improved their argument for a legal requirement of provincial consent in the amending process by invoking section 94 of the BNA Act, for this view encounters the instant objection that this provision constitutes one of the most centralizing features of the Canadian constitution. Sir Kenneth Wheare might have invoked it, along with the powers of disallowance and reservation, federal appointment of all important judicial posts, and the "peace, order and good government" clause, to strengthen his suggestion that the Canadian constitution is not federal at all but merely quasi-federal.[11] But surely the provinces cannot invoke it. Those who seek to advance provincial autonomy would be ill-advised to rest their case upon the very provision intended to deprive the provinces of that autonomy. That, at least, is the orthodox understanding of section 94 as expounded, notably, in Frank Scott's classic essay on the subject.

Himself no friend of provincial autonomy, Scott wrote his essay shortly after, as he said, "the Privy Council judgments of Mr Bennet's 'New Deal' Statutes suddenly exposed the damage wrought by decentralizing judicial interpretation."[12] His express purpose was to point to section 94 as a way "out of the legal impasse into which the courts had led the country."[13] The occasion also provided Scott with an opportunity to advance views which he would develop more fully some five years later in "The Special Nature of Canadian Federalism."[14] That essay contains one of the most centralist interpretations of the Canadian constitution ever written, going beyond even Kenneth Wheare's suggestion that the constitution is merely quasi-federal. In his earlier essay, Scott was only slightly less ambitious. He sought answers to the following questions: "what was the intention of section 94[?] Did it permit the curtailment of provincial sovereignty or did it not? Was 'federalism' an essential part of the Confederation arrangement or was it not?"[15] Scott's answer was that section 94 did permit the curtailment of provincial sovereignty and that federalism was not an essential part of the Confederation agreement. For the federal Parliament could acquire, through section 94, not only many of the powers that the Privy Council had mistakenly allocated to the provinces, but also other powers of merely local interest in the provinces.

To show that there could be no historical or constitutional objections to his proposal, Scott reviewed the evidence. The Fathers of Confederation, he suggested, desiring a legislative union, but being unable to attain one at that time, included section 94 so that in a more favourable political climate "an easy way should be left open for an even closer integration of the provinces."[16] All that would be required to transfer constitutional jurisdiction over property and civil rights, in whole or in part, to the federal Parliament would be that the respective provinces (Ontario, Nova Scotia, and New Brunswick) adopt and enact federal legislation on that subject-matter. Although it cannot be simply assumed that section 94 applies to provinces that have joined Confederation since 1867, Scott argued that it applies to all the now-existing common law provinces.[17] Only Quebec, he insisted, is excluded from its operation. Quebec is, in a sense, "less free than her sister provinces, who may employ section 94,"[18] for "no action under that section can include Quebec even if Quebec wants to be included. Quebec is constitutionally incapable of giving up her legislative powers except by formal amendment."[19]

Scott's understanding of section 94 is not mistaken so much as one-sided. This one-sidedness is highlighted by his reliance on statements by Sir John A. Macdonald to establish the character and purpose of section 94, and especially by his failure to cite even those statements in full. Statements by Macdonald are surely suspect; they cannot be re-garded as politically neutral or as representing the views of the other Fathers. Scott, in any case, fails to cite Macdonald's statement that "to prevent local interests from being over-ridden, the same section [94] makes provision, that ... no change ... should have the force ... of law ... until sanctioned by the Legislature of that province."[20] Macdonald's hope – "that the first act of the Confederate Government should be to procure an assimilation of the statutory law of all those provinces"[21] – proved vain. The common law provinces may have desired uniform legislation, but they desired to retain their autonomy and their juris-diction over property and civil rights even more.

Macdonald's view aside, Scott himself fails to realize adequately that section 94 is a Janus-like constitutional provision, looking not only to the federal centralization desired by Macdonald, but also to the provincial autonomy desired by his opponents. He sees that although section 94 bears the somewhat deceptive heading "Uniformity of Laws," it is not merely such a provision. It is, more significantly, a pro-vision for overturning the decisions of the highest court, for irre-trievably transferring jurisdiction over property and civil rights to the federal Parliament.[22] But he does not grasp all the implications of the other side of section 94, that no transfer of jurisdiction occurs unless federal legislation *is adopted and enacted by the provinces affected*. Since the provinces affected must consent to a change in the distribution of powers, section 94, far from restricting either the sovereignty of the provinces or federalism, gives recognition to them. Had Scott fully acknowledged this feature of section 94, he could not have ob-jected to the decisions in *Citizens Insurance Company v. Parsons*[23] on the ground that "the section intended to remove provincial jurisdiction has been used to enlarge it."[24] Since section 94 does give recognition to provincial sovereignty and federalism, it is hardly surprising that the Privy Council relied on that provision to prevent federal en-croachment upon 92(13) by giving a broad and liberal interpretation to the phrase "property and civil rights in the Provinces."

The provincial consent requirement in section 94 creates difficulties not only for Scott's centralist interpretation of the Canadian constitution, but also for his understanding of formal amendment. "Only the ancient doctrine of Imperial sovereignty," he has suggested, "prevented a full power of amendment vesting in Ottawa's hands. It was not any concept of federalism ... that stood in the way."[25] The most cogent reason for rejecting this interpretation of the amending power is section 94 itself. Scott's understanding of formal amendment can be true only if it is assumed that the Fathers of Confederation committed a constitutional absurdity by including section 94 in the BNA Act. A federal government, committed to uniform law, would surely not proceed by way of a provision that made provincial consent mandatory and excluded Quebec when it could accomplish its objective without provincial consent and include that province through the amending power. This consideration also tells against the argument – originated by Scott and developed by Chief Justice Laskin and Justices Estey and McIntyre – that federalism can have no place in the amending process because the BNA Act "has not created a perfect or ideal federal state" but has "accorded a measure of paramountcy to the federal Parliament."[26] That the Fathers intended to confer a measure of paramountcy upon the federal Parliament cannot be doubted. But they cannot have intended to confer upon it power to modify the division of powers at its whim. Had they intended to do so, they would not have included section 94 in the BNA Act.

The provincial consent requirement creates special difficulties for Scott's explanation of Quebec's exclusion from section 94. If that section were merely a uniformity-of-law provision (a provision for removing comparatively unimportant divergences and inconsistencies in the common law of the provinces), then Quebec's exclusion, given its possession of a system of civil law, would be unproblematic. But section 94 is no such provision. It is a provision for amending the division of powers, for transferring constitutional jurisdiction over property and civil rights to the federal Parliament. And once that transfer is effected, the federal Parliament is not even required to maintain uniform laws since it acquires unrestricted jurisdiction by the transfer. To suggest, therefore, as Scott has, that "the exception of Quebec is understandable for there the law differs in origin and character"[27] is to regard section 94 merely as a uniformity-of-law provision and to neglect its importance for constitutional change. If section 94 is a means of altering the division of powers (as Scott insists), it makes no more, and no less, logical sense to suggest (1) that Quebec is excluded from this section because of its possession of a system of civil law than it does to suggest (2) that Quebec is unable to transfer, through the formal amendment power, its jurisdiction over property and civil rights to the federal Parliament because of its possession of a system of civil law. Since Scott expressly denies the latter, he should, logically, deny the former as well.

But he provides a second reason for Quebec's exclusion without fully appreciating how it differs from the first. He also suggests that "Quebec was excluded from the provision, because the guaranteeing of her control over her own basic law was part of the racial agreement implicit in the constitution."[28] The second reason is not necessarily inconsistent with the first, but it does introduce an additional consideration, namely, that to have included Quebec in section 94 would have somehow diminished (or failed to guarantee) its control over its own basic law. If such were the case, Quebec's exclusion would be understandable. But since, as was suggested earlier, section 94 in no way infringes upon provincial sovereignty because no transfer of jurisdiction takes place without provincial consent, Quebec's inclusion in this provision would not have diminished its sovereignty or its control over its basic law and would not have infringed upon any racial agreement that might have been thought to be implicit in the constitution. Quebec's inclusion in section 94 would no more diminish or fail to guarantee its control over its basic law than would its inclusion in a formal amending procedure that permitted modification, with its consent, of its jurisdiction over property and civil rights.

Quebec's exclusion from section 94 becomes more of a puzzle once it is recalled or assumed (as Scott does) that its jurisdiction over property and civil rights can be transferred to the federal Parliament by formal constitutional amendment. To be sure, aside from the universally admitted proposition that the BNA Act, being a British statute, requires, with some exceptions, action by the British Parliament for its amendment, neither subsequent practices nor judicial pronouncements have put to rest the controversy surrounding formal amendment. But if these difficulties are put to one side, and an attempt is made to imagine an amending formula that does not detract from Quebec's sovereignty, it is reasonably plain that its requirements would not need to be more stringent than those of section 94. Such an amending formula would specify that "Quebec's jurisdiction over property and civil rights cannot be modified without its consent." Yet it is just such a requirement that would have been satisfied had

Quebec been included in section 94. An amending formula that requires Quebec's consent does not afford the province greater protection than section 94 would have; one that requires only "substantial provincial consent"[29] affords Quebec – and the other provinces as well – considerably less protection.

STRUCTURAL REASONING AND SECTION 94

The orthodox understanding of section 94 is unsound, then, for descriptive and explanatory reasons. As a descriptive account, it focuses on certain important aspects of section 94 to the exclusion of other, equally essential features. And its explanatory power is limited because it cannot provide a logically coherent reason for Quebec's exclusion. It is at this point that the role of structural argument in constitutional law becomes important. A formal amending procedure can be inferred from section 94 precisely because that provision supplies a constitutionally sanctioned means of altering the division of powers. That amending procedure, it will be suggested below, takes account of the salient features of section 94 and explains Quebec's exclusion. And because that amending procedure avoids all the difficulties encountered by amending procedures that conflict with section 94, it is superior to them on logical grounds. But it is superior to them on other grounds as well, for a structural argument based on section 94 both illuminates the "intentions" of the Fathers of Confederation and also takes account of the role of the British Parliament in the amending process.

Structural reasoning based on section 94 encounters the immediate objection that such reasoning is bound to be inappropriate because section 94 and formal amendment constitute two distinct heads of constitutional power. Or as Chief Justice Laskin and Justices Estey and McIntyre suggested in a different context, a limited legislature, such as the federal government, is not precluded "from achieving directly under one head of power [formal amendment] what it could not do directly under another."[30] But that objection loses much of its force once it is recalled that the formal-amendment head of power is, at least with respect to the division of powers, largely undefined. And because it is undefined, structural reasoning based on section 94, which provides an explicit and textually based constitutional means of altering the division of powers, is preferable to reasoning based on unclear and contested political or constitutional practices, nondivision-of-powers provisions of the BNA Act, the preamble (federally united) to the act, abstract conceptions of federalism, or the characteristics of the American or Commonwealth federal constitutions. Moreover, the constitutional significance of section 94 is enhanced, rather than diminished, by the fact that the Fathers of Confederation gave only slight attention to the question of formal amendment, regarding it as a problem that could be faced at a later time.[31] For by including section 94, they provided an important indication of what they regarded as a legitimate means of effecting constitutional changes to an essential aspect of the division of powers.

A structural argument based on section 94 relies on the following assumption: since section 94 is a means of altering the division of powers without recourse to formal amendment, the requirements of the latter must be more stringent than those of the former. This assumption is justified on two grounds. First, if the assumption did not hold, section 94 would be constitutionally superfluous because it is difficult to imagine under what circumstances section 94 would be used. Political actors would almost certainly choose the less stringent means over the more stringent ones. Second, the assumption is politically justified because the point of amending formulas is to secure rights to political actors either by making their participation mandatory or, alternatively, by putting certain subjects beyond the reach of the amending power; but if formal amendment were less stringent than section 94, that section could not secure the rights it was intended to guarantee.

All this might be conceded. Yet objection might still be made that "the greater stringency requirement" is satisfied by the mere fact that formal amendment requires action by the British Parliament, whereas section 94 does not. Section 91(1) of the BNA Act might be thought to support this line of argument, for the purpose of that provision was to introduce greater flexibility in the Canadian constitution by enabling the federal Parliament to modify those parts of the constitution that concerned only itself without having to resort (as was the case before 1949) to the British Parliament. But analogical reasoning from section 91(1) to section 94 is almost certainly misleading because, unlike the former, which is essentially a "housekeeping" provision,[32] section 94 is concerned with the division of powers that is the heart of federalism.

In matters of federalism, the rigidity of formal amendment has resulted not from the role of the British Parliament so much as from the role of the provinces. The failure of the Fathers of Confederation to include a formal amendment procedure in the BNA Act implied neither that the British Parliament was intended to modify the Canadian constitution at its whim nor that federalism was to have no place in the amending process. The former was politically, though not legally, unthinkable in 1867. And the latter, as we have seen, can be true only if it is assumed that the Fathers committed a constitutional absurdity by including section 94 in the BNA Act. But federalism was important because, as a recent writer on constitutional amendment has observed, "the Imperial authorities were intended to assume a protective stance in relation to the provinces, a kind of trustee role."[33] The imperial Parliament could not perform that role without consulting the interests of the provinces, and if it allowed the provinces to be deprived of their jurisdiction over property and civil rights without their consent, it would not have performed a trustee role at all.

That role came to an end with the Statute of Westminster, but the British Parliament did not suddenly emerge as the mere agent of the Canadian Parliament.[34] The British Parliament is still free, in British legal theory, to repeal the Statute of Westminster and modify the Canadian constitution at its whim. But in Canadian legal theory, it is not free to do these things because acts of the British Parliament that conflict with the requirements of the Canadian constitution for constitutional change have the same status in Canada as statutes enacted for Canada by the United States. They have, Peter Hogg has suggested, no status at all – they are nullities – because "Canada is no longer a British colony."[35] The British Parliament is free, however, to ignore at least some requests of the federal Parliament for constitutional change because not all such requests can be regarded as proper Canadian requests. But *which* requests it can ignore has remained controversial because the meaning of a "proper Canadian request" is unsettled.[36] If the British Parliament refused to act upon requests that conflict with section 94, it would prevent, as Macdonald said of the consent requirement in that section, "local interests from being over-ridden" by the federal government. Canada would not revert to colonial status because of such action of the British Parliament, but the integrity of its constitution would be maintained.

With respect to section 94, then, a formal amending procedure would have to be more stringent in terms of the role of the provinces. Since that provision requires the consent of the federal Parliament and the provinces, but excludes Quebec, the amending procedure, in order to avoid inconsistency and paradox, would have to require the consent of those political actors. And since only Quebec is excluded from section 94, it seems plausible to assume that it is Quebec's role that must give the amending procedure its greater stringency or rigidity. This greater stringency could be introduced in one of at least three ways: if Quebec's jurisdiction over property and civil rights were an unamendable provision of the constitution; or if Quebec possessed a veto over proposed formal amendments to property and civil rights; or if Quebec's consent and the consent of all other provinces – unanimity – were required for such amendments.

If Quebec's jurisdiction over property and civil rights were constitutionally unamendable, that would certainly demand the province's exclusion from section 94, for otherwise the amending procedure and section 94 would contradict each other. Unamendability also guarantees Quebec's jurisdiction over property and civil rights, but it does so only by restricting that province's sovereignty (or freedom of action). It is hardly surprising, therefore, that Quebec, being the province most concerned with asserting its sovereignty, has never claimed that its jurisdiction over property and civil rights cannot be modified even with its consent. Quebec has proceeded on the opposite assumption and has thrice consented to changes in its jurisdiction over property and civil rights by formal amendment.[37] Both of these facts make this version of the greater stringency requirement unacceptable.

The second version of the greater stringency requirement – a veto for Quebec – not only explains its exclusion from section 94 but also avoids the difficulties connected with unamendability. If Quebec can veto proposed formal amendments to property and civil rights, that province might be excluded from section 94 on the ground that this section is a way around its veto. A veto for Quebec also avoids the difficulties connected with unamendability because it guarantees that province's jurisdiction over property and civil rights without restricting its sovereignty, and such a veto is consistent with the formal amendments to property and civil rights that have occurred. The principal difficulty with a veto for Quebec is a semantic one. It has been suggested, for example, that "the Tremblay commission ... [deplored] changes that have made in the B.N.A. Act without Quebec's consent. The Commissioners' general approach implied that Quebec ... should have a right [of] veto."[38] But Quebec's right of veto seems to imply little more than that its consent is required. If Quebec's consent were required, while every other province need not consent, then Quebec might be described as possessing a veto. But a formal amending procedure constructed from section 94 requires the individual consent of the common law provinces. With respect to section 94, then, Quebec's veto collapses into Quebec's consent.

A formal amending procedure that required the consent of all provinces, including Quebec, would be more stringent than section 94 because the former requires unanimity whereas the latter does not. It explains and justifies Quebec's exclusion from section 94 in this way: if unanimity were required to amend the federal distribution of powers in the BNA Act, Quebec's long-standing belief that its control over its basic law is part of the racial agreement implicit in the constitution would make amendments to the property and civil rights section (92[13]) highly improbable, even though all the common law provinces might favour them.[39] The point of section 94, then, is to overcome this special difficulty of unanimity as applied to 92(13) by enabling provinces other than Quebec to modify, if they so choose, their jurisdiction over property and civil rights. And because Quebec was and still is the province most committed to retaining its jurisdiction over property and civil rights, and to preventing formal amendments to 92(13), it would have made little sense – given the point of section 94 – to have included Quebec in that provision. Moreover, such a constitutional requirement would also be consistent with the formal amendments to the division of powers that occurred prior to the Constitution Act, since those amendments had unanimous provincial consent.[40]

THE SUPREME COURT AND CONSTITUTIONAL AMENDMENT

The Supreme Court took no notice of section 94 in its two decisions on constitutional amendment. Instead, it focused on the role of convention, deciding that while there were no legal restraints on the power of the Senate and House of Commons to request of the British Parliament amendments that affected provincial powers,[41] constitutional convention required substantial provincial consent for such requests.[42] The court also relied on convention to dispose of Quebec's right of veto, ruling that Quebec could not possibly possess a veto because none of the other political actors had ever recognized its alleged veto.[43] Both decisions are surprising because, despite the assertions of Justices Martland and Ritchie to the contrary, sections

91(1), 92(1), and 146 are not the only provisions of the BNA Act dealing with amendments to the constitution.[44] Section 94 deals with
that subject too, and it is more important than any of those provisions
– at least for the issues that were before the court – because it deals
with the division of powers. By requiring only substantial provincial
consent, the court sanctioned a formula that, unlike section 94, allows a common law province to be deprived of its jurisdiction over
property and civil rights without its consent. And by dismissing Quebec's right of veto, the court allowed that province to be deprived of
its jurisdiction over property and civil rights without its consent, even
though Quebec cannot be deprived of that jurisdiction with its consent under section 94. It is surely remarkable that section 94 – the
very provision intended by Macdonald, as Frank Scott put it in a different context, "to remove provincial jurisdiction"[45] – should afford
more protection than two Supreme Court decisions.

The Supreme Court's decisions do, however, afford some protection for some provinces. A constitutional requirement of substantial
provincial consent makes unilateral action by the federal Parliament
politically, though not legally, improbable. And some protection for
some provinces (or states) is all that some conceptions of federalism
require. American federalism, for example, does not demand, except
in one important case, any more than substantial consent: three-
fourths of the states can change the constitution. But substantial consent affords no protection at all for other conceptions of federalism.
"If convention requires only partial [provincial] consent," Chief
Justice Laskin and Justices Estey and McIntyre warned, "it is difficult
to see how the federal concept is thereby protected for, while those
provinces favouring amendment would be pleased, those refusing
consent would claim coercion."[46] Substantial consent may conform to
the logic of the American Constitution, but it manifestly conflicts
with the logic of section 94 of the BNA Act. Section 94 does resemble
one important, though neglected, provision of the American constitution: under Article V, "no state, without its consent, shall be deprived of its equal suffrage in the Senate." That provision implies that
there are limits to substantial consent or majoritarian federalism in
the United States. Section 94 implies that majoritarian federalism has
no application to the division of powers in Canada. And that implication is affirmed by the procedure in the Constitution Act for
amending the division of powers; under it a province cannot be deprived of its legislative power without its consent. If the Supreme

Court's decisions on constitutional amendment are unsatisfactory, it is because their reasoning is unsatisfactory. The court failed to see the implications of an important constitutional provision in the BNA Act, 1867, and it failed to secure the full constitutional autonomy of the provinces because it failed to see the importance of structural argument in Canadian constitutional law.

POLITICAL PERSPECTIVES

As pronouncements on the issue of formal amendment, the Supreme Court rulings have run their course.[47] The decisions made possible the political compromise that led to the Constitution Act, 1982, conferred retroactive judicial legitimacy on it, and thus settled conclusively the patriation issue. Virtually everyone accepts the judicial finality of those decisions and the legality of the Constitutional Act, 1982. What remains unsettled, however, is the question of their wisdom. In essays written in 1983, Donald Smiley and Gil Rémillard accepted the legality of the constitutional changes of 1982, but disputed their wisdom and even their political legitimacy. An exercise in constitutional reform that had as its alleged objective the creation of a more harmonious Canada, Smiley wrote, resulted "in a betrayal of the Quebec electorate, a breach of fundamental constitutional convention, ... and an even more serious Quebec challenge than before to the legitimacy of the Canadian constitutional order."[48] Rémillard expressed similar concerns. For him, however, the crucial issue was the failure of the Supreme Court to give sufficient weight to a democratic conception of legitimacy. Important constitutional changes, he said, were to be judged, not by their conformity to convention, but by their responsiveness to the will of the people. "It should not be concluded that the matter of the 1982 Constitution Act's legitimacy is settled once and for all in Quebec." Only a referendum, he wrote, "could permanently settle the question of its legitimacy."[49]

Pierre Trudeau has also criticized the Supreme Court's patriation ruling. His criticism was written a decade after the ruling, at a time when Canadians were again entangled in constitutional difficulties. The patriation ruling, Trudeau said, produced two sets of problems, which could have been avoided if the Supreme Court had adopted the dissenting opinion formulated by Chief Justice Laskin along with Justices Estey and McIntyre. As Trudeau understood it, the dissenting opinion allowed the federal government to proceed unilaterally with its original patriation amendments. But the majority decided against unilateralism, established a conventional rule of substantial consent, and thereby compelled a new round of political negotiations with the provinces. The majority's ruling, Trudeau said, was unfortunate because it had a detrimental impact on Canada's constitutional development and made the country's existence less secure. As a result of it, the provinces were able to demand changes that included an override clause in the Charter of Rights, an opting-out amending formula, and the removal of the referendum provision. None of the changes, Trudeau insisted, was for the good of Canada.[50] Moreover, the majority's opinion tainted the whole constitutional amendment process with illegitimacy because if a province was left out, it would claim that substantial consent had been denied. Quebec was left out, and according to Trudeau, a fabrication of history has occurred. The fabrication asserts that Quebec "had been humiliated in 1982."[51] In effect, the Supreme Court decision allowed Quebec to become "a political martyr as soon as the memory of the historical events had begun to fade."[52] For Trudeau, these results provided additional evidence that the court should have refused to play a purely political role in the patriation reference and should have allowed the federal government to proceed unilaterally.[53] Part of the difficulty with his conclusion is that it cannot be reconciled either with the logic of section 94 of the BNA Act or with the implicit intentions of the Fathers.

CHAPTER FOUR

Does the Canadian Charter of Rights and Freedoms Rest on a Mistake?

The Canadian Charter of Rights and Freedoms is widely regarded as Pierre Elliott Trudeau's most significant achievement and as the most radical constitutional innovation since Confederation.[1] Early in his career, Trudeau came to believe that Canada needed a charter of human rights, so as to afford greater protection to the inherent and inalienable rights of the individual. But his beliefs have not escaped criticism. As early as 1969, Donald Smiley rejected "the rationale of the [proposed] Charter published under the name of Mr Trudeau" because it was "pretentious, misleading, and intellectually shoddy."[2] Smiley conceded, though, that a stronger case than Trudeau's 1968 statement might be made for an entrenched charter. Twenty years later, in a book that reviewed judicial performance under the enacted Charter, Michael Mandel arrived at a much stronger conclusion. "In every realm, and whether on its best or worst behaviour," Mandel wrote, "the Charter's basic claims have been shown to be fraudulent."[3] What makes such a conclusion important is that it is widely shared by Charter sceptics. Many of those who share it also believe that they should do whatever they can to de-legitimate the Charter.[4]

Not only do Charter sceptics raise important questions about the political role of judges, but they have also exposed what appear to be irresolvable dilemmas in Trudeau's constitutional vision. What may be the central dilemma of the Charter arises because those who supported its adoption were motivated by the desire to promote national unity; yet according to Charter sceptics, rights exaggerate the anti-social aspects of our natures, lead to more rather than less conflict, and are destructive of community.[5] In the very act of enforcing the Charter, therefore, judges and legislators will undermine both its fundamental political objective and the cooperative basis on which our society rests. There is, of course, an easy way out of this dilemma. The Charter does not give absolute protection to rights; it subjects them to reasonable limits and to the requirements of a free and democratic society. Moreover, the reasonable-limits clause (on one understanding of it) enables judges to avoid questions of rights altogether by deferring to democratically elected legislators, who can (by appealing to the same provision) implement not rights but the common good. To solve the dilemma of the Charter, therefore, judges and legislators need only to appeal to the reasonable-limits clause. But this is an odd solution. It supposes that the Charter rests on a mistake and that the reasonable-limits clause is a way around the mistake. The clause becomes a provision for taking away all the rights that the Charter appears to confer.

What such considerations demonstrate is the importance of addressing fundamental questions of political theory if the Charter is to make any sense at all. The crucial provision of the Charter is the reasonable-limits clause; but to make sense of that provision, it is necessary to address the issues that divide rights-based liberals and their critics. Is the reasonable-limits clause a device for saving the Charter from itself, or is it an essential aspect of a coherent and defensible liberalism? Even this question takes too much for granted. The Charter is only one aspect of the Canadian Constitution, and the most recent addition to it. Moreover, the chief architect of the Charter was primarily concerned with the problems of federalism and with how a charter of rights would contribute to their solution. Yet federalism is itself contentious, and that makes understanding the Charter even more difficult. There is, finally, the issue of judicial power, which can frustrate Trudeau's intention in advocating a charter of rights. If the Charter merely transforms judges into policy makers, then they can rely on their own subjective values, and the Charter becomes whatever the judges want it to be.

The Charter raises not one but three theoretical disputes. Behind it are the competing theories of federalism; within it are the issues that divide rights-based liberals and their critics; and presupposed by it are the conflicting images of judicial power. To make sense of the Charter – to see if it rests on a mistake – it is necessary to link these disputes and to seek a common solution to them. The outlines of that solution can be found in Trudeau's political philosophy and in his commitment to a more just society. From the perspective of *his* philosophy, the Charter is not about the centralization of power or the legalization of politics, nor even about nation-building. It is about liberal justice: how a policy of liberal justice can help to solve the problems of Canadian federalism; how liberal justice can serve to unite an increasingly pluralistic and multicultural society; and how the same policy of justice can guide judges in arriving at decisions for such a society.

FEDERALISM, JUSTICE, AND THE CHARTER

For many English Canadians, federalism is either a pragmatic device or a regrettable political compromise or a stage in the evolution to a unitary state.[6] Pierre Trudeau, however, saw federalism as "a product of reason in politics," providing unity in the face of emotional, territorial, religious, linguistic, and other cleavages.[7] Canadian federalism, he told the American Congress, was "a brilliant prototype for the moulding of tomorrow's civilization."[8] But at the very heart of federalism was the "terrible paradox" of self-determination, which threatened to destroy it.[9] The Charter of Rights would contribute to the resolution of this paradox, and it would do so by linking the theory of federalism to the theory of justice. The Charter would take the place of "the glue of nationalism," which threatened to destroy federalism, and it would help to ensure that "the title of the state to govern and the extent of its authority will be conditional upon rational justification."[10]

To think of the Charter in this way is to offer a reconstruction of Trudeau's political theory rather than a literal reading of it.[11] And yet his political theory is taken seriously only if it is reconstructed. For not only were his views expounded over the course of four decades, but some of them belong to Trudeau the journalist, some to Trudeau the political theorist, and still others to Trudeau the statesman and the politician. These differences help to explain why there have already appeared so many different interpretations of the Charter. For those concerned with Trudeau the politician, it is a contrivance for avoiding the real issues that Canada faces, such as intrastate federalism, and it gives Canadians a false contentment with institutions that are in a state of decay.[12] Those concerned with Trudeau the statesman see the Charter as a nation-building device, designed to strengthen national unity by giving force and meaning to Canadian citizenship.[13] But neither view captures Trudeau the political theorist.[14]

As a political theorist, Trudeau was first of all a liberal who found "tyranny completely intolerable."[15] But liberty was itself problematic and figured not in one but in two of the questions that most concerned him. The first problem pertained to the "conditions of progress in advanced societies," which it was the function of political science to seek and define. What form of government secures progress? The second question was the "oldest problem of political philosophy." How, Trudeau asked, "can an individual be reconciled with a society?" How can authority be justified "without destroying the independence of human beings in the process."[16]

It is possible to provide a single answer to both questions, to phrase the answer in terms of federalism, and to see the outlines of it in Trudeau's most famous essay. At the heart of "Federalism, Nationalism, and Reason" is both a paradox and a solution: federalism is made necessary by the principle of self-determination since most states consist of several distinct groups; yet the same principle threatens to destroy federalism since each group can demand a state of its own.[17] To dissolve the paradox, the federal state must be retained, but the glue of nationalism must be replaced by a principle of reason. In that way, federalism still provides the basis for progress since "the combination of different nations in one State is [a] necessary condition of civilized life";[18] yet the state will now be held together not by nationalism but by a people's consensus "based on reason."[19] The crucial principle of reason turns out to be, however, nothing other than functionalism in politics, which is itself "inseparable from any workable concept of federalism." Federalism, therefore, is the principle of reason. It not only ensures progress; it also solves the problem of legitimacy and with it the problem of political obligation.

Yet this is a strained reading not only of Trudeau's famous essay, but of his political philosophy as a whole. It gives too much weight to his belief in federalism and too little to his other commitments.[20] Trudeau was not only a federalist; he was also a multiculturalist. He did not simply believe in freedom and progress; he also valued justice and individual rights. In fact, Trudeau insisted that his most basic concern was not federalism but justice. "The just society," the phrase for which he is no less famous than for his theory of federalism, was no "catchword or cliché." "Justice," he insisted, "is the problem – the one about which I have been concerned the most, stated the most, thought the most."[21] None of this comment suggests that the just state must replace the federal state. But it does suggest that Trudeau's political theory contains distinct elements, to which coherence must be given, and this coherence can be achieved only by giving primacy to his notion of justice.

This view will seem odd to those who do not wish to take Trudeau – or federalism – seriously. For them, "the just society" is simply rhetoric, and federalism is merely a political compromise. When federalism is viewed in that light, few theoretical questions arise. But Trudeau took federalism seriously. His concern was with federalism as a theory of the state, and with how it would implement (or fail to implement) justice.[22] Here is a new question: those who have thought about federalism philosophically have been almost exclusively concerned with its implications for freedom.[23] Yet a theory of the state must have a theory of justice; and if federalism is a theory of the state, then it too must have a theory of justice.

To uncover federalism's theory of justice, it is necessary to consider its theory of freedom. Federalism promotes freedom because, as Trudeau noted, it divides power.[24] In that way, it not only helps to prevent the corruption that power brings; it also ensures that there will be a multiplicity of power-holders in a society. These power-holders represent the fundamental interests that make up a federal society: dividing power secures areas of independence and self-government to those interests and thus protects their freedom. But there are limits to federalism's theory of freedom. As a constitutional device, federalism secures the freedom of provinces or states, and even of the central government;[25] but it takes no account of the other actors that make up a society. It gives no protection to the freedom of the individual, or even to the freedom of groups – other than to those groups that may control a province or state. Federalism simply fails to provide a satisfactory answer to the most basic question of freedom: it shows how to protect freedom, but not whose freedom should be protected.[26]

Of course, Canada is also a parliamentary democracy. And whatever the inadequacies of federalism might be, Canadians can surely put their faith in parliamentary government to protect individual and minority rights. That argument was accepted by the Fathers of Confederation in 1867; Sterling Lyon of Manitoba (among others) asserted it with great conviction when he opposed the adoption of the Charter in 1981, and it continues to be urged by right-wing Charter sceptics.[27] Moreover, the British record on individual rights – which is commonly believed to be better than the American – is frequently relied on to show the superiority of parliamentary government over an entrenched bill of rights. But there is a crucial difference between Canada and Britain. "So simple a method of protecting human rights as the English use," wrote Frank Scott, "depends upon basic assumptions on which we cannot wholly rely in Canada."[28] Britain is (or has been) a relatively homogeneous society, whereas Canada is heterogeneous and is becoming ever more so. This is the reason why there are limits to the appropriateness of democratic decision-making in Canada. For although it makes sense, within a homogeneous community, to refer disputed questions to a vote, in a society that is as heterogeneous as Canada, a democratic vote will often neglect the interests of minorities.[29]

These difficulties expose the crucial weakness in federalism's theory of justice, a weakness that is exacerbated when federal states are also democracies. Any theory of justice must seek to make decisions acceptable to those who would otherwise be opposed to them. "A man may be disappointed at a just decision," J.R. Lucas has written, but "he should not be angry or indignant." If he has been treated justly, he cannot feel that he has been treated "without due consideration, or that the decision shows that society has no concern for him, or that he is as nothing in its eyes."[30] Yet it is precisely this requirement that federalism fails to satisfy. As a theory of justice, federalism may show that provinces or states are treated with due consideration; but it cannot show that individuals and groups are so treated. For it gives no recognition at all to individuals and groups (except for those groups that may control a province or state), and treats them "as nothing in its eyes."

This failure can be remedied by taking account of what federalism overlooks. A society – even a federal society – is not simply made up of provinces or states; it also consists of individuals and groups, whose claims to freedom and justice are no less urgent. Federalism cannot meet their claims, since it lacks the conceptual resources; yet it is not a matter of abandoning federalism either, since federalism contributes to freedom and justice in its own way. That is the reason why a bill of rights is so important in a federal state. Through it individuals and groups are given recognition in a federal system, and their interests are placed on the same footing as those of other constitutional actors. The Canadian Charter of Rights and Freedoms, Thomas Berger predicted shortly after it was adopted, "will offer minorities [and individuals] a place to stand, ground to defend, and the means for others to come to their aid."[31] Not only has Berger's prediction been confirmed by subsequent events, including the defeat of the Meech Lake and Charlottetown constitutional accords, but Canadian political scientists are increasingly recognizing the importance of Charter Canadians as well as Charter patriotism.[32] In its own way, the

Charter contributes to political justice in a federal state. "C'est en vue
de construire une société plus juste," Trudeau wrote in 1970, "que j'ai
proposé d'inclure dans la Charte canadienne des Droits de l'Homme
certaines mesures de protection que notre legislation ne prévoit pas
encore."[33] By creating a more just society, the Charter also provides
the answer to his question of how an individual is to be "reconciled
with a society."

This way of reading Trudeau's political theory not only gives coherence to his deepest commitments; it also yields a reply to one group of
critics. Those who regard the Charter as irrelevant, who see intrastate
federalism as the only issue, have not taken the problems of federalism seriously enough. For even if this type of federalism is instituted,
the problem of justice remains. Canada does not simply consist of
provinces; it is also made up of individuals and groups, and intrastate
federalism does nothing for them. Moreover, thinking of the Charter
in this way provides a new perspective for those who regard it as a nation-building device. For them, Trudeau was engaged in a great constitutional experiment, which sought to redefine Canada in order to
save it. Such may well have been the intention of Trudeau the statesman. However, for Trudeau the political theorist, the principles of
statecraft were dictated by the requirements of justice, and the cohesion of the nation was based on the soundness of its principles.[34]

LIBERALS AND COMMUNITARIANS

Among Charter sceptics, those who embrace communitarian ideals
have made no mistake about Trudeau's moral and philosophical objectives; they oppose the Charter precisely because it is an exercise in
liberal justice. For them, a policy of liberal justice is necessarily a policy of rights, and rights not only undermine community,[35] but also
lead to endless and unreasonable political debate.[36] A society based
on rights is a divided society, and the assertion of a right is an indication that cooperation and compromise are no longer possible. "It
is uncultured people," Hegel wrote, "who insist most on their rights."[37]
At best, the Charter will only displace conflict: federal-provincial conflict will give way to conflict over rights. At worst, both forms of conflict will exist together, and Canada will seem even less desirable to
communitarians. For them, therefore, the Charter rests on a mistake.
It was designed to promote national unity, yet it will only succeed in
pulling Canadians apart.

The very forces that divide Canadians can be used, however, to promote the ideal of community. The problem with federalism, communitarians insist, is not that it fails to secure justice, but that the provinces have become too large. Some of the earliest advocates of federalism saw it as a device for promoting local self-government, for instilling civic virtue and a concern for the public good.[38] What is needed, therefore, is not judicial action to protect individual and group rights, but a devolution of power and the creation of a realistic and democratic federalism.[39] Even the Charter of Rights can be made to fit this strategy, for it contains a reasonable-limits clause, which enables legislators and judges to enforce not rights but the common good and allows them to educate citizens in the necessity of such a policy. To save the Charter from itself, judges and legislators need only to be persuaded of the soundness of communitarianism.

That might seem an easy task, given the attractiveness of the communitarian ideal and the apparent bleakness of a society based on rights. In fact, the rights society, as Charles Taylor describes it, is synonymous with bureaucratization, centralization, alienation, and atomization; whereas communitarianism calls for "political vision and inventiveness."[40] The heart of the rights society is atomism, which ascribes rights to individuals independent of their social membership and defines human dignity as the ability to frustrate "the process of collective decision-making."[41] Such a society cannot sustain itself, and it rests on a conceptual mistake. We cannot ascribe rights, Taylor explains, "without affirming the worth of certain human capacities"; and since these capacities can be developed only in society, "this commits us to an obligation to belong."[42] The malaise of the rights society can be avoided by embracing communitarianism – or, as Taylor calls it, the participatory society – which defines human dignity as "having a recognized voice in establishing the 'general will.' "[43]

At issue are two visions of the future. Yet one of them may not be accessible to Canadians, and the other misdescribes the foundations of liberalism. The participatory society cannot be created by sheer intellectual daring; its principles must bear a plausible connection to the society that is to be transformed. Since the most basic fact about Canada is that it is a federal society, and since communitarians seek to transform Canadian federalism, what is needed is a compelling account of how the new federalism will differ from the old. Communitarians appear to have a ready answer. The problem with Canadian federalism is that its units have become too large, its organizations too bureaucratic, and power too centralized. Solving these problems means solving the problems of federalism. Yet this solution supposes that federalism is primarily a device for coping with size, and it does not give sufficient weight to the fact that a crucial feature of Canadian federalism is its heterogeneity at the local, as well as the national, level.

A federal state, as A.V. Dicey noted, presupposes union but not unity.[44] That is another way of saying that federalism, as a form of the state, makes sense only if those who make up a federal society wish to retain some of their diversity and autonomy. Of course, they cannot wish to retain all of it, for then there would be no need for the common government that federalism presupposes. Moreover, the diversity that is characteristic of a federal society will never correspond completely with provincial or state boundaries, no matter how precisely they are drawn. The provinces or states will often reflect the very diversities that made the federal state necessary, and these same diversities will reappear within the central government. Devolving power will never eliminate the need for a central government, nor reduce the diversity that is characteristic of the units that make up the federal state. These facts are so well known as to seem obvious and even trivial; yet their implications undermine communitarianism as a viable alternative for Canada.[45]

What is central to communitarianism is precisely what must be absent from federalism: a strong and singular sense of community identity. Communitarianism (or the participatory society), Taylor and others have suggested, "clearly presupposes a strong sense of community identity."[46] A federal society cannot have a strong and singular sense of community identity because federalism commonly presupposes territorial, religious, linguistic, and ethnic cleavages or diversities; yet communitarianism requires such an identity since it forms the core of its conception of human dignity. In a communitarian society, as Taylor explains, "special importance attaches to the fact that we as a whole, or community, decide about ourselves as a whole community."[47] But would such a statement about a federal society such as Canada make sense? The most obvious difficulty with saying it is that a federal society is not a single society, but a number of societies, and each citizen belongs to at least two of them. With which of them should the citizen of a federal society strongly identify? And what if the constituent societies pursue different objectives?

Of course, communitarians are aware of these difficulties. Charles Taylor, for example, is certainly aware of the diversity of Canadian society, and he even celebrates it. He can do so because he distinguishes two senses of community identification in Canada. For Canadians, community identity is not simply a matter of participating in a common decision procedure; it is also a matter, as Taylor points out, of being "British" or an "immigrant" or French Canadian.[48] But this distinction restates the problem rather than solves it. To solve the problem, it is necessary to show how a strong identity based on a common decision procedure can be reconciled with an equally strong identity based on ethnicity or religious belief. According to Taylor, decentralized self-rule is the answer. "[K]eeping power at the regional level," he writes, "... is one very effective form of decentralization, ensuring that important issues are within the scope of communities which ... have a higher sense of community identification than the nation."[49] The decentralization of power to a province or region may ease the tensions between Taylor's two types of community identification, but it cannot eliminate them. The very cleavages that exist in national politics are often found in the provinces and even in local communities, and so the tensions between his two types of community identification are likely to reappear once power is decentralized. That is why communitarianism, with its insistence on the importance of a strong and singular sense of community identity, may not be a coherent alternative for a country as diverse as Canada.

Communitarians, in any case, often provide a caricature of the society that they seek to criticize. When they describe a rights society or the kind of society to which the Charter of Rights will lead, they see only atomism, with its instrumentalist conception of society. The Charter, they believe, will serve only individual and selfish ends, and it will not even promote the duty to belong to society. Communitarians base these conclusions on what they take to be the principles of atomistic liberalism, which form the basis of a rights society; yet liberalism – despite what many communitarians say – does not deny the obligation to belong to society. Take the case of John Locke, who must be an atomist if any liberal is. Did Locke deny the obligation to belong? "God," he writes, "having made man such a creature that in his own judgment it was not good for him to be alone, put him under strong obligations of necessity, convenience, and inclination to drive him into society."[50] Of course, Locke denies that this obligation is sufficient to establish a political society, but his purpose in doing so is to protect the individual from illegitimate power, rather than to atomize society. Much the same purpose is evident in Mill's *On Liberty,* another classic of liberalism. In fact, Mill was so far from denying an obligation to belong that he simply took social membership for granted; his central question was not one that an atomist would ask. "How much of human life," he queried, "should be assigned to individuality, and how much to society?"[51]

What makes freedom and rights so important for liberals is that they protect diversity and autonomy. If diversity is replaced by uniformity, then human beings will not flourish. The differences between human beings are such, Mill wrote, that unless "there is a corresponding diversity in their modes of life," they will neither "obtain their fair share of happiness" nor grow up to "the mental and moral stature" of which they are capable. Diversity in modes of life ensures that "things which are helps to one person towards the cultivation of his higher nature" do not become "hindrances to another."[52] Protecting autonomy, on the other hand, is important because of what it means to be human. If a person "lets the world choose his plan of life for him," then he "has no need of any other faculty than the ape-like one of imitation." If "he chooses his plan for himself, he employs all his faculties." Mill recognized the importance of social custom as well as the wisdom of collective experience; but he insisted that, with respect to self-regarding actions, it was "the privilege and proper condition of a human being, arrived at the maturity of his faculties, to use and interpret experience in his own way."[53] When communitarians think of liberal freedom and liberal rights, however, they see only atomism.

As a liberal document that affirms liberal values, the Canadian Charter of Rights and Freedoms does not need to imply an atomistic society. The easiest reply to the communitarian critique is to say that the Charter is not an atomistic document because, unlike the United States Bill of Rights, it expressly protects the rights of groups and disadvantaged minorities.[54] There is also a more complex answer. Liberals want to preserve diversity and autonomy, yet they do not deny the importance of membership in society. Liberal moral ontology, as Will Kymlicka has noted, regards "individuals ... as members of a particular cultural community, for whom cultural membership is an important good."[55] Moreover, there is a fundamental affinity between a rights society and a federal society: both seek to protect diversity, yet neither denies the importance of the social union. That is why both types of society are also incompatible with communitarianism, which seeks not social union but a strong sense of community identification. For communitarians, such an identification may even displace political justice,

given the importance they attach to community decision-making.[56]
For liberals and federalists, however, there is no substitute for justice.
A society that values diversity must ultimately appeal to justice, for it is
only through a policy of justice that the diverse elements which make
up a society such as Canada are given due consideration.

THE POWER OF JUDGES

If diversity is what makes a policy of justice essential, it is also what
makes justice seem unattainable. A society committed to diversity
embraces a plurality of values, yet there is no easy formula for reconciling them. That is why to one government official "Canada is in danger of becoming a rights-ridden country," a country in which there
will be difficulty in "justifying opposition to any kind of right."[57]
Some critics opposed the adoption of the Charter precisely for that
reason. The Charter, they insisted, would lead to the inflation of
rights and would mask the real issue: who should have power in
Canadian society, judges or legislators?[58] Moreover, the enactment of
the Charter has deepened the concerns of the critics, rather than dis-
pelled them. Critics now say that "the Charter has puffed up lawyers
and courts ... [and] has *legalized* our politics."[59] Or they say that it has
created "a rather strange kind of politics, ... employing the language
and techniques of the court room rather than the more familiar
methods of the politicians on the hustings."[60] Ultimately, the concerns of the critics rest on a deep scepticism not only about rights but
about law itself. If the Charter's theory of justice is not accessible to
us, if there is no way of determining which rights claims are valid
under it, or even when rights can be limited, then the constitutional
text must be meaningless. And if that is the case, then the very idea
of a government of law collapses.

Some legal philosophers have not shied away from this conclusion.
For the Critical Legal Studies Movement – which provides the basis
of a great deal of Charter scepticism – the belief in the rule of law, or
what they also call legalism, is a liberal illusion and all government is
the government of men.[61] Law, a member of the movement has written, "is indeterminate at its core, in its inception, not just in its ap-
plications." The rules of law "derive from structures of thought ... that
are fundamentally contradictory," and "the same body of law, in the
same context, can always lead to contrary results."[62] If this view is
sound, then law itself, and not just the Charter of Rights, rests on a

mistake. The best that any society can do is to select decision-makers whose biases and political preferences accord with those of its citizens.

What is central to the Critical Legal Studies Movement is not its attack on law, however. Critical Legal scholars condemn the rule of law (or legalism) because that is the easiest way to discredit liberal constitutionalism. For them, a liberal constitution isolates individuals from each other, deprecates their social obligations, and ignores the tensions inherent in social membership; and it does so because it confers rights. Critical Legal scholars take over, therefore, the communitarian criticism of the rights society. Yet they also extend that criticism. For in their view, rights are themselves insulated from society, and whatever does that is legalism. Legalism – the view that judges mechanically apply predetermined legal rules – is not simply the false consciousness of liberal constitutionalists; it is what ensures that the judicial application of rights will be untainted by other social values. Law and legalism protect the rights society: that is why Critical Legal scholars attack them.[63]

But why must a liberal constitution possess any of the features that Critical Legal scholars find so objectionable? The Canadian Charter of Rights and Freedoms does not isolate Canadians from each other or deprecate the importance of social membership.[64] All of its rights either presuppose society or are membership rights. The right to vote in an election and to move anywhere in Canada are not rights against society; they are rights to be full members of society. The official language rights are not rights against society; they are rights based on the kind of society that Canada is, and they seek to preserve it. Many of the legal rights are rights against the agents of society, such as the police, who often cannot be controlled by any other means. Even the equality rights – the most controversial of all – can be viewed as membership rights. Those who suffer discrimination do so because they are not regarded as full members of society. Put in another way, Critical Legal scholars have mistaken the origins of human separation. "For community," as Robert Kocis has written, "is not destroyed when you claim a right against me but when I put you in a situation where you feel the need to claim a right. It is not the claiming of a right but wrongful action which harms community."[65] In all these cases, those who assert their rights under the Charter do so to regain or to protect their membership in Canadian society, and not because they consider society unimportant.

Nor does the Charter insulate rights from other social values. Not only must its rights be balanced against each other, but they are subject to "reasonable limits" and to the requirements of a "free and democratic society." The Supreme Court of Canada has interpreted that provision to mean that limits on rights are to be based on the fundamental and underlying values which the Charter seeks to protect, such as the inherent dignity of the human person and the commitment to social justice and equality. Moreover, the court has used the reasonable-limits clause to introduce standards of formal rationality. Thus a Charter right can be limited if the objective in doing so is sufficiently important, if the measures adopted are carefully designed to achieve the objective, if they impair the right or freedom in question as little as possible, and so on.[66] None of this adds up, though, to a theory of justice or even to a theory of legal rationality. That is why Critical Legal scholars may still have a case against the Charter. Even if it contained none of the other failures that they have attributed to it, it might simply confer too much discretion on judges and require them to make what are essentially political decisions. "Notwithstanding the pretensions of intellectual rigour and analytical depth," Joel Bakan has written, "constitutional arguments are really just appeals for faith in the institution of judicial review." They do not provide, he adds, "good reasons for the authority of judicial power."[67] In other words, the failure of the Charter may simply be the failure of law itself.

But to arrive at such a conclusion, it is necessary to expect both too much and too little from the Charter. It is to expect too much because it is to equate law with legalism.[68] It is to suppose that the rule of law is possible only if judges adopt a policy of legalism. But this is to set an impossible task for them and to misunderstand the nature of a constitution. A constitution is not, as legalism supposes, a collection of legal rules that judges mechanically apply; it is a statement of a society's fundamental values, which they must interpret and reconcile.[69] That does not imply, however, that there are no differences between judicial and political decisions, or that judges necessarily assume a legislative role when applying the Charter. For not only must they be guided by the constitutional text, but the ultimate test of a judicial decision is its ability to provide a compelling account of what the Charter requires. That is not the test of a political decision: its ultimate test is the public good. The Charter can be law to judges even though its provisions cannot be mechanically applied by them: for it restricts and guides judges and sets standards of reasoning for them.[70]

Yet the Charter could not perform such functions if law were indeterminate at its core. In that case, the Charter would not have a theory of justice; or – what amounts to the same thing – it would be compatible with every theory of justice. Not even Critical Legal scholars make that assumption. Not even they believe that the Charter can be made to yield (for example) a theory of Platonic justice, according to which everyone must do his or her own task.[71] And despite the reference to the "supremacy of God" in the Charter, no one expects judges to enforce the divine will or to seek the Charter's theory of justice in it. Even the most superficial reading of the Charter rules out these and other conceptions of justice. To read it is to see, moreover, that it does not give primacy to any one value, such as democracy, nor does it reduce justice to following procedures. These features rule out other conceptions of justice and show the irrelevance of much American constitutional theory. Many Americans have been preoccupied with demonstrating that judges should enforce only democratic rights;[72] yet democracy is merely one of the values protected by the Charter. What is striking about it is the sheer number of values that it seeks to protect; and how in protecting those values, it responds (as we have seen) to a problem of federalism.

But the deficiencies of federalism are only one aspect of the Charter's theory of justice. Any such theory must not only specify the values (or interests) that are to be protected; it must also show how conflicts are to be resolved. "Justice," wrote Ernest Barker, "is the reconciler and the synthesis of political values: it is their union in an adjusted and integrated whole."[73] The Charter does this through its reasonable-limits clause. Yet to make sense of that provision, it is necessary to see that the Charter is addressed not only to judges and legislators, but also to ordinary Canadians, and that justice under the Charter must not only be done, but it must be seen to be done. A just decision is not something that can be simply imposed; it is, on the contrary, what can be acknowledged as such even by those whose rights (or interests) are adversely affected. That is why, as J.R. Lucas has written, justice "is the condition under which I and every man can identify with society, feel at one with it, and accept its rulings as my own."[74] Because that is so, the Charter's reasonable-limits clause not only guides judges on how to balance rights against other interests; it also articulates a public conception of justice.[75] By demanding that limits on rights be "reasonable," "prescribed by law," "demonstrably justified," and consistent with a "free and democratic society," the Charter attempts to make those limits acceptable even to those who are adversely affected by them.

There exists, therefore, a theoretical, as well as a practical, response to Critical Legal scholars and all those who regard the Charter as a mere transfer of power to judges. The practical response is that judicial decisions under the Charter – as Patrick Monahan, Richard Sigurdson, and others have shown – do not confirm the worst fears of the critics.[76] Judges have not made democratically elected legislators redundant, nor have they behaved (in the famous words of Judge Learned Hand) as "a bevy of Platonic Guardians."[77] The theoretical response is that the Charter is not simply or even primarily about power. Rather, it (as Trudeau insisted) is about justice in a heterogeneous society. Far from dividing such a society, justice is what holds it together. Ever since Plato, it has been commonly recognized that injustice has "the effect of implanting hatred where it exists."[78] Plato saw why justice was crucial, but he failed to see the importance of a public conception of justice; for having discerned what justice was, or what he believed it to be, he contrived to impose it. The Canadian Charter of Rights and Freedoms confers no such mandate on judges. Not only does it constrain judges, but it requires them to justify their decisions to those affected by them. In that way, the Charter and its reasonable-limits clause are expressions of liberalism. The heart of liberalism is not simply a belief in freedom and rights; there is also, as Jeremy Waldron has noted, the belief that "the social [and legal] should either be made acceptable or be capable of being made acceptable to every last individual."[79] Such a requirement places an enormous burden on judges; yet in a country as heterogeneous as Canada, it is a requirement that they cannot afford to neglect if the Charter is to be perceived as an instrument of justice by all Canadians.

CONCLUSION: THE LIMITS OF JUSTICE

There are limits to what the Charter can accomplish. But these limits are not inherent in the concern for justice that ground it. Nor can they be traced to the notwithstanding clause and the other provisions that were included in the Charter as part of the complex political compromise to gain its acceptance.[80] The most basic limits to the Charter's theory of justice are inherent in human nature itself. For although the Charter is about justice, it grants new resources (or powers) to judges and citizens that can and sometimes will be used to frustrate the requirements of justice. That is why some critics, including second-wave feminists, criticize rights discourse as well as the power concealed by legal formalism. "Law," Carol Smart has written, "is so deaf to core concerns of feminism that feminists should be extremely cautious of how and whether they resort to law." Part of the problem with rights, she explains, is that "rights formulated to protect ... the weak against the strong may be appropriated by the more powerful. Hence the Sex Discrimination Act may be used as much by men as by women." Despite such criticism, she recognizes that "it would hardly be preferable to turn the clock back to a time when women had virtually no rights." Ultimately, her objective is not to abolish law, but to demystify it, to limit its hegemony, and to reorient it towards feminist goals.[81] Chaviva Hosek has expressed similar views. She acknowledges that "women are generally perceived as having emerged among the winners" in the process of entrenching the Charter of Rights, yet she also notes that the gains were difficult to obtain and there remains "justifiable scepticism about what has been achieved for women."[82] But such scepticism did not prevent women's groups from subsequently opposing the (failed) Meech Lake and Charlottetown constitutional accords on the ground that their Charter rights would be adversely affected.[83]

What the feminist critique highlights is that the Charter can and sometimes will be used to oppress women or to advantage individuals and groups that do not need its protection.[84] But that is only one perspective on the Charter, and it may be more a reflection of human nature than of the Canadian Charter of Rights and Freedoms. If the limits to justice are inherent in human nature, then those limits will reappear (in one form or another) even in a political system that lacks a charter of rights. It is no criticism of the Charter to show that there are limits to justice in every political system. And although the Charter grants resources to those who wish to advance only their own interests, it also assists those who are concerned with justice. One of the most important changes brought about by the Charter is the judicialization of public issues. Such a change is no guarantee of justice, yet it contributes to a dialogue of justice that all Canadians can share in.[85] And by providing individuals and minorities with explicit standing in the constitutional order, the Charter not only gives greater prominence to their rights, but also remedies a failure of federalism. To think in these terms is to offer a reinterpretation of Trudeau's political thought and to address the ways in which the Charter does not rest on a mistake.

CHAPTER FIVE

Nation-Saving or Nation-Destroying: The Impact of the Charter of Rights on Canadian Federalism

If the Charter of Rights is less problematic than some critics suppose, it is also more problematic than Trudeau was willing to admit. As a statesman, he had as his great political objective to save Canada from the particularisms that threatened to destroy it. Moreover, he wanted Canada to become "a truly pluralistic state" and "the envied seat of a form of federalism that belongs to tomorrow's world."[1] At the centre of his vision was the Charter of Rights, which was designed to unite Canadians by creating an identity that transcended local and regional boundaries. The Charter, Trudeau said, would provide Canadians with new first principles, similar to those enunciated during the American and French Revolutions. Henceforth, Canada would be a nation characterized by "the primacy of the individual" as well as the "sovereignty of the people," and the people of Canada would be united by "a set of values common to all."[2] In this way, the Charter would respond to separatism, provincialism, and other disintegrative particularisms by appealing to "the purest liberalism," which, in turn, would provide Canadians with "a new beginning."[3]

But the Charter has a limited capacity to promote Canadian unity. Writing in 1994, Peter Russell concluded that Canada "might choke on Charter patriotism."[4] Eleven years earlier, Donald Smiley arrived at a similar conclusion; he said that the Charter would be "fragmenting rather than unifying."[5] In the same year, Alan Cairns estimated that the Charter would not be "an unmixed blessing" since it "may contribute to an aggressive rights-conscious individualism hostile to fraternity and solidarity."[6] Other critics have focused on the Supreme Court as a nationalizing and homogenizing institution under the Charter.[7] Such a court, wrote Rainer Knopff and F.L. Morton in 1985 and again in 1992, might well perform a nation-building function, but it would also "engender the opposition of powerful provincialist forces."[8] Political events – including the failed Meech Lake and Charlottetown constitutional accords – have given urgency to the doubts expressed by the critics. Even Trudeau was recently compelled to ask, "[H]ow can the Charter strengthen Canadian unity when its pursuit has caused such discord?"[9]

My objective in this chapter is to assess the adequacy of the Charter as a nation-saving device and thus to provide a tentative answer to Trudeau's question. The way he has attempted to answer his own question is by suggesting that the origins of contemporary disunity are to be traced, not to the Charter, but to those politicians who seek to dismantle Canada in order to promote their own reactionary agendas. Those same politicians, he suggests, criticize the Charter so as to mask their real objectives.[10] But the difficulties raised by the Charter cannot be settled so easily. It is a complex document, containing a multiplicity of provisions and drawing its justification from a variety of moral and political principles. Two dimensions of the Charter require especially close attention, partly because Trudeau attached great importance to them, but also because he wrongly assumed that they would work together to promote Canadian unity. He believed that the Charter would create a Canadian identity based on the possession of rights *and* that it would establish the sovereignty of the Canadian people. The difficulty is that these two dimensions of the Charter have their roots in divergent political traditions, presuppose radically different conceptions of unity, and differ enormously in their implications for Canadian federalism. Not only do these two dimensions of the Charter work against each other, but one of them is nation-destroying. Part of the answer to Trudeau's question is that the Charter has two dimensions, only one of which is nation-saving and consistent with the kind of unity available to Canadians as a people.

TO SAVE A NATION

The political purpose of the Charter sprang from Trudeau's desire to save Canada from the particularisms that threatened to destroy it. He appears to have been aware of the difficulties of the undertaking, so much so that early in his career, he opposed radical constitutional revision. Radical revision, he said, was "a hornet's nest."[11] But Québécois separatists were instrumental in forcing the issue, and Trudeau became convinced that the constitutional debate had to be carried to a conclusion. Moreover, as the struggle intensified, he also realized that "the whole Constitution [was] up for grabs."[12] The novel strategies necessitated by such a situation eventually became the subject of a secret memorandum, which concluded with an ominous quotation from Machiavelli. "It should be borne in mind," he is quoted as saying, "that there is nothing more difficult to arrange, more doubtful of success, and more dangerous to carry through than initiating changes in a state's constitution."[13]

The way Machiavelli attempted to resolve the difficulty he had raised was by reminding the Prince that great things were never the outcome merely of good fortune; they were always the product of good fortune combined with the indispensable quality of *virtú*. Moreover, he reminded the Prince that a people who had become divided among themselves were incapable of recovering their unity by their own efforts. Seldom or never, he insisted, is any republic or kingdom organized well from the beginning, or totally made over at a later date, except when organized by one man.[14] Machiavelli was quick to add, however, that a kingdom or republic that put its trust in the *virtú* of one man could not endure since "the *virtú* departs with the life of the man." What was needed for the salvation of a kingdom or a republic, he insisted, is not so much to have a prince who will rule prudently while he lives, but rather to have one who will so organize it that its subsequent fortunes come to rest upon the virtues of the people.[15] For Machiavelli, the most important secret of statecraft was to know how this could be done.

Machiavelli believed that the Prince could obtain the required knowledge and uncover the great secret of statecraft by consulting the history of republican Rome, whose glorious example he was urged to imitate. The critics have responded by insisting that, since history does not repeat itself, the study of republican Rome can have only limited relevance.[16] Still, Machiavelli retains his importance. He articulated, even if he did not solve, a great problem of statecraft. How can a people who are divided among themselves attain unity and greatness? So stated, it is a problem that has troubled Canada throughout its history. Moreover, Canada represents an especially difficult case of Machiavelli's problem, partly because it is a federal state.

A federal state strives for unity, yet constitutionalizes division. In a country such as Canada, with its vast territory and distinctive regional and ethnic communities, the divisions of federalism, as Trudeau observed, are indispensable since they permit "a balance to be struck between ... the common good and the particular interest."[17]

Canada might not exist at all if federalism had not been invented. But the advantage of federalism is also its peril. Regional consensus and provincial loyalties can work to the detriment of national allegiances, thereby undermining the unity of the federal state. Such a state presupposes the existence of local, as well as national allegiances, but it cannot take the existence of those allegiances for granted, nor can it assume that they will always work harmoniously together.[18] Federalism can become, as Trudeau said, a system of government whose continued existence is the subject of almost daily concern.[19]

Moreover, Canada is a special kind of federal state, containing two distinct language communities that are capable of forming two complete nations. The situation in Canada has no parallel in the American federal experience, and Lord Durham regarded it as so pernicious in its effects that he advocated the assimilation of the French. The alternative to assimilation, he said, was "two nations warring in the bosom of a single state."[20] The Fathers of Confederation rejected Durham, embraced the federal idea, and guaranteed the continued existence of the French nationality. By doing so, they built into Canada a tension that might eventually destroy it, but the same tension could also work to transform Canada into a distinctive kind of civilization. French and English are equal because, as Trudeau has said, each "has the power to break the country." If they collaborate, however, "Canada could become the envied seat of a form of federalism that belongs to tomorrow's world."[21]

The creation of such a Canada is made more difficult by the existence of other problems, not the least of which is the contemporary transformation of the Canadian identity. In the 1960s and 1970s, Aboriginals, women, ethnic Canadians, gays, and visible minorities, as well as other groups, asserted their distinctiveness and demanded official recognition.[22] "Every single person in Canada," Trudeau noted in 1970, "is now a member of a minority group." Moreover, he praised the Canadian mosaic because it gave "richness and variety to Canadian life."[23] But he did not suppose that the mosaic had replaced federalism or that Quebec had become an insignificant fragment of the mosaic. The challenge was to embrace the mosaic and a more pluralistic conception of Canada without destroying either federalism or Quebec's place in it. For Trudeau, such objectives demanded the redefinition of Canada as a multicultural society within a bilingual framework, together with the renewal of federalism through the adoption of a charter of rights.

Trudeau's strategy was to reshape the Canadian identity and thereby to save the Canadian nation. But Canada is an unusual kind of nation, which makes it a difficult one to save. Some countries, such as the United States, are nations because a single ideology dominates and controls their way of life. Such nations are said to be ideological nations.[24] Other countries are ethnic nations: they define their identity by reference to a common language or culture and rely on their particularistic identity to establish ties between members of the nation.[25] Still others are civic nations. As such, they emphasize the instrumental features of social institutions, use legal criteria to determine membership, and rely on utilitarian considerations to bind individuals to the social order and to each other.[26] There are also consociational nations, that is, nations that combine two or more ethnic communities, establish rigid boundaries between them, and rely on élites to negotiate the common policies required for economic prosperity and military security.[27] But Canada cannot be described as a nation in any of the above senses, a fact which has led some critics to suggest that Canada is "a nation that is not a nation."[28]

Trudeau, however, arrived at a different conclusion. Like Ernest Renan before him, he insisted that the essence of a nation was not language or culture or history, but will. "A nation," Renan said, "is a soul, a spiritual principle ... [based] on the desire to live together, and the will to continue to make the most of the joint inheritance." Moreover, the existence of a nation could not be taken for granted, but must ever be renewed. Just as the existence of the individual was "a continual affirmation of life," Renan wrote, so the existence of "a nation is ... a daily plebiscite."[29] Canada was a nation because Canadians had demonstrated the will to live together.[30] But since it was a federal nation, Canadians had also demonstrated the will to live apart. To complicate matters even more, Canada was undergoing a transformation and was becoming an increasingly heterogeneous and pluralistic society. Such a transformation strengthened the will to live apart because it eroded principles that had served as the basis of the Canadian nation since Confederation. Trudeau's response was to introduce constitutional changes designed to save Canada by strengthening the will of Canadians to live together.

RIGHTS AND THE CANADIAN IDENTITY

At the centre of Trudeau's strategy was the Charter of Rights. The Charter is a complex document: not only were its contents ultimately determined by negotiations between a number of actors, but Trudeau has himself offered multiple and apparently divergent accounts of its nation-saving dimensions. No account of the Charter, however, can neglect his understanding of it as the constitutional instrument that most clearly expresses the Canadian identity and thereby strengthens Canadian unity.[31] As early as 1968, Trudeau advocated a conception of Canada that was knit from coast to coast by persons confident of their rights wherever they might live. Such a Canada, he said, would be a country with which the people could identify.[32] More than two decades later, he expressed a similar view. By enacting the Charter of Rights, he insisted, "firm foundations for a national identity had been laid."[33]

Trudeau believed that the Canadianism of the Charter expressed an identity that the people of Canada would readily embrace. In the years before its adoption, the Charter was known as the "people's package," largely because of its immense popularity. The popularity of the Charter was explained, he said, by the fact that ordinary Canadians regarded Canada as "more than a collection of provinces to be governed through wheeling and dealing. To them, Canada is a true nation, whose ideal is compassion and justice."[34] As the "people's package," the Charter's objective was to express this ideal by creating a more just society. As a just society, Canada was committed, Trudeau said, to providing equal opportunities for all Canadians and to the redistribution of wealth between provinces.[35] The just society would also redress the inequalities between the English and French languages, so that both language communities could consider "the whole of Canada their country and field of endeavour."[36] Finally, as a just society, Canada would protect the fundamental rights of the human person, thereby recognizing her or his absolute dignity and infinite value.[37] In these ways, the Charter would contribute to the creation of a more just society, provide Canadians with a national identity, and strengthen their will to live together.

Moreover, the Charter was the constitutional instrument that gave recognition to the fact that Canada was a nation of minorities. Such recognition protected the rights of minorities and provided them with a constitutional status almost equal to that of other constitutional actors. "We must never forget," Trudeau said, "that, in the long run, a democracy [such as Canada] is judged by the way the majority treats the minority."[38] Throughout its history, Canada had witnessed "the intolerance of the English-speaking majority towards the francophones, the intolerance of whites toward the indigenous populations and non-white immigrants, intolerance toward political and religious dissidents."[39] Not only did such intolerance undermine Canada's image of itself as a just society, but it also threatened national unity. The Charter strengthened that unity by providing minorities with a new constitutional status and creating a Canada with which they could identify.

But if the Charter was to unite Canadians, it could not simply strengthen their will to live together. Canadian unity would be promoted only if the Charter strengthened the will of Canadians to live together without undermining their capacity to live apart. A charter that undermined federalism or the autonomy of the provinces or the distinctiveness of Quebec would not unite Canadians. Trudeau attempted to meet this consideration by assuring them that the Charter would not alter the distribution of power, since it would "not involve any gain by one jurisdiction at the expense of the other."[40] Moreover, it would recognize that, since rights often require implementing legislation, the necessary legislation would be subject to the existing division of powers.[41] Such assurances were enhanced by Trudeau's personal commitment to a pluralistic Canada and to a renewed federalism.

However, the issue of federalism cannot be settled so quickly. The Charter has altered Canadian federalism because it has empowered judges to establish uniform national standards on matters that would otherwise be the subject of provincial diversity. As a result, the Supreme Court now decides issues that were previously left to provincial governments, and the national standards established by the court set "limits to the capacities of provincial governments to build distinctive provincial communities based on separate bundles of rights."[42] Moreover, the Charter's constriction of provincialism is magnified by its subtle and pervasive Canadianism. It is commonly recognized that a Canadian value is affirmed whenever the Charter is used to strike down a provincial law or executive order. But a Canadian value, as Alan Cairns has observed, is also affirmed whenever the Charter is used to nullify a federal law or executive order.[43] As a result, the Charter generates a continuous affirmation of Canadian values, strengthens a discourse that defines Canadians in other than provincial terms, and diminishes provincial diversity to a greater degree than Trudeau's formal analysis of the division of powers suggests.

Trudeau may also have underestimated the Charter's impact on Quebec's distinctiveness. Throughout his career, Trudeau regarded himself as the defender of the people of Quebec and as an opponent of schemes to absorb that province into the rest of Canada. But he was also an opponent of Québécois separatists, whom he described as self-interested "counter-revolutionaries" committed to establishing a closed society in Quebec.[44] Unlike separatists, Trudeau wanted the Québécois to open their borders without abolishing them and to regard all of Canada as their homeland. For him, the Charter was a crucial instrument for the promotion of such objectives. Many Québécois, however, believe that a different concern is more fundamental, namely, the erosion of the French-language community within the borders of Quebec. Trudeau wanted the Charter to establish that the choice to speak either French or English belongs entirely to the individual, even within the boundaries of Quebec. For him, the safeguarding of this principle was the most effective response to separatists that he could devise.[45] But such a principle, when combined with a declining birth rate and the apparent unwillingness of immigrants settling in Quebec to learn French, can also weaken the French-language community within Quebec and fuel the separatism that Trudeau sought to discredit.[46] Moreover, although the Charter as enacted makes concessions to the French-language community in Quebec, including the use of the notwithstanding clause, the concessions have not satisfied the concerns of many French-speaking Quebeckers.[47]

Trudeau did not suppose that the Charter would solve all the problems of Canadian federalism; he believed only that its adoption was a "first step toward basic constitutional reform."[48] Instead of providing such a step, the Charter has become a source of division and contention. But the contentiousness of the Charter should not be equated with its objective of promoting a national identity based on rights. Any country, even a country such as Canada, needs a set of common values. "A nation," David Cameron has written, "must ultimately be grounded in a set of common values, shared customs ... and implicit understandings." Such common beliefs are necessary "if the country is not to fly apart."[49] In a country such as Canada, common beliefs and common values express the will of citizens to live together. If such a will did not exist, Canada could not be even a federal nation, since federalism, as A.V. Dicey noted, presupposes the capacity to form "a common nationality." He also observed that the people of a federal state must desire union without desiring unification.[50] They have the will to live together, but retain their will to live apart. The Charter recognizes the existence of both wills, although it fails to solve the enormously difficult problem of how those wills are to be expressed and balanced. As a result, demands for its modification that attempt to correct such a failure are not necessarily inconsistent with its great objective of creating a Canadian identity and a more united Canada.

CAN CANADIANS BE A SOVEREIGN PEOPLE?

For Trudeau, the Charter was not simply an expression of the Canadian identity. He also intended it to provide Canadians with a new beginning by establishing the sovereignty of the Canadian people.[51] What made a new beginning possible was the patriation of the Canadian constitution in 1982. Writing in 1950, Frank Scott predicted that the patriation of the constitution would compel Canadians to formulate a Canadian *grundnorm*. "What," he asked, "will the theory be on which our constitution will then rest?" Will it be, he continued, a divine grundnorm, deriving its authority from God; or a provincial-autonomy grundnorm, based on the compact theory; or an Anglo-French grundnorm, calling itself a treaty between races; or a popular grundnorm, labelled "We, the People."[52] Scott raised the most divisive question that Canadians would face once they severed their constitutional tie with Great Britain. The way Trudeau attempted to answer Scott's question was by appealing to the fundamental and inalienable rights of the human person that the Charter was designed to secure and by using those rights to justify the sovereignty of the Canadian people. Henceforth, he said, Canada would be a country whose people were sovereign and whose unity depended on "equality among all Canadians."[53]

The Charter acquired a radically new dimension when it ceased to be concerned with the rights of the people and became involved with their sovereignty. When Trudeau was concerned with the Charter as a rights document, he spoke of it as an instrument that put specific restrictions on legislative sovereignty and mandated specific governmental action. "An entrenched bill of rights," he said, would place "some restriction on the theory of legislative sovereignty." It would "restrain" the power of the federal and provincial governments "in favour of the Canadian citizen."[54] As a rights document, the Charter had as its objective to add the fundamental rights of the people to the list of characteristics that defined Canada. If it accomplished this objective, it would modify the Canadian constitution, but it would not provide the new beginning promised by Trudeau. For such a new beginning, Canada needed a new principle of legitimacy; the Charter would provide a new beginning if it established the sovereignty of the Canadian people. The struggle over the Charter, Trudeau wrote after the 1982 Constitution was adopted, "was much more than the struggle between two levels of governments. It had been a struggle to establish the sovereignty of the people."[55]

Moreover, that struggle was not primarily to establish the supremacy of the people over their governments, nor was it a struggle intended to teach the ancient democratic message that governments are servants of the people. To be sure, Trudeau, as Philip Resnick has suggested, was more Burkean than Rousseauian in his understanding of the sovereignty of the people.[56] Even so, the people of Canada already possessed supremacy over their governments, de facto if not de jure. What the sovereignty of the people was intended to establish was that Canadians were *one* people. They were one people, Trudeau wrote, because "no one is special" and all Canadians are on "an equal footing."[57] What the Charter implicitly denied with respect to the Canadian people was even more telling. By establishing the sovereignty of the people, the Charter, Trudeau said, rejected the compact theory of Confederation and denied that Quebec had a claim to special status. Because Canada was to be a country for which decentralizing provincialists and Québécois separatists could not speak, Canadians, he added, could dream of one Canada.[58]

Trudeau's appeal to the sovereignty of the people was an effective counter to provincialists and separatists; but it was ill-suited to his other objectives. Canada, after all, is a federal state, and federalism is not easily reconciled with the principle of sovereignty.[59] As a legal principle, the idea of sovereignty is most easily applied to unitary states, which are characterized by the concentration of legal authority in a single body or institution. As a principle of moral legitimacy, the sovereignty of the people makes most sense in a homogeneous society. When a society is heterogeneous, because the people are themselves divided by differences of language or culture or history, appeals to the sovereignty of the people are either ineffectual or illiberal in their implications. In a heterogeneous society, the sovereignty of the people may turn out to mean little more than the tyranny of the most numerous or the most powerful. The way that Trudeau attempted to meet this difficulty was by reformulating the idea of sovereignty. Canadians, he said, were a sovereign people "with a collective will to live as a nation ... under a federative form of constitution."[60]

Such a reformulation represents an uneasy compromise. The compromise is necessary because Canada is a federal state and because

Trudeau was himself a federalist. As such, he admired and repeatedly cited Lord Acton's famous essay on nationality. "The co-existence of several nations under the same State," Acton wrote, "is the test, as well as the best security of its freedom. It is also one of the chief instruments of civilization."[61] In essays written in the 1960s, Trudeau drew on Lord Acton to remind Canadians of the virtues of federalism. But he was also committed to the sovereignty of the people. Initially, he meant by the sovereignty of the people nothing more than that government was the servant of the people.[62] Eventually, he added a new dimension. In an essay written in the 1980s, Trudeau cited Rousseau's general will in an attempt to support the view that Canada "had a will of its own" and that Canadians were one people.[63] He appeared intent on combining a Rousseauian conception of the sovereignty of the Canadian people together with an Actonian understanding of Canadian federalism.

Part of the difficulty with attempting such a reconciliation is that Lord Acton had regarded Rousseau's general will as antithetical to the federal state and as the source of collective tyranny. According to Acton, Rousseau's general will was the basis of a conception of the nation that subordinated all other considerations to the demands of a fictitious unity. A nation founded on the "perpetual supremacy of the collective will" became an "ideal unit" that overruled "the rights and wishes of the inhabitants" and absorbed "their divergent interests in a fictitious unity." Not only was such a conception of the nation "the source of despotism and revolution," but it had virtually nothing in common with what Acton called the English system of nationality.[64] The English system provided for the existence of several nations within the same state, promoted diversity rather than uniformity, and sought to establish harmony instead of unity. Moreover, it recognized that the people were sovereign in the sense that government was the servant of the people; but it denied that they formed a sovereign unity. To conceive of the people as a sovereign unity, Acton said, was "absurd and criminal" because it was ultimately to justify the destruction of the divergent nationalities that made up a state and secured its political liberty.[65]

As a federalist, Trudeau was committed to avoiding the outcome that troubled Lord Acton. But the Charter has taken hold, and Canadians have been willing to regard themselves as a sovereign people. It has even been suggested that the dramatic defeat of the Meech Lake and Charlottetown constitutional accords was a display of the new sovereignty of Canadians.[66] In the case of the Meech Lake accord, it has

been suggested that the people of Canada rose up to defeat the accord
because politicians had negotiated it behind closed doors and without
the participation of the people. "Those who govern," Alan Cairns
wrote in an insightful analysis of the accord, "may have to relearn the
ancient democratic message that they are servants of the people."[67]
But the failure of the accord, as he noted, had a darker side as well.
The people of Canada also rose up to assert their sovereignty, to proclaim the absoluteness of their rights, and to defeat the particularistic
demands of Quebec.[68] Moreover, many Québécois viewed the assertion of such sovereignty as a rejection of their nationality and their
place within Confederation, with the result that separatism acquired
new legitimacy in Quebec. The failure of the two accords may confirm
that government is the servant of the people, but the failures do not
establish that Canadians are a sovereign people in the possession of a
collective will. They are not a sovereign people in this sense partly
because, as Peter Russell has written, "not all Canadians have consented to form a single people in which a majority ... have, to use John
Locke's phrase, 'a right to act and conclude the rest.'"[69]

The patriation of the Constitution was a momentous event, but it
did not transform Canadians into a sovereign people in the possession of a collective will. With the patriation of the Constitution, the
Canadian legal system acquired a greater degree of self-sufficiency
than it had possessed before. As a result, Canada used the occasion to
proclaim its external sovereignty and the people of Canada were able
to share in the declaration. And because the patriated Constitution
contained a Charter of Rights, governments were compelled to recognize that the people had acquired a new constitutional status and
a new means of protecting their rights. In these two respects, the people of Canada can be regarded as sovereign.[70] But Canadians are not
a sovereign people in the sense that they form an indivisible unity or
possess a collective will. To the extent that the Charter has led them
to suppose that they possess such sovereignty, it is a nation-destroying
instrument that has turned Canadians against each other, weakened
their will to live together, and undermined the constitutional principles that they agreed to live by in 1867.

THE CHARTER AND THE CANADIAN
POLITICAL NATIONALITY

So long as the Charter has both nation-destroying and nation-saving
dimensions, it cannot provide Canadians with the new beginning

promised by Trudeau or promote the kind of unity that the Canadian people are capable of achieving. When it was being adopted, its critics believed that it would come into conflict with parliamentary institutions or federalism or the new amending formula. In each case, the Charter was regarded as based on a constitutional principle that conflicted with an opposing dimension of the constitution and thereby promoted disunity.[71] But the key difficulties created by the Charter may be rooted in the Charter itself, and in Trudeau's failure to provide a coherent conception of it. Trudeau spoke of the fundamental rights of Canadians, as well as the sovereignty of the Canadian people; but these two dimensions of the Charter work against each other and exacerbate the disunity of Canadians. If it is to promote Canadian unity, Canadians require a coherent conception of it. Moreover, a conception of the Charter can unite them only if it sustains Canada's distinctive constitutional experience. A country such as Canada cannot completely neglect its past without endangering its future.[72]

If Canadians are to be regarded as a sovereign people in the possession of a collective will, then Canadian history must be viewed as irrelevant and the Charter as a document without roots in Canada's constitutional experience. Writing in 1858, George-Étienne Cartier and two other Fathers of Confederation observed that "the basis of Confederation now proposed differs from the United States in several important particulars ... It does not profess to be derived from the people."[73] In the United States the people were said to be sovereign: they were, as Tocqueville observed, "the cause and the aim of all things; everything comes from them, and everything is absorbed in them."[74] In Canada the people were accorded no such status, and the Crown retained its authority. Moreover, Canadians formed a people in a way that differed from Americans. Americans were a people because, despite their differences, they formed an ideological nation and conferred primacy on individual rights. At Confederation, Canadians also formed a people. They were a people because they arrived at a constitutional settlement that enabled French and English to live together, settled the issue of minority rights, and brought into existence a nation that accepted pluralism, yet recognized the need to sustain a common nationality that would hold Canadians together.

The moral ideal implicit in Confederation received its clearest articulation in Cartier's speech on the Canadian political nationality. Unlike Macdonald, who favoured a unitary state, Cartier was an unequivocal federalist. He saw Canada as an "agglomeration of communities having kindred interests and sympathies." He believed that "dissimilarity [was] the order of the physical world and of the moral world, as well as the political world." Canadians were not of different races for the purpose of warring with each other. "We were of different races," he said, "... in order to compete and emulate for the general welfare." Cartier appears to have supposed that French and English would retain their own ways of life and also develop a common way of life. Canada, he said, would stand for a new nationality; it would be a political nationality, with which "neither the national origins, nor the religion of any individual would interfere."[75] Canadians were a people separated by their diversities, but united by their common sympathies, common allegiances, and common identities.

Confederation also affirmed that Canadians were a people in the possession of rights. Some of those rights (such as federalism itself and the minority language rights) were the expression of the intricate pluralism of the Canadian people; others were the ordinary rights of the citizen protected by the common law.[76] Trudeau appealed to the spirit of Confederation when he observed that "every person in Canada is now a member of a minority group." Moreover, the Charter contributes to the Canadian constitutional tradition by giving greater recognition to the pluralistic dimensions of the Canadian people. In the BNA Act of 1867, Thomas Berger has written, "we made a beginning: in the 1982 Constitution and Charter we have made a most significant advance."[77] If Quebec separates from the rest of Canada, both Quebec and Canada will be compelled to address the same issues of pluralism. An independent Quebec, Berger suggests, "would at once be faced with the very questions that confront Canada today: the rights of a great linguistic minority, the claims of the aboriginal peoples, and the place of numerous ethnic and racial groups in the life of the country."[78] Rights express the Canadian identity, but this identity is not monolithic.

Some of the rights and entitlements protected by the Charter and the Constitution express the pluralism of Canadians; other rights and entitlements attempt to capture what they have in common. Canada could not be a nation if Canadians had no values in common. Trudeau attempted to express those common values by saying that Canada was a compassionate and just society, and that the Charter captured the deepest moral commitments of Canadians by protecting the fundamental rights of the human person. Some of his critics have repudiated even these rights, on the ground that they are not universal ones but only the rights of liberal society and of bourgeois individualism.[79]

As such, they are rights that are said to have little relevance either to the Québécois or to the Aboriginal peoples, both of whom attach more importance to community than to abstract individualism. "Aboriginal peoples," Mary Ellen Turpel has written in a critique of the Charter, "do not advance their claims within the rights paradigm because they do not share it."[80] Moreover, she doubts that the Charter can unite Canadians since Aboriginals embrace cultural values that are incommensurate with the possessive individualism it enshrines.

But the Charter has dimensions that the critics appear to neglect. According to its critics, the foundational value of the Charter is abstract individualism; yet Trudeau himself insisted the struggle for freedom was "yesterday's battle." For him, "the value with the highest priority in the pursuit of a Just Society had become equality."[81] Moreover, Trudeau's liberalism was not that of John Locke, whose possessive individualism critics of the Charter have often repudiated. Rather, Trudeau was a humanistic liberal, who believed in liberal equality and who "found the most useful thinking to be that underlying the liberal philosophies of Lord Acton, T.H. Green and Jacques Maritain."[82] Unlike Lockean liberalism, humanistic liberalism is much more difficult to reject, partly because it embraces values that the critics of the Charter themselves endorse. In the case of the native peoples, humanistic liberalism is what grounds the claims of Aboriginal women for equal treatment with Aboriginal men. And there are similarities between humanistic liberalism and the Four Directions of Aboriginal culture. "Some First Nations," Turpel has observed, "base social interaction on the various teachings of the Four Directions that life is based on four principles – roughly translated as trust, kindness, sharing and strength."[83] Trudeau's humanistic liberalism endorsed similar ideals. "What the world should be seeking and what we in Canada must continue to cherish," he wrote, are the human values of "compassion, love and understanding."[84]

The Charter realizes the values of humanistic liberalism only imperfectly, and such a form of liberalism, in any case, does not exhaust the content of the Canadian identity. Such qualifications do not undermine the significance of the Charter as an instrument for the promotion of Canadian unity. Some critics seem to suppose that it cannot contribute to Canadian unity because it rests on values that are incommensurate with those embraced by Aboriginal Canadians or French Canadians. But no such incommensurability appears to exist, at least not to the extent alleged by the critics. Even in the case of

Aboriginals, there appear to be values and ideals that they share with other Canadians. Aboriginal women's groups, for example, criticized the Charlottetown accord on the ground that it would allow self-governing Aboriginal communities to disregard the equality provisions of the Canadian Charter.[85] Because there are common values, the Charter can be the constitutional instrument that expresses the Canadian identity and promotes Canadian unity. What it can accomplish in principle is not identical to what it accomplishes in fact. As enacted, the Charter gives too little consideration to the particularisms of federalism, contributes to the erosion of the French-language community in Quebec, and fails to resolve the issue of Aboriginal rights. Not only can such failures be corrected by constitutional revision, but their correction can have as its objective the creation of a Canada with which all Canadians can identify, thereby strengthening the Charter's contribution to Canadian unity.

The failures of the Charter cannot be corrected if Canadians regard themselves as a sovereign people in the possession of a collective will. Trudeau proclaimed the sovereignty of the people so that Canadians could be provided with a new beginning; but when formulated in the language of Rousseau, it is a new beginning that conflicts with the foundational principles of Confederation and introduces a contradiction within the Charter. The contradiction also has practical consequences since the sovereignty of the people can form an obstacle to the adoption of constitutional revisions that enable the Charter to express the fragile and evolving identity of Canadians. Trudeau regarded the defeat of the Meech Lake and Charlottetown accords as an affirmation of the sovereign unity of the Canadian people and as a defeat for provincialists and separatist politicians.[86] But the failure of the accords can also be regarded as a defeat for the Charter, at least for the dimension of the Charter that seeks to accommodate the pluralism of the Canadian people.

The sovereignty of the people was Trudeau's political counter to decentralizing provincialists and Québécois separatists. If Canadians are a sovereign people, then Canada is not a country for which provincialists and separatists can speak, and the unity of Canada is assured. In this way, Trudeau arrived at a constitutional strategy that would save the Canadian nation by de-legitimating his political rivals.[87] The Machiavelli of *The Prince* advocated a similar stratagem; his advice was that the Prince should eliminate his rivals. In a country such as Canada, Machiavelli's stratagem, even in Trudeau's diluted version of it, appears to have little relevance.[88] The difficulty with the stratagem is that it overlooks the fact that provincialists and separatists speak for dimensions of the Canadian people which are embedded in the Canadian nation. Canada is an unusual nation because its people have the will to live together and the will to live apart. Separatists and provincialists attempt to speak for the will to live apart; Trudeau sought to speak for the will to live together. If Canada is to exist as a nation, then both wills – as well as those who attempt to express them – must exist together.

CONCLUSION

Trudeau regarded the Charter not only as a nation-saving device, but as the first step in basic constitutional revision and as a new beginning for the Canadian people. His Charter is an imperfect instrument for the accomplishment of these objectives because it rests on contradictory political principles. "The Canadian identity," it has been said, "steadfastly refuses to be expressed in monolithic terms."[89] Such a view of Canada is rooted not only in Canadian constitutional history, but also in Trudeau's liberal pluralism, in his praise of federalism, and in his conception of the Charter as the instrument that expresses the fragile and evolving identity of the Canadian people. But he also conceived the Charter as the instrument that establishes the sovereignty of the Canadian people, de-legitimates the agendas of separatists and provincialists, and provides the foundation for the dream of one Canada. Not only do these two conceptions of the Charter work against each other, but one of them conflicts with the foundational principles of Confederation. In one of its dimensions, therefore, the Charter is a nation-destroying device.

But it also has a second dimension, which builds on the Canadian constitutional tradition and attempts to contribute to the evolution of the Canadian people. This second dimension regards Canada as a nation of minorities united in its effort to create a more just society. Such a conception of Canada is enormously difficult to realize because, as Trudeau observed, the creation of a just society is a task that mortal and imperfect beings "will never finish."[90] In the case of Canada, the creation of a just society is made more difficult by the particularisms of Canadian federalism, which the Charter must accommodate if it is to contribute to Canadian unity. Despite such difficulties, the Charter appears to provide an answer to Machiavelli's great problem of statecraft: how can a people who are divided among themselves attain unity and greatness? By creating a more just society that affirms the kind of nation which Canada can become.

CHAPTER SIX

Reimagining Confederation: Moving Beyond the Trudeau-Lévesque Debate

As founders of a new state, the Fathers of Confederation had imagined themselves to be creating a nation that could take its place among the great nations of the world. "Shall we be content to maintain a mere provincial existence," George-Étienne Cartier asked rhetorically, "when, by combining together, we could become a great nation?"[1] Cartier's sentiment was echoed by Macdonald, McGee, and Brown, as well as by voices in the popular press.[2] But the public imagination has turned away from those who created Confederation. Many Canadians now embrace visions of the future that have been shaped by either René Lévesque or Pierre Trudeau. Lévesque's mission was to persuade Québécois to erase from their collective memory those aspects of their identity that tied them to other Canadians and to remind them of the proud nation that they once were and could still become. Pierre Trudeau, on the other hand, dreamed of a Canadian people more united than many of the Fathers of Confederation were able to imagine. What makes the Trudeau-Lévesque debate so ominous is that it centres on the difficult and explosive issue of language. The contemporary world has witnessed increasing linguistic conflicts, together with the disappearance of minority languages.[3] Québécois fear that their own language and culture will disappear unless radical measures are taken. Other Canadians, influenced by Trudeau's constitutional vision, believe that the changes demanded by the Québécois will undermine the Canada that they have come to cherish.[4]

The Trudeau-Lévesque deadlock threatens a basic principle of Confederation, namely, the belief that French and English can live together and become a great nation. It is also destructive of the federal idea, which is predicated on the accommodation of linguistic and cultural diversity. As Canada's prime minister, Trudeau contributed to the deadlock by defending the applicability to Quebec of a language regime based on individualistic principles; as Quebec's premier, Lévesque fuelled it by endorsing a language regime within Quebec that ultimately appeals to the cultural community. As a philosophical dispute, the Trudeau-Lévesque debate raises difficult, but not irresolvable issues.[5] What has transformed the dispute into a deadlock is the rival political agendas that each has adopted: Lévesque, a sovereign Quebec; Trudeau, a pluralistic and united Canada. Each agenda has enormous moral resonance because it emphasizes a contrasting dimension of community. Trudeau's implicit appeal is to the Canadian community and the universalism it represents; Lévesque's appeal is to the Québécois community and the particularism implicit in it. Ultimately, such appeals represent not a political impasse so much as a moral challenge. The challenge is to imagine a form of federalism that accommodates adequately both the universal and the particular, and reimagines Confederation.

CONFEDERATION:
THE REIMAGINATION OF GREATNESS

Confederation was itself an act of imagination. The Fathers not only imagined a new nation, but wanted it to be a great nation. By associating nationhood with greatness, they accepted a dominant assumption of their age. Like other nation-builders at that time, the Fathers believed that a nation had to be of sufficient size to form a viable unit of development; otherwise it would lack historic justification.[6] Nationhood was also associated with unification, which contributed to its greatness. The principle of nationality, it was said, "is legitimate when it tends to unite ... scattered groups of population, and illegitimate when it tends to divide a state."[7] These principles of nation-building the Fathers of Confederation accepted. What they refused to accept was a consequence that appeared to follow from them. Many of the nation-builders of the nineteenth century believed that smaller nationalities and minority languages were doomed to disappear; yet the Fathers imagined that they could build a great nation without destroying the smaller nationality that would form a part of it. In this way, they rejected an assumption that was dominant in their own time and has persisted into our own.

What the Fathers rejected was the view of nationhood and nationality that had received its most systematic formulation in the political thought of Lord Durham. Writing in 1839, Durham said of French Canadians that they were "an uneducated and unprogressive people ... with no history, and no literature."[8] He proposed a union of the Canadas – under the political control of the progressive English Canadians – in which the French Canadians would be gradually assimilated. Durham retains his importance, not because of his controversial views about French-Canadian culture, but because of his profound analysis of nationality. His assimilation proposals, it has been said, sprang not from prejudice, but from the supposition that "a people hived off ... from the life of the larger nation will surely be vulnerable to exploitation."[9] Assimilation – the creation of a single, homogeneous people – would put an end to intolerance and exploitation; it would also establish equal opportunity and liberal justice for all. For Durham, the alternative to assimilation was not cultural pluralism, but a ceaseless struggle between English and French, in which the weaker nationality would eventually lose. All that he could foresee was ethnic conflict: "two nations warring in the bosom of a single state."[10]

Macdonald announced, indirectly, that the Fathers had rejected Durham. His own preference, he admitted, had been for a legislative union because such a union would be "the cheapest, the most vigorous, and the strongest system of government." But a legislative union, he went on to say, "was impracticable," partly because the people of Lower Canada viewed it as a threat to their language, nationality, and religion. Those who favoured a legislative union "were obliged to modify their views and accept the project of a Federal Union as the only scheme practicable."[11] Cartier added his voice to Macdonald's. "The idea of unity of races," he said, "was utopian – it was impossible."[12] Canada was to be a great nation, yet it would have to reject assimilation and embrace federalism.

But Confederation has also been viewed as a threat to French-Canadian nationality. Federalism, it has been said, is premised on political sainthood. In the real world, governments act in terms of the powers they possess, with the consequence that the English majority will prevail over Quebec and promote its own interests by centralizing power in Ottawa.[13] Such a view of Confederation is buttressed by the fact that the Fathers are believed to have created a special kind of federalism, in which the federal Parliament was granted imperial powers and the provinces were relegated to the status of municipal bodies. If Quebec and the other provinces had wished to preserve their autonomy, Frank Scott insisted, "they would never have entered Confederation at all."[14]

Supporters of Confederation have responded by insisting that the Fathers viewed its creation as a moral compact. Even Macdonald spoke of Confederation as a "distinct bargain," "a solemn contract," a "Treaty of Union."[15] When the French of Lower Canada were called upon to judge the proposed Confederation, the first thing they wanted to know was what guarantees would be offered to secure the future of the French-Canadian nationality.[16] Confederation appeared to them as a kind of *modus vivendi*, a compact of cultures or nations in which French and English each recognized the right of the other party to live according to its own language and culture. Others have supposed that Confederation was a compact of provinces, and the provinces have been viewed as the natural focus of communal values and sentiments.[17]

Act or compact? Was Confederation a legislative act that established a near-unitary state in Canada? Or was it a compact that left intact the moral or cultural sovereignty of the founding units? This question has divided politicians as well as constitutional scholars; yet those who supported Confederation were not overly troubled by it. Instead, they devoted themselves to settling the division of powers, to arranging the composition of the central legislature, and to providing limited guarantees for minorities.[18] Those who supported Confederation believed that its compromises had enabled them to create a great nation and a strong central government without destroying either Quebec's nationality or other local particularisms. Those who have come afterwards have not believed that such objectives can be realized together. Hence, they ask, act or compact?

Such a question seems to suppose that Confederation must be either a disguised unitary state or an association of provincialisms. Those who ask the question appear to reject federalism itself. Like Confederation, federalism involves the union of opposites. "The sentiment which creates a federal state," it has been frequently observed, "is the prevalence throughout the citizens of ... two feelings which are to a certain extent inconsistent." The citizens of a federal state must have both "the desire for national unity and the determination to maintain the independence of each man's separate State."[19] Put differently, the citizen of a unitary state has one overriding attachment, but the federal citizen has two official loyalties.[20] The Fathers of Confederation created a type of union suited to their vision of Canada; yet their creation was a federal state, and it presupposed the union of opposites.

As the union of opposing sentiments and principles, Confederation faced an uncertain future. No one knew how French and English would respond to the creation of a transcontinental state. That is one reason why Macdonald had initially favoured a unitary state. Yet Confederation was predicated on the rejection of Macdonald's unitary-state idea as well as Durham's assimilation proposals. By joining in the larger union, wrote A.R.M. Lower, "the two races surely tacitly agreed to bury the hatchet and to try to live amicably together."[21] Cartier had expressed a similar belief. "We were of different races," he said, "not for the purpose of warring against each other, but in order to compete and emulate for the general welfare."[22] By creating a new nation, the Fathers attempted to come to terms with the Conquest; they also challenged future generations to reconcile the opposing sentiments and principles that the Confederation project presupposed. It was a challenge to embrace federalism, to reject assimilation, and to arrive at a new understanding of greatness.[23]

IMAGINING A QUÉBÉCOIS COMMUNITY

To René Lévesque and other separatists, Confederation was little more than a political dream with "the cross of death on its forehead."[24] Not only has Confederation left its promises unfulfilled, but federalism has compelled the Québécois to "lead a mutilated existence," and bilingualism has turned out to be "a program of mongrelization."[25] Confederation has killed no one, yet the Québécois nation is in danger of disappearing. "Every clear minded individual knows," Lévesque insisted, that the Québécois nation cannot be allowed to disappear because it is almost as vital to the individual's "balance and growth as the family."[26] The most direct political solution is to dissolve Confederation and embrace one of the forms of sovereignty. Sovereignty would enable the Québécois to restore their nationality as well as their language community. As a sovereign state, Quebec would be a small nation, in which common values could sink deep roots. Such a nation, wrote Marcel Rioux, "is an adventure in communal living."[27]

The Québécois nation is not a community in the same way that a face-to-face society is a community. No Québécois will ever meet, let alone know, most of their compatriots. Nor are inequality and exploitation – the great solvents of community – absent from Quebec society. Not only does the actual nation turn out to be less of a community than is sometimes suggested, but separatists have been accused of inventing it and using its symbols to advantage themselves.

All nationalists, Pierre Trudeau insisted, are reactionaries; they want "the whole tribe [to] return to the wigwams," so that they can be its tribal kings and sorcerers.[28] The trouble with such a condemnation is not only that it misdescribes the aims of separatists, but also that it does not account satisfactorily for the persistence of nationalist sentiment.[29] Even if nationalists invent the nation by recasting it, their creation does not thereby become a mere masquerade. The nation, as Benedict Anderson has insisted, is an imagined community; yet it is no less important for being imagined.[30]

As an imagined community, the Québécois nation shares characteristics of other imagined communities. Every nation imagines itself to possess finite boundaries; and no nation believes that it is coterminous with the human race. Nations imagine themselves to possess sovereignty, because every nation dreams of being free, and sovereignty is the symbol of freedom. Each nation views itself as unique in its possession of an irreplaceable culture. Culture gives unity to the nation and binds together its members, who regard themselves as forming a brotherhood and sisterhood of all nationals.[31] "Ultimately, it is this imagining" of fraternity that makes it possible for millions of people "willingly to die" for the nation.[32] The culture of the nation also enables the living to unite with the dead, and those who are not yet born. In this way, the nation is imagined as existing eternally, and those who unite themselves with it have "a satisfying answer to personal oblivion."[33]

For Québécois separatists, the core of their imagined community is the French language. "The French of Quebec," wrote Camille Laurin in a white paper issued by the Lévesque government, "have never believed that their language could be dissociated from the destiny of the entire nationality."[34] For separatists, the first principle is that the "French language is not just a means of expression, but a medium of living as well." Through their language, the French of Quebec realize that they are part of the same group and share similar feelings. The French Language is best understood as "an institution, a way of life, a manner of conceiving one's existence."[35] Language, Charles Taylor has argued, comes to the individual from a community; and it fashions both the self and a world. The French of Quebec are a distinct people because they are members of a distinct language community. "We are Québécois," Lévesque insisted; and "at the core of this personality is the fact that we speak French."[36]

If the language community is healthy, nothing more needs to be said. But French-language communities outside of Quebec have been gradually disappearing, and the French language is insecure even within the boundaries of Quebec. French Quebec, Lévesque wrote, "is, literally, in danger of death."[37] Those Canadians who believe otherwise are oblivious of the facts of linguistic assimilation. Such assimilation, Lévesque suggested, takes place because of the declining birth rate of the French-speaking population, because of emigration of francophones out of Quebec, and because of the arrival of immigrants who do not wish to learn French. Moreover, the federal government is believed to have adopted policies that work against the French language, thereby hastening the destruction of the Québécois community.[38]

But why should a threatened language community want to preserve itself? To this question, it has been said, there is no rational answer, other than the fact that "some communities simply persist in wanting to preserve and improve [their] identity."[39] When their language is perceived as most threatened, Québécois are most receptive to political demands for sovereignty. Somewhat akin to sovereignty are demands for a regime based on the principle of territorial unilingualism within the boundaries of Quebec.[40] Where such a regime exists, as in Switzerland, sharply defined and stable linguistic frontiers can provide the basis for linguistic peace among rival language groups. In the absence of such boundaries, language groups have been known to "fight to the death in the bosom of the state in which they are embodied."[41]

Despite the apparent urgency of their political program and their condemnation of Confederation, separatists have been unable to capture the undivided loyalty of the Québécois people. "For our own good," Lévesque urged, "… Quebec must become sovereign as soon as possible."[42] But many Québécois view sovereignty as a last resort, an option to be embraced only if separation is forced upon them by the intransigence of the rest of Canada. "My own feelings are ambivalent," Léon Dion has written. "When I think of Quebec, my homeland, my heart beats fast; when I think of Canada, my country, reason takes over. Yet in a sense Canada too is my homeland."[43] The way separatists such as René Lévesque respond to such statements is by insisting that the Québécois people have only one homeland. But as many Québécois are unwilling to accept such a response, the imagined Québécois community turns out to be more contentious than separatists appear willing to allow.

The separatist agenda contains, moreover, a tension or ambiguity that affects their imagined community. The tension is not immediately apparent because separatism appeals to a multiplicity of considerations, including a concern for dignity. "Independence for Quebec," wrote Marcel Chaput, "is not the explosion of revenge toward the Conquerors of 1760, but the quest for Dignity which is every people's right."[44] But the appeal to dignity is not exhaustive of the case for separatism. Separatists also justify their political agenda by appealing to the imminent and concrete danger of death that threatens their imagined community. Hence, sovereignty or a regime based on territorial unilingualism is said to be the only means that will secure the survival of their community, given such problems as linguistic assimilation and immigration. Moreover, separatists are often perfectionists as well as survivalists. As perfectionists, they are motivated by a concern for the health and purity of their community, and their fear is linguistic and cultural pollution.[45] Perfectionism (or purism) can affect the content of exhibitions in museums, the selection of historical sites that are to be restored, and the way children and adults think of themselves and their language. When purism is the motivation, sovereignty or a regime akin to it is the device that enables separatists to remove corrupting influences from their language and culture.

But a concern for the purity of the imagined community does not have the same moral and political implications as a concern for its survival. Purism can be objectionable even to those who are otherwise sympathetic to the imagined community because a policy of purism contains elements of state paternalism, attempts to control language and culture in relation to native speakers, and substitutes a reified museum culture for the vitality and spontaneity of the original community.[46] Such objections do not apply to a policy motivated by a concern for the survival of the community's language and culture. When survival is the issue, a government can often justify the adoption of policies that would be otherwise objectionable, provided the policies are rationally connected to the goal of survival. What the survivalist argument requires, however, is an empirical component that will enable it to justify a specific political agenda. Separatists suppose that the French language will disappear unless their agenda is adopted. Not only does such an argument require a precise empirical component, but separatists have to show that measures less drastic than either political sovereignty or territorial unilingualism will fail to secure the survival of the French language.[47]

Separatists have challenged the Confederation project by imagining a Québécois community and seeking to protect it. What makes separatism problematic is not its imagining of community, but its political agenda, portions of which are either inimical to community or unnecessary for its protection. Many Québécois instinctively sympathize with separatism and put to one side the issue of its political adequacy. They do so because Quebec is their homeland and because separatists speak most directly for it. "We are attached," wrote René Lévesque, "to this ... Quebec, the only place where we have the unmistakable feeling that 'here we can be really at home.' "[48] But there are also Québécois who regard Canada as their country, even though they are increasingly coming to view the current constitutional arrangement as detrimental to their homeland. These Québécois are caught between Canada and the imagined community of separatism. Still other Québécois regard Canada as their country, cherish Quebec as their homeland, and believe in the principles of pluralistic liberalism. They believe that language and culture owe their vitality to the people, and they envisage a Quebec that can be a home both for the Québécois and for those whose ethnic and linguistic origins differ from their own.[49] Separatism has raised the most fundamental questions about Confederation and its implications for the Québécois community, yet it has left some of them unresolved.

THE DREAM OF ONE CANADA

Even if Québécois separatism ends up settling nothing, it has already necessitated the reimagination of Confederation. No one has been more aware of this necessity than Pierre Elliott Trudeau. Early in his career, he was an opponent of radical constitutional revision, viewing it as unnecessary and as "a hornet's nest." But separatism was instrumental in forcing the issue, and Trudeau became convinced that "once the debate began, it had to be carried to a conclusion."[50] His goal was not only to discredit separatists by exposing their reactionary agenda, but also to reimagine Canada as a community of belonging in which Québécois and Canadians of other ethnic origins could flourish together. As a result, he rejected the conception of national greatness that associated it with military aggrandizement and cultural uniformity, and called upon Canadians to recognize that the country's greatness consisted of its acceptance of difference and its devotion to basic human rights. "Our image [of Canada]," he said, "is of a land of people with many differences ... but a single desire to live in harmony."[51] In this way, Canada would look to the future and become a model for tomorrow's world.

Trudeau spoke to the Québécois and other Canadians in their

capacity as citizens of a morally harmonious world, of which Canada was but a part. The challenge of the age, he believed, was for people with different values to live together. He frequently spoke of tolerance and justice, and reminded Canadians of the need for love, understanding, and brotherhood. Nothing was unchangeable for him but "the inherent and unalienable rights of man"; yet he detested egoism and warned that "a society of egoists quickly becomes a society of slaves."[52] What he longed for was the just society, in which the warm spirit of justice was always "ready to serve the highest purposes of rational man."[53] As to Canadian federalism, Trudeau viewed it as "an experiment of major proportions," and he wanted it to become "a brilliant prototype for the moulding of tomorrow's civilization."[54] Implicit in his vision of Canada was a commitment to moral universalism that even his critics could respect. Trudeau, wrote Marcel Rioux, was able to "transcend the ethnic peculiarities which afflict almost all of humanity to become a type of *homo sapiens* whose numbers, alas, are all too few in Canada."[55]

The irony of Trudeau's moral universalism is that it has produced a vision of Canada that has exacerbated the very divisions that it was intended to heal. His Canada is widely embraced by English and ethnic Canadians, but is increasingly rejected by those who are assumed to be its greatest beneficiaries. English Canadians suppose that "official bilingualism" has imposed hardships on them so that French Canadians can have what they want. The irony is that English Canadians are hesitant to make further concessions to Quebec, yet many Québécois are indifferent to official bilingualism and believe that it does not address their most pressing concerns.[56] Multiculturalism was adopted for the sake of cultural harmony, yet many Québécois view the policy as a threat to their culture. As to the equality of the provinces, which Trudeau also sponsored, it has become an obstacle even to the symbolic recognition of Quebec's uniqueness and particularity. Not only have his policies failed to satisfy French Canadians, but Canada is more divided than ever on what it means to be a nation.

Trudeau has responded to these ironies by offering reflections on politics, in a manner reminiscent of the years before he held public office. His basic assumption is that Canada was a more just and harmonious society in 1984, but disgruntled and self-interested politicians set out to disrupt the consensus. "The fragmentation of Canada," he has said, "began after the election of Brian Mulroney as prime minister" and after Trudeau himself had left office.[57] He has also blamed provincializing premiers and separatist politicians, many of whom sponsored the failed, but divisive Meech Lake Constitutional accord of 1987 and who further divided Canadians by supporting the failed Charlottetown accord of 1992.[58] Not only has Trudeau condemned these politicians as "perpetual losers," but he has accused them of embracing policies that require Canadians to "say goodbye to the dream of one Canada."[59] Much the same criticisms were levelled against Québécois separatists in the 1950s and 1960s. Separatists were characterized as "counter-revolutionaries" and "a petit-bourgeois minority."[60] They were condemned for embracing the new treason of the intellectuals, which Julien Benda was the first to expose. Like Benda before him, Trudeau believed that the mission of intellectuals was to criticize the injustices of their own society by reference to universal human values. What he refused to grant, both at the beginning and at the end of his career, was that separatists and provincialists spoke for values that his moral universalism was unable to accommodate.

Trudeau refused to grant such a premise because he believed that his vision of Canada accommodated particularistic values. His strategy was to discredit nationalist thinkers, while accommodating particularistic values. When separatists demanded a Québécois homeland, Trudeau responded by inviting the Québécois to embrace all of Canada as "a shared community of belonging."[61] In this way, he drew on moral universalism to recast the demand for a homeland. He added a particularistic dimension by encouraging French Canadians to regard their own historic nation as "the guardian of certain very positive qualities." Particularism, however, was to be combined with liberalism, and Trudeau reminded French Canadians that their own nation was the guardian of values "more private than public, ... more instinctive and primitive than intelligent and civilized."[62] As to culture, he praised it for making "a man what he is," and he insisted that a government should have the power to promote culture, so long as the measures it adopted did not violate the liberty of the individual or the requirements of the open society.[63] In these ways, Trudeau sought to accommodate within his scheme of liberal universalism the values that separatists had used to justify reactionary policies.

A similar strategy was applied to language. Trudeau's position (or what can be taken for it) is set out in a white paper, the philosophical core of which is the distinction between language as an instrument of communication and language as the expression of a way of life. The former relates to the universality of language; the latter to its particularity. What the white paper asserts is that it is unnecessary to choose between universality and particularity: a language can serve both functions. If this point is granted, then Canada can be described as "a country with two official languages, but no official cultures."[64] Moreover, it should strive to become a bilingual country, so that French-speaking minorities can flourish outside of Quebec and the English-speaking minority can flourish within Quebec. As to immigrants, they make the choice to adopt either English or French by coming to Canada. When immigrants and Canadians from other provinces settle in Quebec, they should be encouraged, though not compelled, to learn French. Trudeau ruled out compulsion because he assigned language rights to individuals rather than to collectivities. The assignment of language rights to the individual, he said, "made things awkward for Quebec nationalist politicians because it made them largely redundant"; yet it was "more respectful of the dignity of Canadians" and did not deny "the importance of a linguistic community."[65] Even with respect to language, Trudeau's goal was to accommodate particularistic values within his scheme of liberal universalism.

But the language issue is not settled so easily. Even if Trudeau's assumption about the functions of language is granted, difficulties remain concerning the ascription of language rights. He justified their ascription to individuals by appealing to the dignity of the individual and to the values of the open society. Not only did he assume that such values ruled out policies that restricted the right of the individual to adopt the language of her or his choice, but he supposed that restrictive language policies were motivated by intolerance and racism. As a result, Trudeau opposed Quebec's right to adopt a restrictive language policy and ascribed language rights to individuals. But his assumptions do not hold in all cases. If minority-language speakers are surrounded by more numerous and more prosperous speakers of another language, the pressures of linguistic assimilation will be enormous. The temptation will be to adopt the dominant language for the purpose of career and economic advantage, and the minority language will gradually disappear. Moreover, when a dominant and a minority language coexist, political neutrality is not secured by leaving the choice of language to each individual because such a policy almost always works to the advantage of the dominant language.[66] In some situations, the ascription of language rights exclusively to individuals can have a devastating effect on the minority language; and a community can reject such an ascription without embracing racism or exhibiting intolerance, and without violating the dignity of the individual.

Trudeau's liberal universalism fails to resolve the language issue, but it does state conditions that a solution must satisfy. He stated one such condition when he criticized Québécois separatists for their alleged racism. A language policy motivated by racism is abhorrent, even in a society concerned with the preservation of its language, because a racist policy excludes and stigmatizes those who should be treated with consideration and respect. In Quebec and Canada, racism is an illegitimate reason for restricting language rights or any other right. But a restrictive language policy can also be based on considerations of social peace or economic efficiency or cultural pluralism, in which case the policy is more likely to express the values of liberal universalism than to violate them.[67] A government that appeals to such considerations can legitimate a restrictive language policy even in a liberal society, provided the policy in question is the least restrictive alternative available. A government that neglects the second condition, by placing greater restrictions on individual rights than its objective warrants, unnecessarily violates the dignity of the individual. In these ways, liberal universalism provides conditions that a restrictive language policy must satisfy if it is to be acceptable in a society that abhors racism and respects the dignity of the individual. If Trudeau arrived at a different conclusion, in which individual rights eclipsed the language community, it was because he focused on policies that he regarded as racially motivated and as unduly restrictive of individual freedom.

Trudeau opposed such policies because they undermined his dream of one Canada, which represented his attempt to reimagine Confederation and to provide a model for tomorrow's world. "In Mr Trudeau's view of things," Guy Laforest insists, "there is no Quebec nation or people. There is a single, indivisible Canadian nation, and the people of Quebec are Canadian citizens who happen, more or less accidentally, to live in the territory of Quebec."[68] But Trudeau never dreamed of a Canada or a world that would value uniformity or hate diversity. As a moral univeralist, he imagined a world without war, in which universal brotherhood and human dignity were fundamental values; yet his moral universalism included a deep regard for the uniqueness of individuals and the diversity of cultures. Canada was a better model than the United States, Trudeau believed, because it had rejected the American melting-pot and was becoming a truly pluralistic civilization. As such, Canada would become a community of belonging in which French and English would flourish together with other Canadians. There was, he said, "no such thing as a model or ideal Canadian. What could be more absurd than the concept of an 'all-Canadian' boy or girl?"[69] Not only did Trudeau never renounce these views, but he advocated policies to facilitate their realization. The final irony of his attempt to reimagine Confederation is that some of his own policies have served to undermine the diversity he valued and the harmony he sought to achieve.[70]

FEDERALISM AND THE IMAGININGS OF COMMUNITY

Trudeau reimagined Confederation and hoped that Canada would become a model for tomorrow's world. But the contemporary world has witnessed the re-emergence of ethnic nationalism and the disappearance of multinational states. Canada may face a similar destiny. It may disappear, yet the problems of the polyethnic state are likely to remain. Not only has polyethnicity been the norm in civilized societies, but ethnic frictions, as William McNeill has written, "are a cost of participating in the modern world from which no people or government ... can long remain immune."[71] When viewed from such a perspective, Canada's experience with the English-French conflict takes on a new dimension. Moreover, Canada continues to face difficult questions of constitutional renewal, and many Canadians are seeking to redefine Canada's identity as a nation. Such an activity presupposes that Canadians have available to them principles that will dissolve the Trudeau-Lévesque deadlock and reimagine Confederation itself.

At one level, the Trudeau-Lévesque conflict is much less than a deadlock. It has its origins in divergent political commitments, with Trudeau exalting the individual rights of Canadians and Lévesque focusing on the Québécois nation. Reflecting on this contrast, Charles Taylor has concluded, "The Charter and the promotion of the nation, as understood in their respective constituencies, are on a collision course."[72] The collision can be avoided, he suggests, by building a country based on deep diversity, in which some Canadians can belong as bearers of individual rights and others can have membership through their particular community. Such a proposal has resonance because Canada is a country devoted to accommodating difference. Moreover, the differences to be accommodated are deep but not necessarily antagonistic. Lévesque's fundamental value is the cultural community, but Quebec itself is a liberal society, and the kind of community that is viable in such a society presupposes a measure of liberty and diversity even in relation to language and culture. Trudeau is a liberal, but his liberalism rejects atomistic individualism for liberal pluralism and becomes coherent only if the community can protect its way of life in a manner consistent with liberal principles. Liberty and community create tensions that need to be addressed, but do not result in a deadlock.[73]

Trudeau is not only a liberal; he is also a universalist. And Lévesque was both a communitarian and a particularist. As a particularist, Lévesque regarded the cultural understandings of the Québécois as constitutive of a distinctive way of life. Other Canadians are not members of the Québécois community, although they deserve to be treated with politeness and respect. Paradoxically, a sovereign Quebec would be even more cordial to the rest of Canada since the strong fences of sovereignty would make for good neighbours. Trudeau's vision is different. As a universalist, he believes that all Canadians belong to the same country, have common values, and owe each other the reciprocal duties that common membership implies. All Canadians are members of the just society, which presupposes, he said, "an indispensable partnership between the government and the private sector ... to protect the weak from the strong, the disadvantaged from the well-heeled."[74] From the perspectives of universalism and particularism, the Trudeau-Lévesque debate ceases to be a dispute between a liberal and a communitarian and becomes a deep disagreement about community.

Language is part of the disagreement. For Lévesque, the Québécois were members of the same community because they spoke French. Not only does the French language express a distinctive way of life, but it separates the Québécois from other Canadians, who have a different language and a different way of life. Trudeau, on the other hand, believes that a language regime can be used to unite, as well as divide, the people of a country. "Bilingualism," he has observed, "unites people; dualism divides them." Bilingualism, he goes on to say, "means that you can speak to the other; duality means that you can live [apart]."[75] Unlike unilingualism, however, bilingualism makes demands both on individuals and on the country. These demands are not necessarily destructive of community. In fact, Trudeau regarded the willingness to bear them as an indication of the goodwill that Canadians had toward each other. Even Canadians who were unwilling or unable to learn the other official language could contribute to the Canadian community "by accepting their fellow Canadians who speak the other official language with open minds and open hearts."[76]

Trudeau and Lévesque disagreed about community. It is not enough to say, however, that Trudeau has a liberal conception of community and Lévesque a communitarian conception. Part of the difficulty with such a characterization is that it becomes entangled in the debate between John Rawls and his communitarian critics, including Michael Sandel.[77] Yet Trudeau's liberalism differs from Rawls's because it does not require individuals to abstract themselves from their society or the other circumstances that give meaning to their lives. And Lévesque's communitarianism differs from Sandel's because his goal was not to revive communal traditions so much as to build a Québécois community that was "as progressive, as efficient, and as 'civilized' as any in the world."[78] Rawls and his critics are engaged in a debate about the abstract or disembodied self versus the embedded or communally situated self; Trudeau and Lévesque were concerned about language and culture, together with their implications for membership in a political community. Put differently, the Trudeau-Lévesque debate leads not to the issues that divide Rawls and his critics, but to the difficult subject of ethnic nationalism.

As a dispute about ethnic nationalism, the debate can easily become a deadlock. In fact, Trudeau contributed to such an outcome when he insisted that both Québécois and Aboriginals had to choose between membership in closed ethnic or racial societies and membership in the open Canadian society. If Aboriginals decided to remain in their closed society, they would be safe on their reservations and behind their ghetto walls, but they would risk the awful results that such an existence brings.[79] Even French Canada, Trudeau said, was "too culturally anaemic ... to be able to survive more than a couple of decades" as a closed ethnic society.[80] Québécois and native intellectuals have responded by insisting that their respective societies are or can become thriving and self-sufficient communities. Such a response may meet Trudeau's objection to ethnic nationalism, but it diverts attention from Canadian federalism as a device that attempts to accommodate ethnic and other particularisms within the framework of the morally open society. As a dispute about ethnic nationalism, the Trudeau-Lévesque debate can create a deadlock if it is assumed that a choice must be made between membership in a morally open community and membership in an ethnic community.

Not only did Confederation reject such an assumption, but federalism itself supposes that each individual is a member of at least two communities. By rejecting Durham's assimilation proposals and Macdonald's plans for a unitary state, the Confederation project assumed

that citizens would be members both of their provincial communities
and of the Canadian community. Cartier provided the most explicit
recognition of this assumption when he rejected assimilation, defended federalism, and called for the creation of a new nationality.
Canada would bring into existence, he said, "a political nationality with
which neither the national origins, nor the religion of any individual,
would interfere."[81] Cartier appears to have assumed that the new nationality would exist alongside the nationality to which French Canadians and other Canadians were already committed. Moreover, the new
nationality would not be reducible to narrow economic calculation or
to what contemporary Québécois sometimes call *fédéralisme rentable.*[82]
Like federalism itself, Confederation sought to unite opposites by requiring each citizen to be a member of at least two communities.

But Confederation was a political dream, and the Fathers had a
limited awareness of the moral complexities inherent in the federal
idea. Moreover, there are situations in which the communities presupposed by federalism can come into conflict, and federal institutions can exacerbate the disharmony. Such disharmony does not
necessarily indicate that federalism is a morally incoherent idea, unless it is assumed that undisturbed harmony is the supreme moral
value. Some moral philosophers have made just such an assumption,
yet Henri Bergson challenged it in a seminal work. He did so by drawing attention to the distinction between the open soul and the closed
soul, which he compared in turn to Christian and pagan morality.[83]
Pagan morality was the morality of the city; it strove for moral harmony through homogeneity and regarded foreigners as disruptive of
the social warmth that characterized the city. Christianity, on the
other hand, was characterized by an open soul, preached the humanity of all, and took charity to be the measure of justice. Not only
may it be impossible to choose between these two moralities, since
each individual appears to live both of them; but institutions can be
devised to express each of them.[84] Federalism may be such a device,
since it requires each citizen to be both a member of a distinctive
provincial community and a member of the more open society that
exists at the national level.

The Trudeau-Lévesque dispute creates an irresolvable deadlock only
if it is necessary to choose between the communities of Canadian federalism and the moralities implicit in them. As a particularist, Lévesque
called upon Québécois not only to recover their identity and reimagine their community, but also to dissolve their ties with Canadians who
spoke a different language and lived a different way of life. Trudeau,

on the other hand, is the kind of universalist who seeks to accommodate linguistic and ethnic particularisms, but his concessions to them (especially with respect to Quebec's concern for linguistic survival) are too weak to be fully effective. He illuminates the idea of Canadian community, and Lévesque provides insights into the kind of community that many Québécois cherish; but neither gives sufficient weight to the fact that Canadians belong to more than one community. To give sufficient weight to such a fact is not only to dissolve the Trudeau-Lévesque deadlock, but to make explicit the moral foundation that Confederation and its reimagination presuppose.[85]

FEDERALISM AND THE IMAGINATION

When values collide, politics flourishes, as does the imagination. Moreover, politics is itself concerned with the imagination: no less a realist than Machiavelli conceived of politics as "the engineering of the imagination."[86] As machiavellian figures, the Fathers of Confederation imagined a new nation and secured its constitutional existence; yet they were unable to remove their creation from the political struggle and the rival imaginings of those engaged in it. The Fathers contributed to the imaginings of those who were to come after them by rejecting Lord Durham and creating a federal state. By renouncing Durham's assimilation proposals and institutionalizing the opposing sentiments and principles that federalism presupposes, they added to the conditions under which political imagination and political philosophy flourish. Political philosophy, Isaiah Berlin has said, is possible only in a society in which ends conflict.[87] When ends are agreed upon, only questions of means remain. But political philosophy is also concerned with the reconciliation of conflicting values. The way Canadian federalism seeks to reconcile the opposing sentiments and principles that it institutionalizes is by reimagining community and supposing that each citizen belongs to more than one community. The reimagination of community is also the crucial philosophical issue that Trudeau and Lévesque addressed.

But neither Trudeau nor Lévesque resolved the issue of community. Moreover, it has become more intractable, partly because of the failure of the Meech Lake and Charlottetown constitutional accords. As a result, Canadians are more divided than before and share a heightened sense of crisis. The failures – especially of the Charlottetown agreement in 1992 – have also produced new visions of the future, including a

Three Nations conception of Canada and a proposal for deconfederation. According to the Three Nations idea, English-speaking Canada,
Quebec, and the Aboriginal peoples constitute the "three national
identities [which] uneasily co-exist ... within the Canadian state." The
issue that confronts Canadians "is whether these three distinctive iden-
tifications and aspirations can be reconciled with one another."[88]
Deconfederation, on the other hand, begins with the premise that "the
Canadian experiment has failed," since it is not possible to accommodate the special aspirations of Quebec "within the confines of a single
liberal democracy constituted by immigrants of varied and diverse
backgrounds."[89] Deconfederation also calls for the creation of a
Canada without Quebec, based on strong democracy and the exclusion
of group rights, except for Aboriginal rights. The new visions differ
among themselves, yet a recurring theme is the failure of the Canadian
federation and a growing scepticism about the viability of the federal
idea. The classics of Canadian federalism, Michael Oliver has suggested, no longer enable Canadians to face a future that must recognize deep diversities.[90] In a somewhat similar vein, Alan Cairns has
described a fragmentation of Canadian citizenship, a federalism that is
in retreat, and a Canadian past that "is another country."[91]

The increasing pessimism about the viability of federalism, reflected
in Philip Resnick's *Toward a Canada-Quebec Union* and other important
books, is itself ironic. In 1867 the Canadian constitutional experiment
had as a primary objective the accommodation of deep diversities.
The acceptance of federalism was the great compromise that brought
Canada into existence. "The federal constitution of 1867," Donald
Creighton wrote, "was a characteristic Canadian creation, shaped by
Canadian history, designed for Canadian purposes ..."[92] Yet federalism
is increasingly viewed as an obstacle to the accommodation of Canadian diversities. The change is attributable in part to the Trudeau-
Lévesque debate, which has entrenched an ideology of federalism and
undermined the creative aspects of the federal idea. Lévesque con-
tributed to the ideology by insisting that federalism could not work;
Trudeau added to it by refusing to recognize Quebec's specificity,
even at the constitutional level. Federalism is in retreat, even though
Canada remains, in an important sense, a federal society.

"The federal device," wrote A.R.M. Lower, "must be reckoned one
of the most happy ... of political inventions ... precisely [because of]
its flexibility."[93] In Canada the flexibility of federalism originally consisted of the accommodation of deep diversities, coupled with the

creation of a great nation. Canada is a difficult country. But it is not necessarily an impossible country if it is accepted that identities can be multiple and of different kinds. The Confederation settlement of 1867 took such an assumption for granted. In contemporary Canada, the assumption requires the constitutional recognition of Quebec as a distinct society and a similar kind of recognition for Aboriginal communities. Federalism, however, is not simply about the recognition of deep diversities; it is also about creating common allegiances, developing common identities, and sustaining a community of moral sentiment that includes all Canadians.[94] Trudeau understood common moral sentiments; Lévesque understood deep diversity; but each understood only what the other did not know.

CHAPTER SEVEN

Is Canadian Democracy Special?
Mutual Recognition in a Federal System

Canada began as a federal experiment; it is increasingly becoming an experiment in democracy. Federalism was the great compromise that brought Canada into existence; democracy is what sustains it today. Virtually all the Fathers of Confederation acknowledged the necessity of federalism; yet it is the sovereignty of the people that has become the constitutional ideal which enjoys the widest support among Canadians.[1] The apparent victory of democracy has been accompanied, however, by a crisis of democracy. In the case of Canada, this crisis is not simply a crisis of big government or of citizen disenchantment with élite rule. In Canada the crisis of democracy is also one of national existence and of the gradual de-legitimation of national institutions. So understood, the Canadian crisis is not a new one, nor is it unaffected by the existence and viability of federal institutions. It is, nevertheless, a crisis that challenges prevailing beliefs about democracy.

Canadians sometimes take democracy for granted or consider it less problematic than federalism and the Charter of Rights. What makes federalism and the Charter problematic is that they are widely believed to give primacy to particularistic and individualistic considerations at the expense of collective goods and the common interest. In contrast, democracy is universally applauded and is often regarded as raising only questions about the best means for its maximization.[2] Such a view was not shared, however, by the Royal Commission on Bilingualism and Biculturalism. In their *Preliminary Report*, published in 1965, the commissioners noted that "Canada ... [was] passing through the greatest crisis in its history."[3] Part of the problem, they believed, was that democracy had too often been viewed as "the simple game of majority versus minority." Some English-speaking citizens invoked majority rule "as though they were brandishing a threatening weapon"; some French-speaking people wanted to make use of majority rule "to their own advantage in a more or less independent Quebec." Confronted by such beliefs, the commissioners urged "all Canadians [to] examine closely the concept of democracy itself."4

In Canada, democracy is no less problematic than federalism or the Charter of Rights. Moreover, Canada is an unusual experiment in democracy because it faces distinctive obstacles. The concept of democracy is universal, but its conceptions are particular and respond to specific problems and determinate conditions. In his famous study of democracy in America, Tocqueville attempted to reveal "the image of democracy itself with its inclinations, its character, its prejudices and its passion."5 For him, the essence of democracy was the equality of condition, together with its implications for political liberty. The great danger faced by democracy, Tocqueville said, was democratic despotism, which only the institutions of local self-government could alleviate. In Canada, however, democracy struggles with cultural, ethnic, and local particularisms, which it seeks both to accommodate and to overcome. The great danger faced by Canadian democracy is that citizens will deny each other mutual recognition and destroy the country. Moreover, the Canadian danger is fuelled not by an erosion of local self-government so much as by a failure of federal institutions. In Canada, democracy not only grew out of federalism, but also shares its failures, its aspirations, and its future.

CANADIAN DEMOCRACY: OBSTACLES AND CRISIS

Canada is an unusual experiment in democracy because it faces distinctive obstacles. But it also faces obstacles to democracy that other countries share. Among the common problems is a growing pessimism about the capacities of all Western-style governments to manage their own societies.6 The basis of such pessimism is a perceived disintegration of civil order, coupled with the debility of leaders, the alienation of citizens, and the inability of governments to meet increasing demands for their services. The pessimism extends to society itself. "Contemporary society," Charles Taylor has written, "suffers from a certain malaise of impending breakdown."7 As he understands it, the malaise is intimately connected to the bureaucratization and centralization of modern societies, which lead to increased atomization and alienation. A centralized and bureaucratized society, Taylor goes on to say, can either continue along the path it has adopted or it can decentralize power in an attempt to re-establish a concern for the common good through increased citizen participation.

As a cure for the modern malaise, radical decentralization has its most direct relevance for a country such as the United States. This is so, partly because the United States has its ideological origins in a debate about national versus local democracy, together with proposals for their reconciliation. Thomas Jefferson, for example, sided politically with the supporters of the extended republic, but articulated powerful justifications of local democracy. The New England townships, according to him, were "the wisest invention ever devised by the wit of man for the perfect exercise of self-government and for its preservation."[8] Unlike Jefferson, James Madison defended central authority; but he did not thereby reject the spirit of localism. The Madisonian constitution postulated an extended republic, recognized the independence of the states, and embedded localism in the central government.[9] It was Alexander Hamilton who spoke contemptuously of the people and advocated imperial government. But he himself said that "no man's ideas were more remote from the [United States Constitution] than his were known to be."[10]

Although Canada also suffers from a modern malaise, its ideological origins are different. The United States emerged after experiencing a revolutionary war and debating the character of democratic republicanism; Canada experienced the Conquest of 1760, witnessed what Lord Durham called the war of races, and was compelled to consider the remedies for ethnic and racial conflict.[11] Moreover, the Fathers of Confederation studied American republicanism and rejected it. Republicanism was rejected because American democracy was believed to be less stable, less principled, and more homogenizing than the scheme of constitutional monarchy favoured by the Fathers. Canadian Confederation, it is often said, had a centralized and authoritarian character. In consequence, Canadians have not debated the nature of democracy so much as lamented its absence, chronicled its failures, and listed obstacles to it. Writing in 1946, Frank Underhill recalled the conservative character of Confederation and lamented the weakness of radical democratic sentiment in Canada.[12] Almost forty years later, Reginald Whitaker concluded that the Canadian "balance-sheet" on democracy remained "mixed to poor."[13]

In 1958 Pierre Trudeau arrived at a similar conclusion, although his focus was ethnic conflict and the obstacles to democracy created by it. "Historically," he wrote, "French Canadians have not really believed in democracy for themselves; and English Canadians have not really wanted it for others."[14] Through historical necessity and as a means of survival, French Canadians "felt justified in finessing at the parliamentary game." The same considerations had induced French Canadians to value nationalism more than democracy, even within the borders of Quebec. As to English Canadians, they wanted democracy for themselves, but were unwilling to pursue a common good that included the welfare of French Canadians or to grant them "absolute equality of political rights." English Canadians, Trudeau said, had done much "to instill a distrust of representative government in French Canadian minds." Such were the inadequate foundations on which Canadians "absurdly pretended to be building democratic forms of government."[15]

Trudeau identified obstacles to democracy in Canada. Almost a century earlier, John Stuart Mill had pointed out similar kinds of obstacles in a famous study of representative government. According to Mill, representative government presupposed numerous conditions for its operation, among them a sense of "fellow-feeling." But the existence of fellow-feeling, he went on to say, could not be taken for granted, especially in a country made up of nationalities that spoke different languages. In fact, he believed that representative government was "next to impossible" in such a country, precisely because of the lack of fellow-feeling. In such a country, "mutual antipathies are generally much stronger than jealousy of the government." Mill also recognized the unique justification that such antipathies provided for the nationalist state. Where the sentiment of nationality existed in any force, the nationalist state could legitimate itself simply by appealing to the consent of the governed, because the governed would ordinarily choose to unite with members of the same nationality. "This is merely saying," he wrote, "that the question of government ought to be decided by the governed."[16] He had no easy solution to the problems he identified, other than his belief that mutual antipathies would disappear in a stage of civilization more advanced than his own.

Unlike Mill, Trudeau was more dismissive of nationalist sentiment, partly because he regarded the nationalist state as already obsolete and partly because he had a deep commitment to cultural pluralism. Canada faced obstacles to democracy, he reasoned, but they were surmountable if French and English acknowledged the rules of democracy. Trudeau focused on French-English relations, yet Canada has also experienced other failures of democracy. Among them is the inability of central institutions "to provide regional representation or to encompass the regional diversities of Canadian life within the process of national decision making."[17] The new failure has also been characterized as a failure of intrastate federalism and as a failure of the Canadian Senate to meet even the minimal expectations of the Fathers of Confederation.[18] The failure has been experienced most intensely in western Canada and has fuelled western separatism. As a result, territorial particularisms have increasingly found outlets in provincial governments, regional conflict has been exacerbated, and parliamentary institutions have failed to unite Canadians. "Rather than helping to draw the country together," Roger Gibbins has written, "parliamentary institutions drive it apart."[19]

Democracy is a difficult form of government even under the best of circumstances. Canada, however, faces unique obstacles to democracy, as well as difficulties common to other countries. Like other democracies, it is suffering a modern malaise, is experiencing a crisis of big government, and is witnessing increased citizen disenchantment with élite rule. The contemporary crisis of democracy has produced, in Canada as elsewhere, increasing demands for the radical decentralization of power. The starting-point of political organization, it has been said, should be "as far as possible from the national level – in those places where men [and women] meet face to face."[20] Such a proposal might alleviate the crisis of democracy were it not for the additional obstacles that Canadians confront. Canada has a heterogeneous population and a fragile sense of its existence. Under such conditions, radical decentralization can produce political fragmentation rather than enhanced citizen participation. Fragmentation can also occur within the borders of Quebec, given the increasing heterogeneity of its population. Too much centralization creates obstacles to democracy, but too much decentralization simply exacerbates the obstacles that already exist.[21]

CONCEPTIONS OF DEMOCRACY AND ASPIRATIONS OF EQUALITY

The crisis of Canadian democracy does not consist simply of obstacles to democracy. The Canadian crisis is deeper because Canadians also disagree about the meaning of democracy. For some Canadians, local government forms the heart of democracy. For other Canadians, democracy is more effectively realized at the national level, where prejudice and intolerance are easier to combat and equal citizenship is more secure.[22] For some, democracy has come to be associated with increased citizen participation in constitutional matters and the vigorous assertion of the sovereignty of the people. For others, élite bargaining of the kind engaged in by the Fathers of Confederation remains the only viable means for resolving constitutional difficulties because "no one in Canada has so far found a more democratic method."[23] There are Canadians who embrace Lockean ideas of democracy and emphasize individual rights; there are also Canadians who endorse a Rousseauian conception of democracy and favour the cultural community. Other countries also experience disagreements about the meaning of democracy. In Canada, however, such disagreements become entangled with the obstacles to democracy and exacerbate the crisis.

The crucial Canadian disagreement about the meaning of democracy has been the long-standing disagreement between French Canadians and English Canadians. In 1966 Ramsay Cook took notice of the disagreement and called it the Canadian dilemma. There was, he suggested, a "basic difference in public philosophy that divides Canadians."[24] English Canadians, benefiting from their majority position, defended individual rights and equal opportunity. They embraced a Lockean conception of democracy and believed that the only fair way to run the country was according to the majoritarian principle of "one person, one vote." French Canadians, on the other hand, being both a conquered people and a political minority were, as a consequence, concerned with group rights, espoused a public philosophy that was Rousseauian in character, and expressed the general will to survive.[25] In a more recent essay, Charles Taylor has arrived at a similar conclusion. The individualistic premises of the 1982 Charter of Rights, he suggests, facilitate the expression of the English-Canadian identity, but collide with Quebec's concern for its survival as a nation.[26]

Solutions for the dilemma have also been proposed. One solution requires political élites to embrace consociational democracy; another appeals to Lord Acton's critique of nationalism. The consociational solution supposes that French and English exist in two solitudes, with little contact between their divergent ways of life. Consociationalism also requires political élites to be committed to the existence of Canada, to arrive at compromises that are mutually beneficial, and to be able to persuade citizens to accept the negotiated outcomes.[27] Lord Acton's solution, on the other hand, is theoretical rather than practical. His objective was to expose the oppressive character of modern nationalism and to demonstrate the moral superiority of English liberty. For Acton, the test of liberty and of civilization was the ability of several nations to live under the same state. He did not specify the details of his theory and he did not apply it to Canada, but his ideas are often taken to justify a type of state in which French and English are accommodated and the Canadian dilemma is dissolved.[28]

One difficulty with both proposals is that they do not take seriously enough the democratic dimensions of the Canadian dilemma. In fact, both proposals rely on principles that are not constitutive of democracy and may even conflict with it. Consociationalism postulates the political wisdom of élites and the political apathy of the masses. It also assumes that the masses are intolerant and unenlightened.[29] As to Lord Acton, he was a liberal rather than a democrat. He was dismissive not only of the democratic ideals of the French Revolution, but also of Jeffersonian democracy. He defended the multinational state because it expressed liberal principles and constrained the absolutism and intolerance that he took to be inherent in democracy. In Canada the increasing acceptance of popular sovereignty diminishes the relevance of proposals that repudiate democracy or conflict with important dimensions of it.[30]

The dilemma may simply be irresolvable. What makes the Canadian dilemma so intractable is that it involves two conceptions of democracy, both of which are integral to the Western democratic tradition. Canadians may have no alternative but to live with the dilemma. In a seminal essay, W.B. Gallie implicitly supported a conclusion of this kind. Disputes about democracy, he suggested, are not resolvable by argument because democracy is an internally complex concept that generates multiple conceptions and allows each conception to be supported "by perfectly respectable arguments and evidence."[31] Concepts such as democracy are, in other words, essentially contested concepts. Gallie went on to say that an essentially contested concept presupposes an "exemplar" or a core belief, which is reaffirmed by each of its conceptions. In the case of democracy, the core belief or aspiration is "a demand for *increased* equality."[32]

However, the aspiration of equality may be more complex than Gallie and others have been willing to allow. Not only is it embedded in a tradition of democratic discourse, but it also responds to the differing circumstances of democratic countries. As a consequence, a country may possess a distinctive aspiration of equality, such that its aspiration differs significantly from that characteristic of other democratic countries. Although such a contention may seem obvious or even trite, it was brilliantly denied in *Democracy in America*. In fact, Tocqueville attributed virtually universal and nearly divine significance to the manifestations of equality in America because he regarded that country as the greatest and the most advanced democratic experiment in the modern world.[33] What he found in America was not simply a system of democratic government, but also a democratic society characterized by the equality of condition. Such a society, Tocqueville said, was animated by a passion for social equality that pervaded every aspect of life. What he regarded as immutable was the aspiration of democracy; what he questioned and considered alterable was its political form. "The universal aim," wrote J.S. Mill in a review of *Democracy in America*, "... should be, so to prepare the way for democracy, that when it comes [to other countries], it may come in [its] beneficial shape."[34]

Like the United States, Canada is also a democracy, but its aspiration is different. For Tocqueville, the aspiration of equality revealed itself through the great contrast between the status hierarchies of medievalism and the social equality of America. As a result, he took for granted the existence and development of homogeneous societies in the modern world.[35] But Canada does not fit his model, because it is an ethnically or culturally divided society. Tocqueville also assumed that the passion for social equality would lead to a great conflict with liberty. "The question," he said, "is ... how to make liberty proceed out of that democratic state of society in which God has placed us."[36] In Canada, however, the tension is between liberty and community. Canadians and Americans share a concern about equality, but they confront different problems and possess distinct aspirations. Put differently, the Canadian aspiration of equality is initially concerned not with social equality so much as with mutual recognition in an ethnically or culturally divided society.

Both aspirations can end in failure. For Tocqueville, the great danger was that a democratic people would eventually and voluntarily succumb to democratic despotism. The great danger faced by Canadian society is that French and English will deny each other mutual recognition, treat one another as strangers, and destroy the country. No one has described the Canadian danger more vividly than André Siegfried. "Canadian politics," he wrote, "is a tilting-ground for impassioned rivalries ... [because] an immemorial struggle persists between French and English." "Like brothers that hate each other," he continued, "French and English ... dwell under one roof."[37] Moreover, Siegfried could find no real solution to the rivalries between French and English, and he regarded them as "one of those deep and lasting antipathies against which all efforts of conciliation are vain." French and English were often together and might even pretend that no racial hatred existed. But it would be a mistake, he added, to accept such "deliberate optimism."[38] What Siegfried described was the denial of mutual recognition.

"André Siegfried," wrote Frank Underhill, "is the Tocqueville of Canada."[39] But he was a Tocqueville who focused exclusively on the failures of Canadians. Siegfried also assumed that failure was unavoidable, in view of the depth of racial antipathies and the apparent impossibility of mutual recognition. All French Canadians, he observed, "would unite together as one man in defence of what they regard as the inalienable patrimony of the race."[40] The Fathers of Confederation accepted such a premise, but arrived at different conclusions. In the years before Confederation, Canadians witnessed racial and ethnic antagonisms, and Lord Durham, writing in 1839, recommended assimilation. But the Fathers rejected Durham. Confederation was based on the assumption that racial and ethnic hatreds were eliminable if French and English granted each other mutual recognition. For the Fathers, such recognition consisted of the adoption of a distinctive scheme of federalism and the acceptance of minority rights. Canadian Confederation, wrote W.R. Lederman, consisted of a partnership between the political leaders of English Canada and French Canada and provided "security for the French-Canadian way of life."[41]

Confederation addressed the issue of mutual recognition, but did not permanently settle it. The Fathers also left to future generations other problems of democracy, including the sovereignty of the people. Despite their anti-democratic rhetoric, the Fathers of Confederation, it has been said, "were *liberal* democrats."[42] Such a view draws attention to assumptions implicit in Canadian Confederation. What the Fathers rejected was not democracy so much as mob rule; what they accepted was constitutional monarchy, partly because it provided an ordered liberty that enabled French and English to live together. Put differently, they accepted both liberty and community, as expressed through a complex scheme of federalism and minority rights. Historically, Canadians have not had to face a dilemma of democracy because their constitutional settlement attempted to recognize liberty as well as community.[43] If they are forced to choose between liberty and community, they confront a situation that can have tragic results. Such a choice would not simply compel them to choose between the democratic theories of Locke and Rousseau. There is, in addition, the aspiration of equality, which for Canadians initially requires mutual recognition between people who speak different languages or have different cultural identities. Neither Lockean nor Rousseauian democracy recognizes such an aspiration.

WAYS OF LIFE AND THE WILL TO LIVE TOGETHER

Democracy presupposes an aspiration of equality. In Canada this aspiration initially focuses on mutual recognition between French Canadians and English Canadians, but it is not confined to them. Mutual recognition is also a key presupposition of Canadian federalism. Many French Canadians, wrote A.R.M. Lower, accepted Confederation "because Cartier was able to assure them that the guarantees ... for their language and religion were adequate."[44] Confederation assumed that, with certain mutual guarantees, French and English could put the Conquest behind them and live amicably together. But mutual guarantees can become ineffective or obsolete, and federalism can itself become an obstacle to democracy if federation becomes associated with over-centralized and unresponsive government or with the suppression of cultural particularisms. Canadian federalism and Canadian democracy share an aspiration of equality, with the result that a failure of federalism can become a crisis of democracy.

Virtually everyone agrees that contemporary Canada is experiencing a failure of federalism, yet there is almost no agreement as to the character and cause of the failure. Some, including Pierre Trudeau, blame Québécois separatists and provincializing premiers, and accuse them of embracing reactionary political policies aimed at the fragmentation or disintegration of Canada. In consequence, they are sceptical about demands for the decentralization of power, oppose recognition of Quebec as a distinct society, and regard the 1982 Canadian Charter of Rights and Freedoms as responsive to the needs of ordinary Canadians and as expressive of the will to live together.[45] Others, including the Parti Québécois, believe that federalism inevitably ends in failure, at least in Canada. This is so because the

Canada-Quebec conflict is not simply an administrative or regional conflict, but a clash between two nations or two cultural communities or two ways of life. Quebec, it has been suggested, cannot exist within Canada without "Quebecers [asking] ... English Canadians to undermine and dismantle their national institutions."[46]

Each of the above views illuminates crucial aspects of federalism in Canada. Trudeau's account draws attention to the will to live together. For him, and for those who share his views, federalism is an arrangement based on reason, which celebrates the will to live together and presupposes a consensus that must be constantly renewed.[47] Federal failure occurs when political leaders adopt reactionary political objectives and fail to renew the will to live together that exists among ordinary people. The Parti Québécois, on the other hand, focuses on the idea of a way of life. Those who share such a focus believe that the will to live together is not enough; there are also the requirements dictated by the cultural community and the need to sustain a way of life. Federalism is not rejected so much as considered an instrumental value; it is judged by the interests and aspirations it serves.[48] Federal failure, according to this view, occurs when federation becomes destructive of cultural identity or too constrictive of a way of life.

A way of life versus the will to live together? Such a question captures important dimensions of the Canadian crisis, but it also obscures ironies and ambiguities in the Canadian situation. Canadian federalism is faltering, yet Canadians have more values in common and more common concerns than ever before. "Ironically, at the very moment we agree upon so much," Charles Taylor has written, "we are close to breakup."[49] There are, of course, differences of language. Language is important, not only because it contributes to a sense of identity, but also because it can create barriers between communities. In Canada, French is the language of a minority and is increasingly regarded as threatened even within the once secure borders of Quebec. Such concerns fuel separatism. But Quebec is itself a liberal society, and Quebeckers embrace a plurality of commitments. These include respect for the rights of all people within the borders of Quebec, including the rights of Aboriginals, who themselves have distinct and vulnerable ways of life. There are, in addition, Quebeckers who believe that even an independent Quebec should have ties with the rest of Canada. In both Quebec and Canada, the need to sustain distinct ways of life is entangled with – rather than opposed to – the will to live together.

None of this is to deny that there are situations in which the will to live together can become too burdensome. In Canada, federalism was adopted for the purpose of preventing such an outcome. The Fathers of Confederation made such an assumption; Pierre Trudeau has made it as well. The Fathers, wrote Donald Creighton, regarded "the 'federal principle' ... [as] the great concession ... to French Canada."[50] In some respects, Trudeau went beyond them. As a liberal pluralist, he did not simply make concessions to Quebec's distinctiveness; he celebrated it. As a federalist, however, Trudeau believed in the equality of the provinces and rejected Quebec's claims to recognition as a distinct society.[51] For him, it was provincial equality that sustained a vision of Canada as a liberal society committed to the equal rights of all citizens. Part of the difficulty with such a vision is that it can frustrate the will to live together. Not only does it give little consideration to cultural identity, but it also affords few remedies to groups concerned about the disappearance of their way of life.[52] When Trudeau's vision is applied to Quebec's concern about the disappearance of the French language, it may also violate the "federal principle," if federalism in Canada is assumed to have as an objective the protection of Quebec's specificity.

The Fathers of Confederation not only acknowledged Quebec specificity, but also relied on it as a key justification for the adoption of a federal system. The frustration of their objective is not simply an implicit rejection of Confederation; it also fuels Quebec separatism, turns a failure of federalism into a crisis of federalism, and defeats the aspiration of equality presupposed by Canadian democracy. "Multinational societies," Charles Taylor has suggested, "can break up, in large part because of a lack of (perceived) recognition of the equal worth of one group by another." "This," he adds, "is at present ... the case in Canada."[53] The Canadian case is of course complex because it raises difficult questions about mutual recognition and connects them to equally difficult questions about federalism, about equality, and about democracy. When Americans are troubled by fundamental questions, they frequently turn to their original constitution or to an interpretation of it. But the constitution of 1867 has come to perform a more limited role, and Canadians must increasingly turn to first principles.

In Canada the appeal to first principles is itself problematic, not only because Canadians disagree about such principles, but also because they increasingly focus on the experience of other countries.

Federalism is one example; equality is another. English-speaking Canadians have increasing difficulty recognizing Quebec's distinctiveness, even though federalism was initially regarded as a response to that province's specificity. One reason for the difficulty may be the pervasive influence exercised by American federalism.[54] American federalism is a conception of political federalism that assumes the essential equality of the states and a relatively homogeneous country. Canadian federalism is different, partly because of the distinctiveness of Quebec.

Beliefs about equality have also created difficulties. Equality is increasingly associated with the possession of uniform individual rights and with a refusal to protect (or favour) ways of life.[55] So conceptualized, it has received its most powerful articulation in the United States and is sometimes known as the "colour-blind" constitution. But such an understanding of equality takes for granted assumptions that may not hold in all cases. If rights are to be undifferentiated, then ways of life should be equally vulnerable. A more vulnerable way of life, if granted undifferentiated rights, experiences disadvantage rather than equality.[56] Such a conceptualization of equality also neglects historically based claims to rights.[57] Aboriginals, for example, make claims to rights based on treaties and unjust dispossession; they deny, as do many French Canadians, that government should be blind to the requirements of different ways of life.

The issue is mutual recognition. Historically, Americans have not had to concern themselves with it because of their social uniformity. "I do not know of any European nation, however small," wrote Tocqueville, "that does not present less uniformity ... than the American people."[58] He regarded the existence of uniformity as essential for the success of American federalism; its absence as a factor in the failure of federalism elsewhere. Uniformity created difficulties for political democracy, but supported federalism. Canadians often reverse Tocqueville's assumptions, at least with respect to federalism. Historically, they have associated federalism with diversity. Such a reversal of assumptions has reflected the crucial differences between Canadian and American society. Canada, Tocqueville observed, was a country "divided into two inimical nations."[59] In consequence, federalism acquired a significance in Canada that it did not possess in the United States.

American federalism, as Tocqueville noted, was closely associated with republican liberty and local self-government. Federalism was adopted in the United States because Americans wanted both the

commercial advantages of a large country and the republican liberty
of a small nation. But federalism is not simply about commercial advantages and republican liberty; it also divides sovereignty and requires, as a result, a patriotism capable of sustaining the federal
union. In the United States, such a patriotism consisted of "an aggre-
gate or summary of the patriotic zeal" of the separate states. "Every
citizen," wrote Tocqueville, "transfers ... his attachment to his little republic into the common store of American patriotism."[60] When patriotism is so described, a single or common way of life is taken for
granted.[61] In the United States, federalism divided sovereignty, but
presupposed a single patriotism sustained by a common way of life.
Canadian federalism is different because Canada is composed of two
or more ways of ways of life, with the result that both patriotism and
sovereignty are divided.

What sustains Canada is not a singular patriotism but mutual recognition, as the Fathers of Confederation acknowledged when they
adopted the federal system in 1867. Of course, they also made other
assumptions, some of which supported centralized power and sustained constitutional monarchy. The constitution of 1867, wrote
Donald Creighton, "was a characteristic Canadian creation, shaped
by Canadian history, designed for Canadian purposes, and deliber-
ately different from the constitution of the United States."[62] The
Canadian federation differed from the American federation, not only
because it was more centralized, but also because it responded to the
existence of two nations. As a result, it had to sustain distinctive ways
of life as well as an allegiance that supported a common government.
In the Confederation debates of 1865, Cartier spoke of such an allegiance, called it the Canadian political nationality, and imagined it as
a nationality with which neither religion nor race would interfere.
Canadians were different among themselves, but were regarded as
possessing enough common interests and sufficient mutual sympathy
to sustain a single country.[63]

MUTUAL RECOGNITION AND
CANADIAN DEMOCRACY

Canada is increasingly becoming an experiment in democracy, but it
has not ceased to be a federal experiment. Federalism is important in
Canada not only because it accommodates territorial particularisms,
but also because it protects ways of life and expresses a will to live
together. Ways of life sustain a sense of community or belonging and

satisfy the individual's need for a particularistic identity.[64] The will to live together is also important, although it rests on different moral and psychological assumptions. In John Rawls's understanding of it, the will to live together requires individuals and communities to adopt "the virtues of tolerance and being ready to meet others halfway, and the virtues of reasonableness and the sense of fairness." So understood, the will to live together makes fair social cooperation possible on a footing of "mutual respect" and stands for "*very great* virtues."[65] In Canada, mutual recognition is initially expressed through the federal idea; the institutions of federalism, as a result, attempt to provide guarantees both for ways of life and for the will to live together.

Assimilation and separatism are the most commonly discussed alternatives to mutual recognition. Assimilation received its most sophisticated defence in Lord Durham's *Report*, but was a largely unrealizable goal even in 1839. What Durham failed to appreciate was that the French-English crisis was in fact too serious to be addressed by the means he proposed.[66] More recently, similar conclusions have been reached in regard to Aboriginal Canadians, with the result that assimilation is no longer regarded as a defensible or sustainable policy in relation to them. Separatism may be a more realizable goal, but it too encounters difficulties. In the case of Quebec, separation dissolves ties with the rest of Canada without resolving fundamental questions about the pluralism of Quebec society. In several respects, Quebec's pluralism parallels Canada's, and both raise questions about mutual recognition that assimilation and political acts of separation fail to resolve satisfactorily.

This is so because mutual recognition is presupposed by democracy as well as by federalism. In Canada, democracy has displaced federalism as the primary source of legitimacy, with the result that options such as assimilation and political separatism are increasingly judged according to democratic principles. Such principles do not lead, inevitably, either to assimilation or to political separatism. Embedded within the democratic tradition is a complex discourse of mutual recognition that emphasizes the equal worth and equal dignity of human beings. The discourse is often associated with Rousseau and Marx, but it is not confined to them. In the case of Rousseau, the demand for mutual recognition was a protest against the indignities and inequalities of aristocratic societies; the wounds were to be remedied by the creation of a democratic society infused with "equality, reciprocity, and unity of purpose."[67] Marxists are also concerned with "the *common good* of mutual recognition." They associate mutual recognition with "the moral promises of democracy" and oppose it to the social classes and status differentials of a capitalist society.[68] In a culturally or linguistically divided society, mutual recognition acquires a new character. In such a society, an increase in equality comes through the recognition of difference. Divergent identities are recognized because the suppression of minority identities creates a sense of inferiority and a loss of self-worth. In culturally plural societies, as Charles Taylor has implied, the "equal recognition" of divergent identities is necessary for the existence of "a healthy democratic society ... [since] the withholding of recognition can be a form of oppression."[69]

The denial of recognition can also create antagonistic cultural solitudes, a phenomenon familiar to Canadians. According to Jeremy Webber, the challenge faced by Canadians is not to eliminate those solitudes so much as to sustain a democratic dialogue between them. "A viable allegiance [to Canada]," he writes, "can be compatible with the express recognition of difference as long as we remain willing to continue the national conversation across cultures."[70] The mutual recognition implicit in such a conversation is not easily realized. One obstacle is the complexity of Canada; another is the sheer difficulty of the issues that confront Canadians, which range from decentralization and Senate reform to Quebec's status as a distinct society and demands for Aboriginal self-government. However, failures of mutual recognition are not always attributable to the complex circumstances of Canadians. In a study of Canadian constitutional negotiations, published in 1983, Alan Cairns observed that no one, not even the prime minister, viewed it as his task to accord a generous place for the ambitions and concerns of others. On the contrary, constitutional actors regarded "the clear-sighted pursuit of self-interest [as] the governing consideration," even though there was "no evidence of an 'invisible hand' at work."[71] In subsequent studies, occasioned by the (failed) Meech Lake and Charlottetown constitutional accords, Cairns has drawn attention to the additional consideration of constitutional morality. What the long-term existence of Canada presupposes, he suggests, is not the unbridled pursuit of self-interest, but "reciprocal sensitivity and a build up of trust" among all those "who have stakes in the constitutional order."[72]

The appeal to constitutional morality is not merely or even primarily a moralistic appeal. Rather, it is a restatement of the principles that sustain Canada. Canadians are different among themselves, but they have also demonstrated a will to live together. They have distinct ways of life; they also possess common values, common allegiances, and common ways of life. Such beliefs provide a focus for constitutional morality and reveal some of the dimensions of mutual recognition in Canada. Moreover, the difficulties that confront Canadians are not inherent either in federalism or in democracy. Kenneth McRae, for example, has suggested that many of the difficulties can be traced to an increasing "prevalence of majoritarian attitudes," which have produced demands for equal or uniform rights. "For anyone familiar with Canadian history," he goes on to say, "the repeated refrain of equal rights for all has an ominous ring to it" because it often means that specific "rights are in imminent danger of being overridden."[73] In Canada, majoritarianism and uniform rights are not easily reconciled either with the aspiration of mutual recognition or with the goals of constitutional morality.[74]

Historically, the alternative to simple majoritarianism is a federalism that recognizes diversity. Federalism based on diversity is closer to asymmetrical federalism than to the equality of the provinces. In the case of Quebec, asymmetrical federalism requires the constitutional recognition of Quebec as a distinct society within Canada.[75] When applied to Canadian Aboriginals, it accords a similar kind of recognition to Aboriginal communities.[76] But asymmetrical federalism is not an unmixed blessing.[77] In the short run, it may increase Canadian difficulties because its acceptance appears to imply a complex restructuring of Canadian institutions and may even require a rethinking of representative government in Canada. The precise nature of the change depends on the degree of asymmetry. On the other hand, Canada is already characterized by asymmetry, and asymmetry has been extended in recent years through non-constitutional agreements. Many of those who espouse asymmetrical federalism believe that, although short-term difficulties may increase, long-run prospects are improved. The recognition of Quebec as a distinct society, Christian Dufour suggests, facilitates the solution of the Senate problem because a Quebec secure in its identity would have a far greater commitment to the reform of central government institutions.[78] Asymmetrical federalism presupposes that Canada is experiencing failures that Canadians have the will to resolve.

But Canada may be experiencing a kind of failure that is unrelated to federalism or democracy or constitutional morality. When the Royal Commission on Bilingualism and Biculturalism, in its *Preliminary Report*, counselled Canadians to re-examine the concept of democracy, the unstated assumption was that they still possessed a will to live to-gether. Such a will cannot be taken for granted. There are those who believe that contemporary Canada is experiencing its own gradual dissolution, coupled with the slow emergence of two or more homogeneous nations, each incapable or unwilling to recognize the other(s).[79] Homogeneous nations also encounter obstacles to democracy. The danger they faced, according to Tocqueville, is that citizens will gradually relinquish their rights of self-government.[80]

CHAPTER EIGHT

A Dialogue of Democracy:
Aboriginal Self-Government and
Canadian Federalism

The rights of Aboriginal peoples present Canadians with a moral, as well as a theoretical challenge. The most visible manifestations of the moral challenge are the dismal statistics of Aboriginal poverty, the inadequacies of Aboriginal education, and an Aboriginal suicide rate far in excess of the Canadian average.[1] A theoretical challenge also exists because Aboriginal rights reveal inadequacies in political orthodoxies and compel a re-examination of first principles. The issue is deeper than the failure of the Fathers of Confederation to make adequate provision for Aboriginal peoples: even a reconstituted Canada may be incapable of responding fully to their aspirations.[2]

First among the aspirations is the right to self-government, which includes the recognition of the unique ethnicity or nationhood of the Aboriginal peoples, as well as the territorial and other resources flowing from such recognition.[3] The right to self-government is widely regarded as a basic or fundamental right and is sustained by a concern for the dignity and revitalization of Aboriginal peoples. Moreover, this right was recognized by the (failed) Charlottetown constitutional accord and was widely regarded as the accord's most important innovation. Self-government remains, nevertheless, the most controversial right possessed by Aboriginals. What makes it so controversial is that it has the capacity to dissolve moral and political ties between Aboriginals and other citizens, a result that disadvantages all Canadians. The same right has, in addition, the potential to "twice marginalize" those who live off a suitable land base and who constitute as much as 75 per cent of the Aboriginal population in Canada.[4] Self-government is the strongest right to independence possessed by Aboriginal people; yet its recognition and its implementation presuppose, paradoxically, the continuing interdependence of Aboriginals and other Canadians.[5]

Much the same paradox can be expressed by saying that the right to self-government creates a challenge for Aboriginal peoples: "to develop a model of self-government that is acceptable to the Canadian government and that gives Indians internal self-government without compromising fundamental traditional values."[6] The challenge for Aboriginals as well as for other Canadians is to accept Aboriginal self-government without dissolving ties between Aboriginals and other citizens and to acknowledge the interdependence of all citizens without diminishing the dignity of Aboriginals. The challenge created by the demand for self-government is usually discussed as an issue of liberalism and almost as often as a problem of federalism. But neither liberalism nor federalism provides a satisfactory starting-point. Self-government is, after all, a democratic right and it sustains a democratic challenge. What Aboriginals demand is more democracy for themselves; what they question are the democratic credentials of a society that has failed them. The failure not only gives urgency to demands for self-government, but also creates a challenge to recognize the democratic aspirations of Aboriginal communities without undermining Canadian democracy and the place of Aboriginals in it.

LIBERALISM, FEDERALISM, AND ABORIGINAL CRITICISM

Democracy is not the usual starting-point for the discussion of Aboriginal issues: ordinarily, Aboriginal rights are discussed as issues of liberalism. Such a starting-point provided the basis for the 1969 Statement on Indian Policy, a document issued by the Trudeau government that relied on distinctive liberal doctrines in an effort to ameliorate the life situation of Aboriginals. The declared intention of the 1969 policy was to "open the doors of [equal] opportunity" to Aboriginals by eliminating their anomalous legal status.[7] For most Aboriginals, however, Trudeau's recommendations revealed the irrelevance of liberalism and the perniciousness of an ideology that justified "a thinly disguised programme of extermination through assimilation."[8] Liberalism is also at the centre of the debate about the 1982 Constitution Act, which includes the Charter of Rights as well as provisions recognizing the rights of Aboriginal peoples. The key issue in the contemporary debate is the alleged inability of liberalism to come to terms with the incommensurability of cultures. In consequence, the Charter is viewed as an instrument that postulates the existence of fictitious human rights and that establishes the cultural hegemony of Western civilization over Aboriginal peoples. For those Aboriginals who embrace such a view, the alternative is to reject liberalism, so that Canada can be redefined as a country in which Aboriginal peoples and other "incommensurable communities" are held together by the toleration of differences.[9]

But liberalism is a complex philosophy, and its very complexity has allowed liberals both to absorb Aboriginal criticisms and to offer new solutions to Aboriginal grievances. As a liberal, Pierre Trudeau initially advocated an integrationist policy. When the policy was overwhelmingly rejected by Aboriginals, he responded by recognizing Aboriginal distinctiveness.[10] Trudeau's intention aside, such a change can be regarded as a principled change because liberalism attributes a more important status to cultural membership and cultural minorities than is usually recognized.[11] Within liberalism, individual freedom and personal identity occupy a privileged position. But freedom and identity are neither abstract nor atomistic. Rather, they presuppose cultural membership because, as Will Kymlicka has noted, culture provides the context of choice within which individuals create valuable lives for themselves. "Shared membership in a cultural community," he writes, " ... doesn't constrain individuality. On the contrary, membership in a cultural structure is what enables individual freedom, what enables meaningful choices about how to lead one's life."[12] Those who are forcibly assimilated often lead tragic lives and experience stunted personal development. Consequently, liberals can reject forcible assimilation.[13] They can also rely on cultural membership to justify special protections for minorities and disadvantaged cultures, including the right to self-government.

What makes the right to self-government so important is that it prevents non-Aboriginals from interfering in the affairs of Aboriginal communities. Such protection is crucial. Without it, Kymlicka writes, "the very existence of aboriginal cultural communities is vulnerable to the decisions of the non-aboriginal majority around them."[14] In the absence of self-government, Aboriginal communities could be outvoted or outbid on resources crucial to the survival of their communities. For much the same reason, self-government is needed to protect Aboriginals from the preferences of transient workers who may be resident in Aboriginal communities. Those are some of the legitimate objectives of self-government. But it should not have as its objective the entrenchment of Aboriginal majorities nor allow Aboriginal majorities to tyrannize over Aboriginal minorities. On the contrary, each member of the Aboriginal community, Kymlicka writes, should have "the same ability to use and interpret her cultural experience as she sees fit."[15]

Such are the main features of a liberal conception of Aboriginal self-government. Those who subscribe to it often assume, in addition, the existence of a country based on liberal political principles. "In a liberal democracy like Canada," Kymlicka writes, "aboriginal rights would be more secure if they were viewed, not as competing with liberalism, but as an essential component of liberal political practice."[16] The difficulty with such an assumption is that Canada is not solely a liberal society; it is also a democracy and a federal nation. Moreover, liberalism is not accorded the primacy in Canada that it appears to enjoy in the United States, a fact that has important implications for Aboriginal rights. In the United States, Aboriginal rights almost inevitably confront individualistic liberalism and must either be reconciled with it or regarded as justified exceptions.[17] But in Canada the strongest protest made by Aboriginals is unrelated to liberalism. Canadian Aboriginals insist that they have been accorded far less favourable treatment than French Canadians, even though their status as a founding people is similar. As a result, they reject a dualistic Canada composed of French and English because it assumes that "the peoples of the First Nations never existed." Aboriginals do not deny the distinctiveness of Quebec within Canada. On the contrary, they demand a similar recognition for themselves. "If anyone is more distinct," wrote Chief Georges Erasmus, "surely it is the peoples of the First Nations."[18]

Behind such a protest is an understanding of Aboriginal rights that appeals to the historic equality of peoples and builds on Canada's commitment to it. That is another way of saying that a liberal defence of self-government is inadequate because it neglects both Aboriginal history and the special nature of Canada. The foundation of Aboriginal rights "is not grounded in some abstract notion of the need to respect Aboriginals as members of vulnerable cultural minorities," but in the concrete need to respect Aboriginal treaties, to provide compensation for the violence against Aboriginals, and to restore the dignity of Aboriginal peoples.[19] Recent decisions by the Supreme Court of Canada have arrived at similar conclusions. In those decisions, the court acknowledged the historical foundations of Aboriginal rights by upholding a right that was exercised "from time immemorial before European settlers came." The court also acknowledged that the history of Canadian Aboriginals could not be told "with much pride" because Aboriginal land rights were for many years "virtually ignored."[20]

Aboriginal history tells the story of Aboriginal peoples before and after European contact. What was once the most common version of the story degraded Aboriginals and justified European dominion over them; it portrayed them as immature children or worse and regarded their cultures as inherently primitive.[21] A more recent story restores the dignity of Aboriginal peoples, but disparages European civilization. Aboriginal societies before European contact are described as "orderly, satisfying, serene," whereas European civilization is portrayed as producing pathological societies.[22] Part of the difficulty with both stories is that they make assumptions about the inferiority or superiority of particular cultures. There is, however, a retelling of Aboriginal history that avoids such assumptions. It received near-classic formulation in the United States Supreme Court decision of *Worcester v. Georgia* and more recent expression in the Canadian case of *Regina v. Sparrow*.

Decided in 1832, *Worcester* described Aboriginals before European contact as "a distinct people, divided into separate nations ... [and] governing themselves by their own laws." Moreover, it regarded Aboriginal nations as having entered into treaties with European settlers and as subsequently governing themselves under the Crown's protection.[23] What *Sparrow*, decided in 1990, adds to *Worcester* is the idea that the Crown's protection implies a fiduciary obligation, such that "parliament is not expected to act in a manner contrary to the rights and interests of aboriginals." *Sparrow* requires "government, courts and indeed all Canadians ... [to] be sensitive to the aboriginal perspective itself on the meaning of ... [aboriginal] rights." In *Sparrow* the primary objective is to take Aboriginal rights seriously, so as to uphold "the honour of the Crown."[24]

Sparrow enunciates legal principles, retells Aboriginal history, and reveals inadequacies in prevailing understandings of Aboriginal rights. The right to Aboriginal self-government is often conceptualized as one that erects walls between Aboriginals and other Canadians. Behind the conceptualization is the belief that Aboriginal cultures are vulnerable cultures or the supposition that Aboriginal values are incompatible with Western values. The former view forms the core of a liberal defence of Aboriginal self-government; the latter is crucial to the incommensurability thesis. When self-government is so understood, Canada becomes a country of solitudes, so that the

French and English solitudes are to be joined by an Aboriginal solitude. Such a conception of Canada is difficult to reconcile with *Sparrow*, which presupposes, not the existence of solitudes, but the necessity of mutual respect and cooperation between Aboriginals and other Canadians.

Although the precise legal issue in *Sparrow* was the length of a fishing net, the dispute could not be settled without addressing difficult questions about the Musqueam way of life. The Supreme Court acknowledged the need to sustain that way of life. It also recognized that the Musqueam band existed within Canada, which created the need to share the salmon. As a lower court held, the Musqueam right to fish has not remained static over the centuries because "the world has changed." The Musqueam are now Canadian citizens and live in the wider context of "an industrial society with all of its complexities and competing interests." What such a change implies, the lower court added, is the necessity of regulating salmon fishing "with due regard to the interests of all."[25]

Not only does the "interests of all" become an almost empty phrase in a country of solitudes, but federalism itself becomes problematic in such a country. The way First Nations understand their relationship with Canadians, Ovide Mercredi and Mary Ellen Turpel have written, is through "the two-row wampum, which signifies 'One River, Two Vessels.'" Such a relationship, they add, is "a co-living agreement." What the relationship envisages is that "the two vessels would travel down the river of life in parallel courses and would never interfere with each other."[26] Part of the problem with such an image is the difficulty it creates for federalism. Federalism is frequently suggested as a solution to Aboriginal difficulties because a federal division of powers can secure to Aboriginal communities a degree of autonomy essential for self-government.[27] Ideally, federalism secures autonomy for Aboriginal communities, facilitates the development of Aboriginal identity, and expresses the status of Aboriginals as a founding people through the federal compact. In other words, it is the solution to Aboriginal grievances because it nurtures diverse allegiances and diverse identities. Yet federalism also presupposes a common allegiance and a common identity.[28] The difficulty with regarding Aboriginal communities as "incommensurate communities" and Aboriginal values as totally antithetical to Canadian values is that federalism then ceases to be an option for the resolution of Aboriginal issues. Transforming Canada into a country of solitudes dissolves the common bonds of citizenship, a result that undermines a key presupposition of federalism and works to the disadvantage of the most vulnerable members of Canadian society.[29]

A DIALOGUE OF DEMOCRACY

Neither liberalism nor the incommensurability thesis provides secure foundations for Aboriginal self-government. Both misunderstand the Canadian political morality, which rejects cultural assimilation as well as cultural solitudes. The challenge is to find a secure foundation for self-government without dissolving moral ties between Aboriginals and other Canadians. Ultimately, this challenge requires a reassessment of democracy. The kind of reassessment required was partly anticipated by C.B. Macpherson. In *The Real World of Democracy*, he reminded Canadians that the word "democracy" should not be confined to "our unique Western liberal-democracy." Other systems, he said, also "have a genuine historical claim to the title democracy."[30] For Aboriginals, democracy is crucial because self-government dispels the legacy of paternalism and restores Aboriginal dignity. Democracy is no less crucial to other Canadians. What results is not only a demand for self-government, but also a dialogue of democracy in Canada.[31] The dialogue is sustained by the existence of diverse ideals of democracy and by the interdependence of Aboriginals and other Canadians.

But a dialogue has not always existed, and even its contemporary manifestations are often fragile. Despite a lengthy process of consultation, it was the absence of dialogue that finally characterized the Statement on Indian Policy.[32] As Trudeau later admitted, the document was not "understanding enough" since it betrayed the "prejudices of small 'l' liberals, and white men at that."[33] An absence of dialogue also characterized the failed Meech Lake Constitutional Accord, which Aboriginals opposed because it did not address their concerns. The Charlottetown accord represented a new turn towards dialogue, yet its rejection has renewed concerns about the fragility of dialogue in Canada. Aboriginals believe that their own culture takes dialogue more seriously, and they recommend their cultural ways to other Canadians. "It would be good for all the people of Canada, not just the First Nations," an Aboriginal report has stated, "if governments adopted the principles by which our peoples historically governed themselves." Those principles include "consensus, not conflict; inclusion, not exclusion; ... generosity, not selfishness."[34]

Implicit in the recommendation is an understanding of self-government and its value to Aboriginal peoples. Self-government is often contrasted with alien rule, and the objective is to re-establish home rule by ousting the colonizer. When self-government is so understood, it is by no means identical with democracy because a society may have self-government, but be governed autocratically.[35] However, Canadian Aboriginals reject such an understanding of self-government. For them, self-government is associated with democracy, which in turn is identified with consensus and a face-to-face society. "Indians," Menno Boldt and Anthony Long have suggested, "traditionally defined themselves communally ... [and emphasized] sharing and cooperation rather than private property and competition." Political decisions, they continue, were made in traditional Indian societies, but the method used "was direct participatory democracy and rule by consensus."[36] Ovide Mercredi and Mary Ellen Turpel have arrived at similar conclusions. Traditional Aboriginal society, they write, based political discipline on "the principle of consensus for government," which is "the most perfect form of democracy known because it means that there is no imposition of the rule of the majority."[37] At the heart of the demand for self-government is neither an incommensurability thesis nor a thesis about cultural vulnerability. The ultimate appeal is to Aboriginal democracy.[38]

Chief among the ideals of Aboriginal democracy is the concern for the dignity of Aboriginal peoples. For many Aboriginals, self-government is virtually synonymous with dignity because it removes their badge of inferiority and establishes their equality. Equality is established because self-government demonstrates the equal capacity of Aboriginals to govern themselves. As a result, self-government not only dispels the harmful legacy of paternalism, but also begins the process of revitalization by allowing Aboriginals to heal themselves through participation in their own communities.[39] Participation heals partly because it enables Aboriginals to take responsibility for their own lives and partly because Aboriginal communities have traditionally exemplified the "values of respect, caring, sharing and strength." What they have traditionally rejected are "power-grabbing, money-grabbing, exploitation," values that are ruinous to Aboriginal peoples.[40]

Not only does Aboriginal democracy provide foundations for Aboriginal self-government, but it also rearticulates crucial ideals of democracy. A similar kind of rearticulation occurred in the democratic vision of Jean-Jacques Rousseau. As he understood it, democracy was possible only in a face-to-face society, a society in which citizens shared common beliefs, regarded each other as social equals, and devoted themselves to the public good rather than to the pursuit of particular interests.[41] Other kinds of democracy were sham democracies: they created a people that was neither free nor virtuous. Rousseau's famous advice to the government of Poland was that almost all small states prosper "because they are small," because "their citizens know each other," and because their governments can see for themselves "the harm that is being done and the good that is theirs to do." By contrast, large nations, he added, "stagger under the weight of their own numbers, and their people lead a miserable existence," characterized by apathy, corruption, and selfishness.[42]

The issue of democracy is not settled as easily as Rousseau seemed to imply. Part of the difficulty is that a face-to-face society realizes some, but not all of the ideals of democracy. There are ideals that flourish only in the kind of society disparaged by Rousseau and other advocates of a face-to-face society. Those ideals can be variously described, but their central appeal is almost always to some vision of an open society. In one version, an open society stands for a transition from the closed society to "a new faith in reason."[43] The basic contrast is between the tribalism and collectivism of a closed society and the rationalism and individualism of an open society. As a result, the guiding principles of an open society are personal freedom, social tolerance, and democratic pluralism. In another version, the focus is on the morality of an open society, and the basic contrast is between a closed soul and an open soul. A closed soul restricts morality to the primal group, "caring nothing for the rest of humanity." The open soul confers "inviolable rights" on all men and women, embraces an expansive fraternity as "the essential thing," and envisages a democracy capable of transcending "the conditions of the 'closed society.'"[44]

By articulating democratic values neglected by Aboriginal democracy, the idea of an open society refocuses the issue of Aboriginal self-government. In Canada the idea also has historical relevance since it provided a foundation for the Statement on Indian Policy, issued by the Trudeau government. Not only did that statement describe Canada as "our open society," but it insisted that Canadian society was capable of accommodating Aboriginal cultures through its commitment to multiculturalism. At the same time, the white paper recognized "the need for changed attitudes" among Aboriginals and other Canadians, so that "a truly open society" would be created.[45] Such a society would put an end to injustice by making Indians full and undifferentiated members of the Canadian community. The white paper implied that Aboriginals would have to choose between the closed society of their reservations and the open Canadian society. "Canada is at a cross-roads," wrote the chief architect of the Statement on Indian Policy, "... [and] the Canadian Indian has to choose." Aboriginals could remain "a nation within a nation" and lock themselves behind "ghetto walls," or they could accept "equal citizenship" in Canadian society and share in the advantages of the modern world.[46]

By requiring Aboriginals to decide between membership in their own communities and membership in the Canadian community, the Statement on Indian Policy not only forced on them a choice that was unnecessary, but it also de-legitimated the idea of an open society. Forced to choose, Aboriginals rejected the idea of an open society, asserted the unique importance of membership in Aboriginal communities, and eventually buttressed Aboriginal nationalism with a thesis about the incommensurability of cultures. What the Statement on Indian Policy failed to grant to Aboriginals was a federalist option, such that they could be members of Aboriginal communities and members of a more open Canadian society. Such an option was what many Aboriginals seemed to demand. As Harold Cardinal stated, "the Indian cannot be a good Canadian unless he is first a responsible and a good Indian." Indians, he added, must discover their own identity "before they can begin to work creatively with others."[47]

Similar sentiments are recorded elsewhere. According to a special report of the Assembly of First Nations, "Native youth, like young people everywhere, want the best of both worlds: the formal training to succeed in the white world, and education in their own language, culture, and traditions."[48] What such a statement suggests is that the values of Aboriginal democracy do not exhaust the aspirations of Aboriginal youth. Aboriginal youths also value membership in Canadian society and participation in its institutions. They implicitly reject what Rhoda Howard has described as the ethnocentrism of cultural absolutism. "Cultural absolutists," she writes, "are the real ethnocentrists. They not only argue that no one's sense of justice can transcend the boundaries of her own culture, they also argue that one ought not to transcend them."[49] By rejecting cultural absolutism, Aboriginal youths often experience within themselves the dialogue of democracy that sometimes occurs within Canada. The dialogue is often unrecognized, and it becomes more difficult to recognize if Canada is described as a country of solitudes, if cultures are held to be incommensurable, or if the focus is the vulnerability of cultures. When Canada is redescribed in these ways, the ideals of democracy are constricted and Aboriginal emancipation becomes more difficult to achieve.

STRATEGIES FOR EMANCIPATION

Aboriginal self-government has as its goal Aboriginal emancipation. When Aboriginals and other Canadians repudiated the Statement on Indian Policy, they explicitly rejected assimilation and implicitly accepted Aboriginal emancipation. "In some ways," Ovide Mercredi and Mary Ellen Turpel have written, "the White Paper was the First Nations' equivalent of the Lord Durham Report."[50] But the rejection of the white paper has not solved the problem of Aboriginal emancipation. Part of the difficulty is that Aboriginals and other Canadians have accepted the goal of emancipation without specifying its content. There are also rival conceptions of Aboriginal emancipation that compound the difficulty. In some accounts, it takes on the characteristics of decolonization, and the ultimate objective is analogous to national independence. In other accounts, emancipation is associated with treaty federalism or municipal status for Aboriginal communities. The proposals are almost infinite. Yet there are also constraining factors, among them the moral and factual context presupposed by Aboriginal emancipation. These factors give substance to the goal of emancipation and direction to the strategies for its attainment.

Those concerned with their own emancipation are not likely to focus much attention on the issue of context. Their first and overriding concern is to assert their independence. They want to remove from their lives the fear, the inferiority, the servility, and the despair that they have endured. For them, a colonial model and a decolonization strategy have obvious attractions. As developed by Frantz Fanon, the colonial model portrays an unwilling people who are forced to embrace alien values and who eventually experience total dehumanization. In the mind of the colonizer, wrote Fanon, "the native ... represents not only the absence of values, but also the negation of values." Colonial domination is so insidious that it attempts to persuade native peoples that "if the settlers were to leave," the result would be "barbarism, degradation, and bestiality." Once a people has been subjected to colonization, only the most vigorous process of decolonization can restore its humanity and dignity. Colonized peoples, Fanon added, "were quick to realize that dignity and sovereignty were exact equivalents, ... a free people living in dignity is a sovereign people."[51]

Because of the parallels between the situation of Canadian Aboriginals and the one described by Fanon, a colonial model and a decolonization strategy have relevance for Aboriginal emancipation. The parallels have not escaped the attention of Canadian Aboriginals. In a special report issued by the Assembly of First Nations, Aboriginal peoples are described as "crying for renewal, ... for the casting off of the yoke of oppression, colonization, and assimilation." Aboriginals were coerced into accepting "white culture and values, which our peoples did not want." The result has been "an ungodly mess" characterized by "suicide, poverty and welfare." Aboriginals experienced "the loss of land, language, culture, spirituality," which eventually created "self-hatred, low self-esteem, abuse." To restore their social vitality and their dignity, they need to be free of the control of the dominant society and to take control of their own education and justice system. Aboriginals must assert the right of self-government: it is a right, they say, that "we have never given up."[52]

In a decolonization strategy, the right to self-government is part of a larger political program that has as its objective the removal of the colonizer and the re-establishment of a genuine native culture. Often there is a focus on the pre-colonial past. The "secret hope," wrote Fanon, is to discover a "very beautiful and splendid era whose existence rehabilitates us both in regard to ourselves and in regard to others."[53] Canadian Aboriginals have also discovered a past inhabited by Aboriginal peoples "healthy in body and mind ... [and] in harmony within themselves, between themselves, with nature itself." As a result, Aboriginal self-government has come to be regarded as a restoration of native ways and native concepts. In the absence of such a restoration, Aboriginals "cannot expect any justice." Such a belief also implies that the Canadian Charter of Rights and Freedoms should have no applicability to Aboriginal communities. Far from offering a solution to Aboriginal concerns, the Charter of Rights would not have been necessary "if Europeans ... had learned from [natives]."[54]

The rejection of the Charter is a key component of the decolonization strategy, yet it is also the component that most clearly reveals the limitations of that strategy. The Charter is rejected because of its (alleged) individualism, and individualism is rejected because it is antithetical to Aboriginal communalism. Western values, in other words, are rejected because they are destructive of the communal way of life cherished by Aboriginals. But such an understanding of the decolonization strategy does not withstand scrutiny, at least not with respect to the Charter of Rights. For although the decolonization strategy rejects the Canadian Charter, it also acknowledges that Aboriginal communities are likely to require their own charters. "The notion," Menno Boldt has written, "that Indians need protection for their human rights from the Canadian government and society, but do not need protection from injustice and abuse by their own government and communities, is unsupportable." The introduction of Indian self-government, he adds, "does not obviate the need to protect band/tribal members from injustice and abuse; it merely moves it to another level."[55] Those who embrace the Aboriginal decolonization strategy believe that there is an easy way around such considerations. Aboriginal communities can reject the Canadian Charter, but they must adopt Aboriginal charters.[56] Although such a solution may be satisfactory in itself, reliance on it changes the terms of discourse. The Canadian Charter was initially rejected because of its (alleged) individualism. It is now rejected because it is Canadian. Put differently, the decolonization strategy turns out to be less coherent than it at first appears: the strategy begins as a defence of Aboriginal communalism, but ends up as a plea for Aboriginal solitudes.

The decolonization strategy also encounters other difficulties, not the least of which is the fact that many Aboriginal women refuse to support crucial aspects of it. The lack of support among Aboriginal women was made evident during the debates that preceded the defeat of the Charlottetown accord. As Mercredi and Turpel have written, "the Charlottetown experience was an historic breakthrough: all governments accepted the inherent right of self-government."[57] In effect, the accord proposed a third level of Aboriginal government, exempted Aboriginal languages, cultures, and traditions from the Canadian Charter of Rights, and granted Aboriginal peoples access to the notwithstanding clause in the Constitution Act, 1982.[58] "The extent and openness of the accord's response to Aboriginal peoples," Alan Cairns has written, " ... both astonished and gratified academic students of Aboriginal issues." To law professor Douglas Sanders, for example, the accord's "Aboriginal provisions ... [were] a hallmark of tolerance and generosity."[59] But many Aboriginal women did not share the enthusiasm displayed by academic commentators. Not only did they complain about their exclusion from the negotiations that preceded the Charlottetown accord, but the Native Women's Association insisted that the Canadian Charter should apply even to self-governing Aboriginal communities. The Charter, it was suggested, "simply sets out the same minimum standards of protection as those recognized in international law as applicable to all self-governing nations." The Native Women's Association also objected to the notwithstanding clause on the ground that it allowed "a band or First Nation ... to discriminate against Native women."[60]

The sharp cultural divisions and rigid moral boundaries of the decolonization strategy are also difficult to reconcile with the tactics of Aboriginal emancipation in Canada. As described by Fanon, decolonization is a violent process in which natives "vomit up" white values. He believed that the sole interest of the colonizer was in the maintenance of the colonial relationship, a fact that demonstrated the colonizer's hatred of the native population and justified in turn the violence of decolonization.[61] The situation in Canada is different, as Aboriginals themselves recognize through the tactics they most frequently adopt. In tactical terms, Aboriginal peoples usually seek to achieve their objectives by employing what Noel Dyck has called the politics of embarrassment. They construct and make relevant to governments and the Canadian public alike "a set of moral claims" that are intended to appeal to non-natives.[62] The politics of embarrassment takes for granted precisely what a decolonization strategy denies: the existence of a moral community composed of Aboriginals and other Canadians.

The result is that Aboriginal emancipation has paradoxical qualities. Canadian Aboriginals are victims of colonization, yet their emancipation presupposes the rejection of decolonization. Aboriginals often demonstrate an awareness of the paradox both by the tactics they adopt and by the outcomes they seek to obtain. They frequently insist that they own much of Canada, or all of a particular province, because they were its original inhabitants and have not renounced their rights to it. Chief Gosnell, for example, believed that Natives own British Columbia.[63] Aboriginals also claim ownership of substantial parts of Quebec, a claim that creates difficulties for Quebec separatism.[64] Although various Aboriginal peoples have made such claims, they usually refuse to draw the conclusions that appear to follow from them. Thus Chief Gosnell insisted that Aboriginals did not wish to reclaim British Columbia for themselves; they only wanted a decent and fair settlement. In the case of Quebec, many Aboriginals insist that the rights of all parties should be respected. "Theoretically,

the First Nations have the right to ignore both the federal government and the provinces." But most Aboriginal peoples, it is said,
"want a voice in the process and a place at the table, to contribute
their own perspective and to protect their interests."[65] What Aboriginals appear to want is not decolonization as such, but equal partnership in a reconstituted Canada.

Equal partnership is an ideal, the precise content of which remains
to be determined and negotiated. However, the broad outlines of a
partnership favoured by Aboriginals are often subsumed under treaty
federalism.[66] As commonly understood, treaty federalism represents
a new covenant between Aboriginals and other Canadians. Through
such an approach, the paternalistic, colonialist, and insulting assumptions of the Indian Act are replaced by a covenant that regards
all parties as equals. Treaty federalism is attractive to Aboriginals because it focuses attention on Aboriginal consent and provides guarantees for Aboriginal distinctiveness.[67] It also expresses the inherent
dignity of Aboriginal peoples and restores to them substantial portions of the self-government they possessed before European contact.
At the heart of treaty federalism is the historic sovereignty of Aboriginal peoples, which in turn enables treaty federalism to assume many
of the characteristics of a compact theory of federalism.

But a compact theory captures only one side of federalism. A federation sometimes originates in a compact of peoples or nations, but
even such a federation presupposes common citizenship, common allegiances, and a common frame of government. Federalism, it has
been noted, "is a device designed to cope with the problem of how
distinct communities can live a common life together without ceasing
to be distinct communities."[68] In the case of Canadian Aboriginals,
the common community is not less important than the distinct communities, even if its importance is less often recognized. Community
gives substance to the demand for equal partnership; it also is presupposed by Aboriginals in some of the other demands they make on
non-Aboriginal Canadians. Virtually all proposals for Aboriginal self-
government, according to Roger Gibbins and Rick Ponting, "assume
some continuing *fiscal support* from the Government of Canada."
Without such support, self-government "would be a trap rather than
an opportunity."[69] But if the Canadian community disappears, fiscal
support might disappear with it. Moreover, many Aboriginals do not
live in Aboriginal communities; others have a special attachment to
the Canadian community. The Métis, for example, have traditionally

been more interested in obtaining an effective voice in the government of Canada than in proposals for Aboriginal self-government. There are also Aboriginals who live in large cities: almost 10 per cent of the Aboriginal population resides in Toronto. For them, the common community of Canadian federalism has a significance that no proposal for Aboriginal self-government can eliminate.

The complexities of federalism can promote Aboriginal emancipation, while recognizing the social and moral constraints on it. These constraints not only expose the inadequacies of a decolonization strategy; they also illuminate a key foundation of the Canadian constitutional order. The Canadian Constitution is unlike that of the United States partly because individualistic notions of legitimacy have a less significant role in it. "The legitimacy of our Constitution," Brian Slattery has said, "is grounded primarily in our factual and moral interdependency as members of Canadian society."[70] If such a premise is granted, then important conclusions follow for Aboriginal self-government. Aboriginals are distinct members of Canada, but they also share a factual and moral interdependency with other Canadians. The difficulty with some prominent theories of Aboriginal self-government is that they are unable to accommodate both Aboriginal distinctiveness and the interdependency of Canadians. Those theories insist on the incommensurability of cultures, or ignore the fact that Aboriginals are Canadian citizens, or reimagine Canada as a country of solitudes. When interdependency is acknowledged, Aboriginal self-government becomes part of a way of life that expresses the multiple dimensions of Aboriginal existence, including membership in the Canadian community. "Aboriginal societies," Alan Cairns has written, " ... are penetrated societies. Their members live in many worlds at once, and relate to more than one community."[71] Such a way of life has affinities both with federalism and with the dialogue of democracy that sometimes occurs in Canada. In both cases, moral pluralism replaces moral exclusiveness, different ways of life exist together, and each individual can share in more than one way of life.

CONCLUSION: BETWEEN IDEAL AND PRACTICE

A large part of the appeal of Aboriginal self-government is the promise it makes to Aboriginals and other Canadians. For Aboriginals, self-government promises to restore the dignity and vitality they possessed before European contact and to remove the vestiges of colonialism that encumber their lives. "What," it has been asked, "is more humiliating than being ruled by foreigners, and being treated by them as inferiors in your own country?"[72] For other Canadians, self-government promises to solve the Aboriginal problem. Many Canadians, it has been suggested, believe "that a debt of guilt is overdue to be paid to Indians and Inuit."[73] Self-government promises to lessen or even to remove the guilt.

But there are pitfalls to be avoided. In a seminal work on racism – a work that inspired Fanon's early writings on decolonization – Jean-Paul Sartre observed that the victims of racism often engage in behaviour that is overdetermined. Victims of racism, he said, are often "poisoned by the stereotype that others have of them, and they live in fear that their acts will correspond to this stereotype."[74] As a result, they engage in behaviour that has as a primary objective the negation of the stereotype. Aboriginal self-government is not overdetermined behaviour. The same cannot be said of some of its justifications. Justifications that appeal to the incommensurability of cultures, or to the superiority of Aboriginal culture, or to a conception of Canada as a country of solitudes, appear to have as a primary objective the negation of the stereotypes of colonialism. The difficulty with such justifications is that, by neglecting the factual and moral interdependency of all Canadians, they provide inadequate understandings of Aboriginal emancipation and the mechanisms for its realization. The alternative is to recognize the legacy of colonialism without denying the interdependency of Canadians.[75] Aboriginal emancipation remains the key issue, but it is conceptualized differently. Such a reconceptualization of Aboriginal self-government makes explicit the democratic foundations to which it appeals and the dialogue of democracy to which it contributes.

The dialogue of democracy is substantially a dialogue between Aboriginals and other Canadians, but it is also a dialogue between Aboriginals. Not only do Aboriginal communities differ one from the other, but many of them are troubled by internal rivalry and unresponsive leadership. There are also Aboriginals who are not members of Aboriginal communities, either by their own choice or because they have been excluded. "There is," Noel Dyck has written, "not a single, 'correct' Native voice but a diversity of perspectives on a wide range of issues." He believes that academic commentators should "tell it like it is" and should avoid "a retrospective and decidedly romantic vision of the nature of aboriginal cultures and societies."[76] Alan Cairns has arrived at similar conclusions. Noting that Aboriginal self-government is in danger of becoming a taboo subject, about which only supportive and laudatory opinions can be expressed, he warns that it will provide no easy solution to many of the problems faced by Aboriginals. Moreover, he believes that, because of the absence of frank and open discussion, "the attempt to entrench a right of self-government in the constitution for aboriginal peoples may have been misconceived."[77] What both the ideal and the practice of self-government require is more, rather than less, dialogue.

CHAPTER NINE

The One and the Many: Pluralism, Expressivism, and the Canadian Political Nationality

"Canada, without being fully conscious of the fact, is passing through the greatest crisis in its history."[1] So stated the *Preliminary Report* of the Royal Commission on Bilingualism and Biculturalism, published in 1965. Since then Canadians have become acutely aware of the precariousness of their country. A dominant understanding of the crisis has also emerged, at least among scholars. This understanding is variously expressed, but its common themes are the fragmentation of Canadian citizenship, the wrenching transformation of the constitutional order produced by the public expression of divergent identities, and the struggle for recognition created by the existence of deep diversities within Canada.[2] Abstractly stated, the contemporary crisis is understood to spring from the pluralism of values and romantic expressivism, with the result that "the many" displaces "the one."[3] For some, pluralism and expressivism represent conditions that must be overcome because they substitute ethnic fragmentation and invidious group entitlements in place of the good of all.[4] For others, they are irreducible elements of the Canadian condition.

But pluralism and expressivism represent only one side of the Canadian condition. The other side is less often discussed, more frequently misunderstood, and more difficult to describe adequately. Some of its most important dimensions can be traced at least to Confederation and to George-Étienne Cartier's vision of a new Canadian nationality. As Cartier understood it, the new nationality did not displace pluralism and expressivism but existed alongside them, and it represented values that neither pluralism nor expressivism captured adequately. What the new nationality brought into existence was a country with which all Canadians could identify because common bonds and common citizenship were sustained without suppressing particularistic identities and local affiliations. Cartier drew attention to neglected features of the Canadian condition and revealed the moral complexities inherent in it.

The contemporary crisis is well understood in terms of the disintegrative forces that fuel it. But it is less well understood in terms of the resources available for its resolution. As a result, Canadians experience a heightened sense of fragmentation and exhibit increasing pessimism about their future. The Canadian political nationality does not resolve the contemporary crisis, but it does draw attention to the bonds that unite Canadians, and it does refocus attention on the Canadian identity. It provides a foundation for the Canadian identity, which in turn distinguishes Canada from other types of countries. Canada is a country with an identity because, in its refusal to choose either "the one" *or* "the many," it has developed a distinctive understanding of "the one" *and* "the many."[5] The refusal has also produced novel understandings of community, with the result that traditional conceptions of community are increasingly irrelevant in Canada. Pluralism and expressivism illuminate "the many," but they fail to understand "the one," and they fail to come to terms with the Canadian crisis.

THE CANADIAN POLITICAL NATIONALITY

The contemporary crisis is a new one, but it is also a crisis that has deep roots in Canadian history. It is new because it has eroded long-accepted beliefs about federalism and has undermined the dominance of British values in Canada. Canada can no longer be regarded as a country in which territorial particularisms exist easily together, and Canadians can no longer be described as a people who accept passive citizenship or subscribe to British notions of governance.[6] The contemporary crisis may also represent, in its more distant implications, an Americanization of Canadian society, or a transformation of Canada into a mini–United Nations, or even a dissolution of Canada into three or more distinct nations as represented by Quebec, Aboriginals, and other Canadians.[7]

Whatever its ultimate significance, the contemporary crisis has already necessitated the reimagination of Canada. Some scholars suppose that the crisis is altogether unique, with the result that proposals for the reimagination of Canada disassociate the future from the past. Others ascribe overriding significance to what Canadians have already become; they believe that "the renewal of the Federation does not ... require some basic change in the character of the Canadian people."[8] There is also a third view. This view regards the contemporary crisis as a human situation, defined both by the circumstances of Canadians and by the values they bring to it. When the crisis is so understood, it acquires important historical dimensions because many of the circumstances and values of Canadians are revealed in history. It retains its distinctiveness, although it ceases to be an isolated phenomenon and becomes part of a series of crises that can be traced backed to the Conquest of 1760.

"Of all our clashes," wrote A.R.M. Lower, "who will deny that the deep division between French and English is the greatest, the most arresting, the most difficult."[9] According to Lower, the Conquest of 1760 created the primary antithesis of Canadian history because it brought into conflict historic ways of life and left each succeeding generation to cope with the consequences. But the Conquest also had another side, which initially consisted of the absence of cruelty. It has even been suggested that the conquerors of 1760 were (as conquerors go) more kind than cruel,[10] although it was humiliating to have to be grateful to a kind conqueror. What the kindness of the Conquest created in the French people, Christian Dufour has suggested, was a love-hate relationship for the English.[11] Moreover, the Conquest has profoundly affected the identity of Quebec: each generation reinterprets its meaning and attempts to live with its consequences or to move beyond them. The challenge for contemporary Quebec, writes Dimitrios Karmis, is to transcend the Conquest by recognizing that it is capable of forming a complete society in a manner that accepts social pluralism and rejects the monolithic identity of the old nationalism.[12] The Conquest and its kindness have also affected the way English Canadians understand themselves. For them, the Conquest made Quebec part of Canada, and the Canadian identity was subtly shaped by the French component.

The Conquest brought French and English together, but it did not permanently settle the issues that divided them. Writing in 1943, A.R.M. Lower suggested that virtually "every political fight from 1791 to the present day has had as its fundamental, if unexpressed issue, the English conquest."[13] Such an assessment may also apply to the failed Meech Lake and Charlottetown accords, which had as their darker side an inability "to find a place for [Quebec] nationalism within a tolerant Canada."[14] Quebec separatists believe that such failures are inevitable because French and English constitute distinct nations and cannot exist within the same state. They suppose that the Conquest was not merely a deep humiliation of the French people and a disruption of Quebec's development. Far more important is their belief that the Conquest created a country based on a contradiction. English Canadians often arrive at a similar conclusion; they suppose that the tensions between French and English will be obliterated only when "lesser allegiances" are relinquished for the sake of "a common Canadianism."[15]

The deep issue is not the Conquest as such but the kind of country created by it. The Conquest can be regarded as the foundational event of Canadian history, not because it represents the military victory of one people over another, but because it brought together peoples with different ways of life and necessitated the creation of a country that accommodates more than one way of life. When it is so regarded, the difficulty encountered by both Quebec separatism and the idea of a common Canadianism is that they can make no sense of such a country. Both regard as anomalous a type of country that is by no means uncommon and that Lord Acton celebrated in his famous essay on nationality. The combination of different nations within the same state, he said, was a necessary condition of civilized life as well as a test of political freedom. Acton believed that the alternative to such a country was monolithic or assimilationist nationalism, which he described as a potent source of despotism and as a cause of "material as well as moral ruin."[16] For those schooled in the political theory of Lord Acton, the kind of country created by the Conquest is anything but anomalous.[17]

However, Acton's objective was to celebrate the multinational state rather than to unravel its complexities. He used the multinational state to criticize the despotic character of monolithic nationalism, but he ignored the understanding of nationalism that bases itself on the possession of a distinctive identity or an admired way of life or fraternal bonds among citizens. Nor did Acton devote much attention to the unity or cohesion that would be possessed by the kind of country he celebrated.[18] A multinational state that fails to develop a sense of common citizenship is far more problematic than he seemed to suppose. What is missing from Acton's essay is a clear understanding of the distinction between a multinational state and a federal state, with the result that the most difficult questions are simply not addressed by him. Those questions cannot be avoided once the distinction is made. Moreover, a federal state is predicated on the assumption that the nationalities which compose it have both the desire for national unity and the determination to maintain their independence. Since those objectives can easily produce tension and conflict, the difficult challenge faced by a federal state is to minimize the inconsistency.[19]

In Canada the federalist challenge acquires special importance because of the deep tensions between French and English; yet the challenge is obscured rather than resolved by appealing to Lord Acton. It was addressed at Confederation, which required an agreement between French and English. It was George-Étienne Cartier who was instrumental in securing the agreement required and who provided the deepest understanding of federalism. Cartier understood federalism to be a device that enabled different nationalities to live together because it allowed them to retain their own distinctive nationality and to create in addition a new sense of common nationality.[20] As a result, he was able to assure French Canadians that Confederation respected their nationality through its recognition of local loyalties and distinctive identities. Confederation also created a new nationality. He called it a political nationality; it was a nationality with which "neither the national origin, nor the religion of any individual, would interfere."[21]

Cartier addressed fundamental questions. But such questions, as Isaiah Berlin has demonstrated, can have no final solutions so long as human beings disagree about ultimate values.[22] What Cartier did provide is the outline of a distinctively Canadian understanding of federalism, which rests on foundations altogether different from those of American federalism. In the United States, federalism is usually discussed as an issue of freedom and as a corrective for the corruption inherent in centralized power. James Madison, for example, regarded federalism as a device that secured freedom in large republics.[23] Cartier regarded it as a device that, by dividing the allegiances of citizens as well as the powers of government, enabled different nationalities to live together. That is another way of saying that Canadian federalism was intended as a response to nationalism. For Cartier, federalism accommodated crucial nationalist objectives; it also promoted values that nationalism neglected. As a result, it was a device for maximizing values because it protected values inherent in distinct ways of life and also allowed common values to flourish.

The common values nurtured by federalism were what Cartier called the Canadian political nationality. Some of the values were common in the sense that they were embedded in the Canadian situation. That is why he was able to insist that French and English shared many of the "same sympathies." Those common sympathies implied a rejection of the American way of life and opposition to union with the United States.[24] Other values were regarded as common because they could be made so. In a discussion of Cartier's ideas, Donald Smiley insisted that "the concept of a Canadian political community – or nationality – means that Canadians as such have reciprocal moral and legal claims upon one another." Canada, he explained, is not simply an arena in which competing cultural and regional interests vie for power. Rather, it is a political community, and Canadians are required to "find and commit themselves to a group of common objectives."[25] The assumption shared by Cartier and Smiley is that Canadians have common values and are able to arrive at additional common values once they make adequate provision for their differences. The contemporary crisis has not undermined such an assumption, even if it has diverted attention from it.

COMPARATIVE PERSPECTIVES

But Canada may not be a country worth preserving, at least not in a recognizable form; and the Canadian political nationality may turn out to signify nothing at all. What makes the contemporary crisis more difficult to resolve is that many Canadians embrace such assumptions. They suppose that "Canada is a nation that is not a nation" or that it "preserves nothing of value." Canada, it has been said, represents "the *absence* of a sense of identity, the *absence* of a common life."[26] Even those who are sympathetic to the Canadian experiment often experience anxiety about the future. "The disadvantage of a synthetic state like ours," wrote John Holmes, "is that it lacks the visceral drive to achievement" and engenders "anxiety about national survival [based on] fear of our own failure of will." The "central problem" for Canada "is to find a reason for the country's existence."[27] Canadians often attempt to solve their central problem by appealing to Lord Acton's account of the civilizing virtues of the multinational state. There is an alternative to Acton. Canadians frequently compare Canada to other countries. Not only do such comparisons reveal important dimensions of the Canadian identity, but they also provide reasons for the country's existence that cannot be found in Acton's account of the multinational state.

The most frequent comparison is with the United States. In fact, Canadian Confederation rejected the American model, partly because that model was associated with political instability and partly because its underlying principles were regarded as destructive of provincial identities and cultural pluralism. The latter belief has become a Canadian orthodoxy. George Grant, for example, appealed to it when he criticized John Diefenbaker's vision of one Canada, a vision based on equal rights for all citizens irrespective of religion or race. Not only did one Canada presuppose an "interpretation of federalism [that was] basically American," but it was also "inconsistent with the roots of Canadian nationalism ... [in its] failure to recognize the rights of French Canadians, *qua* community." The difficulty, according to Grant, was that Diefenbaker had relied on "a principle ... more American than Canadian."[28] Others contrast the intolerance of the American "melting-pot" with the liberal freedoms inherent in Canadian pluralism.[29] Still others suppose that the rejection of the American model is the elemental bond that can hold Canada together. French and English, it has been said, need each other to survive, because "Quebecers dread being assimilated by the Anglophones: Anglophones do not want to become Americans."[30]

However, American scholars have not viewed their own society in the way that Canadians have frequently seen it. Traditionally, they have described the United States not as a melting-pot but as a society devoted to natural rights. Nationalism in the United States, it has been suggested, differs from the usual pattern because it presupposed the birth of a "new man," someone who had left his past behind.[31] The "new man" discarded ethnic and religious rivalries, possessed inalienable rights, and regarded other citizens as equally endowed with rights. Natural rights also created an American civil religion because the rights of man came from God and their religious dimension contained a transcendent goal for the political process. The goal was "to carry out God's will on earth," which required "a struggle against the common enemies of man: tyranny, poverty, disease and war." At its best, the civil religion provided an "apprehension of universal and transcendent reality as seen in ... the experience of the American people."[32] Through their devotion to natural rights, Americans attempted to found a country that particularized the universal.[33]

American scholars have also provided a sobering interpretation of Canadian pluralism. The United States and Canada are both federal states; yet the American union, as John Ranney wrote, "was based on a remarkably high degree of cultural, social and political community."[34] Slavery was of course the great exception, but it was a problem that the

Framers left for later generations to resolve. Much the same point might be expressed by saying that "the United States was a federation of states which were defined politically not ethnically; Canada was a federation of peoples, organized into different provinces."[35] The traditional direction of American society has been toward a society with a common identity based on common ideals. The implicit goal is the creation of "the larger fraternity of all Americans, in which people are tied to one another in what they feel to be a common good society."[36] In contrast, Canada has been described as "a confederation of groups," with group membership so central and permanent that it is unrealistic "to envisage ... these group identities weakening in time to be replaced by a common citizenship."[37] For American scholars, Canadian pluralism is not a model to be emulated. Rather, it is a reminder of the dangers of balkanization because it allows groups to struggle for special treatment and fails to develop common bonds among citizens.[38]

Although such criticisms dispel complacency, they misunderstand the Canadian experiment. In fact, their most telling application is to Lord Acton's unqualified celebration of the multinational state. What the criticisms expose are the inadequacies of a pluralism that takes unity for granted and assumes the existence of a spontaneous harmony among divergent groups or nationalities. Acton was able to provide an enthusiastic defence of the multinational state precisely because he ignored the problems that confronted it, including the issue of ripeness. If a state is to contain more than one nation, "ripeness is all." A union "too tight for the circumstances increases tensions dangerously ... and may turn mean, nasty, and aggressive."[39] There are circumstances that preclude two or more nations from combining within the same state. Acton was unable to envisage such circumstances, even though in modern history cultural diversity has more commonly produced conflict and tension than tolerance and harmony.[40]

The Canadian union is by no means identical to Acton's multinational state, nor does it exemplify the uncompromising liberalism to which he subscribed. Rather, Canadian Confederation was an arrangement based on mutual concessions between peoples with different ways of life. This is why the Fathers of Confederation are often described as men who avoided abstract principle and aimed at pragmatic consensus. Of course, Confederation also had great objectives, among them the creation a continental state so as to increase economic prosperity and bolster military security. To achieve their objectives, the Fathers created a new nation, but they also attempted to preserve the smaller nationalities and the local identities included in it. What was taken for granted is that Canadians are members of at least two communities; they are members of a more open national community and also members of a more distinctive local community. In this way, the Fathers attempted to avoid the balkanization that American scholars have mistakenly identified with Canadian Confederation.

Next to the United States, a country to which Canada is often compared is Switzerland. The comparison usually focuses on the issue of language and attempts to demonstrate that, although Canada has witnessed linguistic conflict, peace can be achieved in a multilingual federation. "Switzerland," according to Kenneth McRae, "really does deserve its reputation ... as a highly successful example of linguistic co-existence."[41] The foundations of linguistic peace in Switzerland are complex, but a factor that receives special attention is the Swiss policy of territorial unilingualism. The policy was authoritatively described by Walter Burckhardt, who understood it to imply that each locality should be able to retain its traditional language regardless of immigration and consequently that linguistic boundaries once settled should not be shifted. "Each group must be sure that the others do not wish to make conquests at its expense and diminish its territory." Burckhardt regarded territorial unilingualism as so vital to Switzerland's existence as a nation that he described it as "an obligation of Swiss loyalty" and as "one of the foundations of our state itself."[42]

Territorial unilingualism becomes far more controversial when Canada is the country under discussion. In Switzerland, territorial unilingualism contributes to linguistic peace and buttresses national unity. But in Canada there is no agreement as to whether territorial unilingualism is likely to strengthen national unity or to erode it. One view supposes that Confederation would be far more acceptable to French Canadians if their language community enjoyed the security provided by a territorially unilingual Quebec. Strong fences make for good neighbours.[43] However, there are also those who believe that territorial unilingualism would fuel Quebec separatism and exacerbate the divisions that exist among Canadians.[44] For them, a personality principle is the only acceptable basis for language policy in Canada because only such a principle promotes an open society and respects the right of each Canadian to choose between the official languages.

In Canada, demands for territorial unilingualism meet their antithesis in the personality principle, and a clash of values occurs. The irony is that although many Canadians have felt compelled to choose between these two principles, neither principle satisfactorily addresses the issues that have bedevilled Canada. Historically, language policy in Canada has not centred on the choice between territorial unilingualism and the personality principle. Rather, it has had to confront the even more difficult problems raised by the complex dispersal of language minorities. French is a minority language within Canada, but English is a minority language within Quebec, and there are French-speaking minorities within English-speaking provinces. Moreover, the problem of language minorities can be traced back to the Conquest of 1760, which rejected assimilation and laid the foundation of a distinctive multinational state. What such a multinational state assumed was that French and English could live in close proximity and without strong territorial walls to separate them, provided each respected the rights of the other. "Language rights," wrote Frank Scott, "must be respected if you wish to have domestic peace." For Scott, respecting language rights entailed a policy of bilingualism "sensibly applied." By recognizing language minorities, such a policy had the "realism [of] accepting facts."[45]

A language policy presupposes facts, but it also appeals to moral values. This is another way of saying that language policy chooses between conceptions of the good life and has implications for the kind of life that citizens can live. In Switzerland, territorial unilingualism has often been regarded as part of a more general concern about boundaries and borders. In a classic essay on Swiss self-awareness, Karl Schmid observed that the Swiss concern for boundaries "goes down deep within us, just as deep as the feeling that from outside our borders danger threatens."[46] Similar kinds of observations have been used to establish that Switzerland cannot provide a model for Canada. Noting that "Switzerland seems to achieve harmony by the device of mutual ignorance in water-tight cantons," Charles Taylor concludes that " ... we Canadians ... [require] our own model."[47] The Canadian model rejects not only the model of "mutual ignorance" but also that of a monolithic identity. Behind the rejection is a distinctive conception of nationhood as well as a complex understanding of community.

PHILOSOPHICAL DIMENSIONS

When Canada is compared to other nations, the Canadian identity turns out to presuppose distinctive values, principles, and commitments. But Canadians often experience difficulty in understanding the kind of country Canada is. The difficulty is sometimes attributed to a failure to grasp fully the distinction between ethnic or cultural nations and political or civic nations, a distinction that classifies countries into those that possess a single language or a common culture and those that base membership on legal criteria.[48] But the problem goes deeper: Canada is regarded as a difficult country to justify, even by those who accept the distinction and understand the implications of civic nationhood. Because this is so, the very concepts and ideas that have been used to justify Canada's existence as a nation require re-examination. The irony is that ideas intended to legitimate Canada's existence have made it a more difficult nation to justify.

Both the Canadian understanding of pluralism and the corresponding Canadian version of civic nationhood have contributed to such a paradoxical outcome. Canada is commonly celebrated as a pluralistic civilization or as a cultural mosaic because it allows diverse ways of life to flourish. In Canada, it is said, "there is no official culture ... [because no] ethnic group takes precedence over any other."[49] Corresponding to pluralism is civic nationhood. As described by a prominent Canadian scholar, civic nationhood emphasizes the instrumental dimensions of societal institutions, bases community on individual interest, and postulates that "the attachment of individuals to the social order is primarily utilitarian."[50] Although pluralism and civic nationhood are often regarded as justifications of Canada, they fail to provide adequate foundations for it.

The failure is not immediately apparent, partly because pluralism and civic nationhood are sophisticated philosophical positions and partly because they are presented as correctives to doctrines that are destructive of Canada. Take the case of pluralism. In some of its versions, pluralism is as old as philosophy and provides an alternative to the monism of Plato. According to Isaiah Berlin, monism is the belief that "all genuine questions must have one true answer," and "true answers when found must necessarily be compatible with one another and form a single whole." Pluralism, on the other hand, regards the notion of a perfect whole as "conceptually incoherent" because "values can clash" and individuals "are doomed to choose."[51] Moreover, important political values appear to be implicit in the dispute between monists and pluralists. Monism, or "the one," seeks a final solution and supposes that "no cost would be too high to obtain it, ... [including] the slaughter of individuals on the altars of the great historical ideals."[52] In contrast, pluralism, or "the many," is "the more humane ideal" because it allows for a measure of negative liberty, produces a more tolerant society, and recognizes diverse ideals of human life.[53]

Behind Canadian pluralism is a set of beliefs not unlike those defended by Berlin. That is why pluralists describe Canada as a tolerant society or as a society in which different ways of life flourish. For those who oppose pluralism, Canada preserves nothing of value and promotes a corrosive moral relativism.[54] What many critics envisage is a different type of society, one based on a comprehensive vision of the good. There are also critics who recommend the rigorous "evaluation" of diversity in order to establish the best possible life.[55] For all of them, moral relativism is a poor alternative to a society based on the good. Pluralists respond to such criticisms by insisting that they too acknowledge the objectivity of values. Where they differ from the critics is in their recognition "that there are many different ends that men may seek and still be fully rational."[56] Pluralists, in other words, reject a comprehensive good and recognize the diversity of goods. Such a belief gives depth to the mosaic; it makes philosophical pluralism an attractive, although still ultimately unsatisfactory, justification of Canadian nationhood.

Corresponding to pluralism is civic nationhood. Its philosophical roots can be traced to the Enlightenment. What civic nationhood assumes is that the cohesion of the state and the citizen's loyalty to it depend on its capacity to ensure the welfare of the individual.[57] Opposed to civic nationhood is ethnic nationalism, which regards the nation as "a community bound by spiritual ties and cultural traditions."[58] Fichte described such a nation as an organic unity, advocated a new education system to mould the people into a corporate body motivated by a common interest, and regarded language both as a common bond and as a distinctive way of thinking. Others – including Herder – have embraced a more open conception of cultural nationhood, but even they have despised the multinational state.[59] In itself, the rejection of the multinational state is unproblematic. However, in areas of mixed populations, cultural nationalism can produce tensions and mutual hatred, resulting in the creation of second-class citizens, in demands for cultural purification, and in the election of corrupt governments. When such results occur, civic nationhood is not difficult to defend, and "the verdict of Lord Acton ... [appears] prophetic, temperate and just."[60]

In Canada, civic nationhood is often associated with the virtues of the multinational state. It has even been suggested that Canada's "sense of national mission" owes much to "Lord Acton's famous declaration."[61] Canadians rely on Acton to expose the evils of ethnic nationalism and the contradictions in it. Thus Québécois separatists and other opponents of the multinational state have been dismissed as a minority who want their tribe to return to the wigwam so that they can be its kings and rulers. Similarly, nationalistic government has been described as "intolerant, discriminatory, and ... totalitarian."[62] The result is that cultural nationalism is portrayed as a doctrine that rests on little more than the tyranny of the majority.[63] In contrast, civic nationhood and Acton's multinational state are offered as the direction Canada must take if its cultural and ethnic conflicts are to be resolved. Since nationalism is not dead, the purpose of Canada, it is often said, should be to tame and civilize it.

What pluralism and civic nationhood have in common is the rejection of monism. However, the rejection of monism does not establish the truth of pluralism. In fact, pluralism and civic nationhood are beset with their own difficulties, many of which spring, ironically, from the wholesale rejection of monism and from the failure to distinguish its negative and positive aspects. In Isaiah Berlin's most influential essay on philosophical pluralism, there is a section entitled "the one and the many," but the discussion is about the one *or* the many.[64] Missing from the essay is a concern for the one or the whole. A similar kind of omission often occurs in discussions of civic nationhood: the focus is on individual welfare to the neglect of community. By avoiding the least-attractive features of monism, pluralism and civic nationhood do not thereby provide a substitute for community.

The solution to the difficulty is, of course, to rediscover community. Not only has a such rediscovery occurred, but community has acquired enormous significance, even among those who initially diverted attention from it. In recent essays, Isaiah Berlin has drawn attention to Herder, largely because "the notion of belonging is at the heart of all Herder's ideas." Herder believed "that men are made miserable" not only by poverty and disease, but also because they are "outsiders or not spoken to, that liberty and equality are nothing without fraternity."[65] He celebrated the cultural community and hated all that is associated with monism. For Berlin, Herder provides a crucial illustration of how pluralists are to understand community. Similar attempts have been made to introduce community into civic nationhood, at least in Canada. In essays published in the 1960s, Pierre Trudeau provided a sophisticated justification of civic nationhood, understood in utilitarian and functionalist terms.[66] But in later writings, he spoke of Canada as a community of belonging and regarded measures he advocated as "good for Canadian patriotism because they give Canadians a sense of belonging to one nation."[67]

Community reappears, and yet difficulties remain. The appeal to Herder may settle the issue of community for some countries, such as those with a single language and a single culture. Countries with two or more language groups are another matter because they are simply outside the range of communal possibilities envisaged by him. Not only do such countries appear to "make a nonsense of Herder's romantic verities," but the idea of belonging cannot be confined to cultural membership if a country such as Canada is to be taken seriously.[68] Trudeau's attempt to rescue civic nationhood results in a similar kind of difficulty. The difficulty arises because his measures for strengthening the national community are widely regarded, among those most affected by them, as corrosive of local communities and as destructive of cultural distinctiveness.[69] The problem of community is not solved in a country such as Canada either by an understanding of belonging that fails to make sense of the national community or by a conception of the nation that erodes particularistic identities.

Missing from both accounts is adequate recognition of the complexities of community. Pluralism and civic nationhood are unsatisfactory justifications so long as they neglect community, but they are not made satisfactory by appealing to orthodox understandings of community, at least not in Canada. The difficulty is that orthodox accounts suppose that community is singular, whereas in Canada it is multiple. In Canada, federalism was instrumental in creating a single country and in multiplying community. In some countries a multiplication of community takes place because federalism "divides the people against themselves," and the objective, as Reg Whitaker has noted, is either to overcome the atomization of mass societies or to prevent the tyranny of the numerical majority.[70] In Canada a more basic consideration operates because federalism has had as its objective the creation of a Canadian union. Because Canadians began as a people divided against themselves, a multiplication of community was necessary for them to become more than a divided people.

Implicit in Canadian nationhood is the assumption that community is not only multiple but of different kinds. Confederation took such an assumption for granted, and George-Étienne Cartier articulated it through the idea of a Canadian political nationality. Behind his concept was the belief that Confederation could recognize particularistic identities, while creating a country that was a complex social union. Almost three decades before Cartier, J.S. Mill attempted to made explicit some of the assumptions inherent in a social union. What such a union presupposed, he said, was "a strong and active principle of nationality." However, Mill distinguished the principle of nationality from "nationality in the vulgar sense" and associated it with a "common feeling of common interest among those who live under the same government." Where such a principle of nationality existed, he added, "one part of the community shall not consider themselves as foreigners with regard to another part." Instead, citizens believe "that their lot is cast together, that evil to any of their fellow-countrymen is evil to themselves."[71] When citizens subscribe to such a belief in a country such as Canada, they implicitly acknowledge that community and fraternity apply not only to those who share the same language or the same culture, but also to those who speak a different language and have a different culture. Community is multiplied and a political nationality is sustained, so that Canadians can both recognize their differences and overcome them.

The contemporary crisis has created new obstacles for the Canadian political nationality. Canadians increasingly focus on their differences and have a diminished understanding of their reciprocal obligations and shared commitments. Difference as such is not the root cause of the contemporary crisis, however. Difference has a positive value because it provides individuals and groups with distinctive identities and contributes to the meaningfulness of their existence. But Canada has witnessed far more than the articulation of new differences. What has occurred is a virtual explosion of identities, such that women, gays, ethnics, and Quebec and Aboriginal nationalists vie one against the other. Reflecting on the contemporary situation, Raymond Breton has concluded that "pluralism involves a sort of jockeying for status and power ... [and] a process of invidious comparison."[72] Others, relying on similar observations, predict the demise of Canada or call for the imposition of a monolithic Canadian identity. One response to such predictions and such demands is to say, with Reg Whitaker, that fears about the imminent breakup of Canada are exaggerated. This is so because, he writes, "the most economically powerful sections of civil society do not always find it in their interests to support the disintegration or balkanization of Canada." On the contrary, they often start with a provincialist agenda but end by building pan-Canadian corporations and "spreading a nationalist gospel."[73] A different kind of answer focuses on the additional issue of pluralism and the implications that follow from it. Pluralism is not a new issue in Canada; its roots are as deep as the Conquest. It was also a key issue at Confederation, although many of the arrangements and institutions of Confederation have lost their meaning or fallen into disuse. The erosion of Confederation has compelled Canadians to reimagine themselves as well as their country, and questions about identity have again become inescapable. In Canada such questions almost always raise the issue of difference and distinctiveness, and lead just as surely to the issue of unity and oneness. Not only have Canadians as a people experienced more than one crisis of identity, but each crisis has compelled them to come to terms with their distinctiveness and their sense of community by reimagining the one *and* the many.

CHAPTER TEN

Recovering the Moral Foundations
of Canadian Federalism

Implicit in Canadian federalism are moral assumptions about the kind of life that Canadians can and should live. These assumptions provide an understanding of how Canadians, who have different ways of life, can also live a common life together. There is, said Socrates, no more important question than how we should live.[1] Canadian federalism responds to such a question; yet discussions of federalism normally focus on other issues. Historically, the most important issue has been the federal principle, and the apparent failure of the Canadian constitution to correspond to it. Much attention is also directed to the conflictual dimensions of federalism, with the result that it becomes redescribed as federal-provincial diplomacy. When the moral dimensions of federalism do receive attention, the usual objective is either to remove moral issues from the public agenda or to diminish the moral standing of one or the other of the two levels of government. The former objective is characteristic of consociational federalism; the latter is a feature of Pierre Trudeau's renewed federalism. Many of the most prominent images of Canadian federalism either diminish its moral dimensions or fail to recognize them altogether.

Neglecting the moral foundations of federalism is unproblematic so long as the practice of federalism is accepted. But Canadian federalism has been called into question, most forcefully by Québécois and Aboriginal nationalists. Many of them consider it an illegitimate form of polity, regarding it as an affront to their dignity as peoples as well as a source of moral and social harm. They believe that the disintegration of Canada is to be welcomed because it will allow healthy nations to emerge. They also disparage justifications of federalism that appeal merely to economic values or that celebrate political freedom and social diversity at the expense of community. For them, a federalism that appeals to instrumental values is at best an arrangement based on convenience, to be abandoned as soon as circumstances permit.

When the moral foundations of Canadian federalism are neglected, Canada becomes a country that is more difficult to understand and harder to sustain. A federalism without foundations is more easily transformed into the local sovereignties envisaged by Québécois and Aboriginal nationalists or into the kind of centralized unitary state advocated by Durham and Macdonald. The alternative is to recognize that the practice of federalism in Canada has deeper foundations than is usually recognized. Those foundations can be traced at least to Confederation and to Cartier's defence of it. What his defence contains is a new image of federalism that differs significantly from American models. For Cartier, Canadian federalism recognized the existence of different ways of life and also envisaged a common way of life. Such an image of federalism not only captures the distinctive moral foundations of Confederation, but it also has implications for contemporary controversies. The very image of Canada changes if federalism is regarded as a way of life.

CANADIAN IMAGES OF FEDERALISM

The most prominent contemporary images of federalism view it as a constitutional arrangement that divides power and raises almost no moral questions. Moreover, Canadian federalism is often viewed cynically: governments are portrayed as ceaselessly vying for jurisdiction, while the federal system is characterized as possessing either no legitimacy at all or only the kind of legitimacy that derives from instrumental considerations. The cynical understanding of federalism has roots that can be traced to Confederation. In the debates of 1865, Macdonald boasted that Canadian Confederation was superior to the American union because it "avoided all conflict of jurisdiction and authority."[2] But his boast was immediately challenged. Henri Joly, for example, warned that all federations contained some fatal vice; he also predicted that the two nationalities would disrupt Confederation.[3] Similarly, Christopher Dunkin refused to "prophecy smooth things" because Confederation contained much to quarrel over. The provinces, he said, "cannot possibly work harmoniously together long; and so soon as they come into collision, there comes trouble, and with the trouble, the fabric is at an end."[4]

The debate between Macdonald and his critics also foreshadowed developments after Confederation. The four decades or so after 1867 are usually portrayed as the years that witnessed the eventual defeat of the Macdonaldian constitution. In most accounts, the defeat is ascribed to the genesis of provincial rights and the articulation of the compact theory of Confederation. According to Ramsay Cook, it was Oliver Mowat who originated the provincialist version of the compact theory of Confederation; Henri Bourassa developed the idea of a cultural compact.[5] Macdonald envisaged a project of nation-building that would gradually reduce the provinces to administrative units of the central government. In contrast, the compact theory insisted on the essential sovereignty of the provinces, regarded the central government as their creature, and justified a vigorous program of province-building.[6] The compact theory reversed Macdonald's assumptions and shattered his belief that a highly centralized constitution would eliminate discord and conflict.[7]

In itself, the failure of the Macdonaldian constitution is neither a tragic event nor enormously difficult to understand. Writing in 1933, Norman McL. Rogers suggested that the failure was rooted in federalism itself. "The controversy over provincial rights," he observed, "is inherent in every federal constitution ... [because] from the moment of its birth a federal state is put in a posture of competition with the states or provinces of which it is composed."[8] Such a conclusion is supported by Robert Vipond's study of the provincial rights movement in Ontario. According to Vipond, the Macdonaldian vision failed partly because it did not fit the self-identities that existed and partly because it neglected the fact that federalism "was essentially competitive."[9] The self-identities included a powerful commitment to local self-government as well as a desire to preserve local distinctiveness.[10] In 1867 Macdonald achieved a temporary victory over such self-identities, only to witness their re-emergence in a strong provincial rights movement.

With the failure of the Macdonaldian constitution, alternative images of federalism emerged. Unlike Macdonald's quasi-federalism, classical federalism ascribes sovereignty to both levels of government when they act within their spheres, with the corollary that neither level of government is subordinate to the other. Moreover, classical federalism was largely the creation of the judicial committee of the Privy Council, whose performance has been the subject of enormous controversy. According to Alan Cairns, "the really dramatic cleavage between the supporters and opponents ... [was over] the governmental pluralism of the federal system."[11] Opponents not only appealed to Macdonald's original vision of Canada, but also adopted a position similar to Harold Laski's famous pronouncement about the obsolescence of federalism. "The epoch of federalism is over," wrote Laski in 1939, "... [because] only a [centralized] system can effectively confront the problems ... of giant capitalism."[12] Supporters, on the other hand, argued that the provincialist orientation of the Privy Council accurately reflected the sociological realities of Canada. If the Privy Council had not leaned in the direction of the provinces, surmised Pierre Trudeau, "Quebec separatism might not be a threat today; it might be an accomplished fact."[13]

In Canada as elsewhere, classical federalism is the image that grounds the most celebrated justifications of federalism. The justifications include Alexis de Tocqueville's association of federalism with republican liberty, Lord Bryce's belief that it allows "experiments in legislation and administration which could not be safely tried in a large centralized country," and James Madison's conception of federalism as a device for the prevention of governmental tyranny.[14] Canadian versions of these justifications are not difficult to find. Donald Smiley, for example, stated that "provincial autonomy, indeed federalism itself, finds its major justification in liberal views about the desirability of dispersing political power." He also identified other justifications, one of which is crucial for Canadian federalism: "the desire to preserve certain territorially-defined particularisms."[15] The existence of such particularisms provides a distinctive justification of local autonomy. "It is wrong to assume that the same laws are suitable for all peoples," wrote Louis-P. Pigeon, "... [because] laws have a cultural aspect." The central government, he explained, is tied to "the need of military, political, and economic strength, which larger units only can offer." In contrast, provincial autonomy "is linked up with the preservation of [a distinctive] way of life."[16]

One difficulty with the classic justifications is that they are easily disputed. Franz Neumann, for example, denied that federalism maximizes freedom on the ground that federations often suppress freedom and sometimes deny it altogether. He also believed that federalism was incapable of guaranteeing the kind of local self-government that was "the indispensable cornerstone of a large-scale democracy."[17] William Riker deepened Neumann's critique; he suggested that a federal division of powers "may actually promote tyranny by its constant frustration of majorities which, in their frustration, come to behave tyrannically."[18] In Canada, the classic justifications are sometimes subject to a more oblique and potentially more devastating criticism. By focusing on the kind of institutions that actually existed, students of federalism increasingly discovered, in the years after 1945, that the model of classical federalism was difficult to apply to the Canadian situation. Not only did such a conclusion require Canadians to develop new models of federalism, but it also brought into question the validity of the classic justifications.

In an influential study of constitutional adaptation from 1945 to 1967, Donald Smiley concluded that "the old classical federalism ... has no relevance today."[19] Classical federalism, as J.R. Mallory said, was displaced by a type of federalism in which "there is close contact and discussion between ministers and civil servants of both levels of government so that even changes in legislation are the result of joint decisions."[20] The new arrangement was usually labelled cooperative federalism, although it was also called administrative federalism or executive federalism. "The term cooperative federalism," Edwin Black wrote, "was appropriated more for its favourable value connotations than for any descriptive precision it might convey."[21] Others, including Richard Simeon, suggested that the new arrangement was characterized more by conflict than by cooperation.[22]

Institutional conflict is at the centre of what Alan Cairns has called political federalism.[23] His essay "The Government and Societies of Canadian Federalism" builds on "A Different Perspective on Canadian Federalism," written with Edwin Black, and both provide the foundation for "The Other Crisis of Canadian Federalism." The earliest essay, first published in 1966, discovers province-building: "since 1867 Canadians have been engaged in more than the construction of a new state; they have been building provinces and complex series of relationships between governments and societies as well."[24] The next essay not only unfolds the logic of province-building, but also introduces the important idea of competitive federalism, which Cairns understands as "a peculiar Canadian version of the American separation of powers." Moreover, the Canadian version is more difficult to operate because it involves not just the separate legislative and executive strata, "but governments, conscious of their historic position, jealous of their prerogatives, and aggressively enterprising in the performance of their managerial responsibilities for their societies."[25] The last essay, published in 1979, explores federalism in crisis, a crisis that Cairns describes as being "of recent vintage – essentially a product of the last two decades." Canadian federalism has produced big governments, which in turn have produced a crisis of federalism. The crisis exists partly because "the working constitution ... can no longer control and channel the activities of government in order to minimize their self-defeating competition with each other." What the existence and magnitude of the crisis suggest is that, "even if we leave the Québécois nationalist pressures aside, ... the grounds for optimism are slim."[26]

Unlike political federalism, consociational democracy focuses not on conflict so much as on its management, in an attempt to discover the conditions of political stability in divided societies. "The essential characteristic of consociational democracy," Arend Lijphart writes, "is not so much any particular institutional arrangement as the deliberate effort by elites to stabilize the system." Consociational democracy, he adds, "means government by elite cartel designed to turn a democracy with a fragmented political culture into a stable democracy."[27] A key corollary is that consensus should not be sought at the grass-roots level.[28] Although Lijphart regards the Austrian Second Republic as the best example of consociationalism, the model also has implications for countries such as Canada. William Ormsby, for example, has traced the successful beginnings of the federal concept in Canada to the partial acceptance of consociationalism in 1839–45.[29] S.J.R. Noel, on the other hand, has focused on contemporary Canada, drawing attention to the strength of the consociational model as "a way of viewing the Canadian political process which accounts for its successful maintenance yet requires no dubious assumptions about the role of political parties and posits no chimerical notion of an 'underlying' national identity."[30]

The strength of consociationalism is that it provides an alternative to American models, such as Madisonian pluralism, which are unable to accommodate the most distinctive features of Canada. Consociationalism also corrects political federalism by focusing attention on the sources of continuing political stability in Canada. But the consociational model is not without limitations. With respect to contemporary Canada, many of the limits are identified in Richard Simeon's study of federal-provincial diplomacy, published in 1972. Noting that Lijphart's model requires that there must be considerable deference of non-élites to élites, as well as that the élites must themselves share important overall goals (including a commitment to maintaining the system itself), Simeon suggests that "neither of these conditions are fully met in Canada, ... less so in the early seventies than they were in the early 1960s."[31] Similarly, William Ormsby has noted that the gradual failure of the consociational solution in the 1850s was what made Confederation necessary. "The only alternative," he writes, "was a proper federal union and this was the solution adopted in 1867."[32]

The constitutional achievement of 1867 was due in no small measure to the labours of Macdonald. But Macdonaldian centralism engendered powerful counter-images such as the provincial rights movement and the compact theory. What eventually emerged was a pattern of federal-provincial conflict that bears some striking similarities to political federalism. Confederation was not solely the work of Macdonald, however. As Garth Stevenson and others have suggested, it was Cartier who, despite Macdonald's misgivings, insisted on significant autonomy for Quebec and hence guaranteed federalism. "One must attribute to Cartier and his followers," Stevenson adds, "the fact that Canadian provinces ... were also given exclusive and substantial powers of their own."[33] Cartier also drew attention to the moral dimensions of federalism. Contemporary discussions frequently refer to him, yet they only rarely grasp the significance of his contribution. The result is an impoverishment of federalist theory at a time when the practice of federalism faces serious challenges.

CONTEMPORARY CHALLENGES

The questioning of federalism is not new in Canada. What is new is that federalism appears to have fewer supporters than before, partly because of the strength of the contemporary challenges to it and partly because of the weaknesses inherent in the most prominent contemporary images of federalism. In 1867 the sharpest ideological conflict was the one between those who supported a new union on the ground that it would provide opportunities for commercial expansion and those who rejected it because of their desire to maintain traditional ways of life.[34] There was also the French-English conflict, the severity of which provided the immediate and most urgent reason for a new union so far as Canada was concerned.[35] The contemporary challenges are different. Part of the difference is the rise of a new kind of nationalism in Quebec, which has produced novel arguments against federalism, especially as it is currently practised. Another difference is that the conservatism of the Fathers of Confederation has been displaced by a brand of liberalism potentially more hostile to federalism than Macdonald ever was. The new nationalism and the new liberalism support, in turn, a number of other challenges, with the result that Canadian federalism appears increasingly irrelevant and Canada's existence seems increasingly difficult to justify.

What is new about nationalism in Quebec is its association with the state. Whereas the old nationalism was tied to the church and a traditional form of society, the new nationalism regards the government of Quebec as a major instrument for the modernization of society. Moreover, the old nationalism often concerned itself with the purity of the French race: a concern that received classic expression in Lionel Groulx's *The Iron Wedge*.[36] Groulx focused special attention on what he regarded as the evils of mixed marriages, from which no happiness or meeting of souls could result and which produced children with disordered thinking, low intelligence, and incoherent personalities.[37] Behind such beliefs was his theory of the iron wedge: "the psychological and moral personality, the true one, cannot be composite ... [because] its law is unity."[38] The new nationalism is different. Its beginnings can be traced to the early 1960s, and it is most appropriately described as a nationalism of growth. According to Léon Dion, "the nationalism of growth basically rests on the assumption that Quebec lies on the threshold of gigantic development in every sector of thought and development."[39] The new nationalism is concerned far more with the dignity of Quebec than with its purity, and its affinity is with the cultural flourishing celebrated by Herder.[40]

The new nationalism also adopts a new approach to Canadian federalism. The old nationalism, as articulated in the Tremblay Report of the mid 1950s, accepted federalism so long as it was understood as a type of classical federalism that enabled Quebec to preserve its traditional way of life. Federalism was perceived as an arrangement that allowed French and English to live side by side, with minimal interaction between them. Accordingly, Confederation became unsatisfactory only when Ottawa attempted to legislate for Quebec under the guise of universal standards in areas such as social security, or interfered with education through a program of conditional grants, or attempted to control culture for the purposes of Canadian unity.[41] Power over such matters was to reside in Quebec, even if the power was unexercised, or exercised for reactionary objectives.[42] The new nationalism, on the other hand, seeks powers that can be vigorously exercised for the purpose of creating a more progressive society. Those who embrace the new nationalism, wrote Michel Brunet, not only renounce "their forefather's illusions ... [but] have the will to organize inside Quebec's borders a new society."[43] For many of them, the new society implies a rejection of federalism, partly because federalism as it is practised in Canada denies Quebec the powers it needs and partly because it misdirects politics by institutionalizing conflict. "For us the most disastrous aspect of the present regime," wrote René Lévesque, "... certainly is ... the incredible 'split-level' squandering of energy."[44]

The new nationalism reconceptualizes politics and culture according to expressivist principles. Herder's expressivism, as Guy Laforest has suggested, can provide a powerful justification of the new nationalism.[45] But it also has implications that are difficult to reconcile with that nationalism. Herder believed that a natural community such as a *Volk* had no need for a sovereign authority exercising supreme power, but his belief is decisively rejected by the new nationalism.[46] Moreover, he coupled expressivism with assumptions about homogeneity and the avoidance of ethnic intermixture, a view that has only limited application to Quebec. According to F.M. Barnard, Herder believed that "if all nations remained where they were originally 'planted,' one could look upon the world as a garden of diverse national plants, each flowering according to its own nature and development."[47] Not only does Quebec exist in a different kind of world, but its own population, as Quebec nationalists increasingly recognize, reflects plurality and intermixture within a society whose majority is French-speaking. Reflecting on the internal diversity of Quebec's population, Michael Ignatieff has noted that, on balance, "modern Quebec nationalists are at pains to differentiate their conception of the nation from the ethnic idea that they associate with the catastrophe of Yugoslavia."[48]

Once the social pluralism of Quebec is recognized, expressivism acquires new dimensions as well as new difficulties. It is used not only for the purpose of criticizing federalism as it is sometimes practised, but also to defend Quebec's right of self-determination. But the right of self-determination encounters serious difficulties once social pluralism is accepted. According to Donald Lenihan, Gorden Robertson, and Roger Tassé, the acceptance of pluralism and the recognition that Quebec is a modern society takes "the punch" out of romantic arguments for self-determination. What remains, they postulate, is an unconvincing and "perfunctory moral imperative to the effect that 'the people' should control their own destiny."[49] A different kind of difficulty arises once the logic of self-determination is coupled with the fact of social pluralism. Pluralistic societies, as Iris Young and others have noted, consist of different social groups that have different needs, cultures, histories, experiences, and perceptions of social relations; these differences, in turn, "influence their interpretation of the meaning and consequences of policy proposals."[50] In Quebec there are groups that either do not share the aspiration of independence or believe (as do some Aboriginal Canadians) that a principle of self-determination should be extended to French-speaking Québécois only if it is also extended to them. In such a situation, the unqualified and consistent application of expressivist principles may simply exacerbate political conflict and social fragmentation.[51]

Corresponding to the change within Quebec from the old to the new nationalism was a shift within English Canada from conservatism to liberalism. A once-common complaint about Confederation was that Macdonald and other Fathers had infused it with conservative principles. Writing in 1946, Frank Underhill believed that the conservative tone of Confederation not only diminished the Canadian imagination but also impoverished Canadian politics. "One reason for our backwardness," he suggested, "... has been the weakness of the Radical and Reform parties of the Left in our Canadian history." Underhill associated the deficiencies of Canadian politics with the absence of an Enlightenment in Canada and a corresponding neglect of the doctrine of the rights of man. "How can such a people," he asked rhetorically, "expect their democracy to be dynamic."[52] Almost two decades later, John Porter's *Vertical Mosaic* expressed a similar concern. "Canada," Porter wrote, "has no resounding charter myth proclaiming a utopia against which, periodically, progress can be measured." Echoing Underhill, he regretted the absence of "creative politics" in Canada.[53]

The Vertical Mosaic is a complex book. Its declared purpose is to dispel "one of the most persistent images that Canadians have of their society," the image of Canada as a classless society. But Porter's objective was not to abolish social classes. On the contrary, he believes that classes, together with the "ranking of individuals or groups in an order of inferiority or superiority is a universal feature of social life."[54] The real trouble with Canada is not that classes exist, but that class membership depends on inappropriate considerations. In Canada, ethnic affiliation substantially affects the life chances of an individual, yet such a result violates "the [liberal] egalitarian ideology ... [which holds] that individuals should be able to move through this hierarchy of skill classes according to their inclinations and abilities."[55]

The remedy, according to Porter, is to remove the social and psychological barriers to equal opportunity, which in Canada requires a reconsideration of federalism. Federalism, he suggests, is an obstacle to equal opportunity. By infusing Canadian politics with a conservative tone, it impedes the adoption of redistributive measures necessary for the creation of a liberal egalitarian society. Moreover, federalism works against equal opportunity because it tends to legitimate differentiation based on ethnicity. As for its most often discussed benefit, Porter insists that federalism frequently fails to protect freedom. It finds its only and very limited justification in Quebec's cultural particularism. But even Quebec's particularism is merely a short-term consideration because "as Quebec becomes more industrialized it will become culturally more like other industrialized societies."[56] Although Porter denies that he is calling for the complete abandonment of federalism, he does insist that a liberal democratic society "may require a breaking down of the ethnic impediment to ... the equality of opportunity."[57]

A strong commitment to equal opportunity is not unique to John Porter. No less a liberal than John Stuart Mill regarded the principle of equal opportunity as a distinguishing characteristic of the modern world and used it to argue against the continued legal subordination of women.[58] Lord Durham is also relevant because his assimilation proposals have been traced to the liberal demand for equal opportunity.[59] What is remarkable about the principle of equal opportunity is not its popularity but the apparent ease with which its complexities are overlooked. The simplest and most absolute formulations of the principle create the greatest difficulties. Historically, the principle was understood to require the removal of unjustified legal disabilities. But such an understanding proved unsatisfactory because it neglected the social obstacles to equal opportunity. Consequently, the principle was often reformulated so as to require a substantial and constant redistribution of wealth. But even this formulation proved unsatisfactory. As Plato knew, an absolute commitment to equal opportunity required nothing less than the abolition of the family. "Attractive as the phrase of equality of opportunity at first sounds," F.A. Hayek observed, "... any attempt concretely to realize it [is] apt to produce a nightmare."[60]

In Canada a liberalism grounded on an absolutist conception of equality encounters an additional difficulty: it comes into conflict with the new nationalism. The result is that a conception of equality clashes with an understanding of dignity. Canada's contemporary constitutional difficulties are often traced to the emergence of a new nationalism in Quebec. "It is generally recognized," Gilles Lalande has suggested, "that Quebec precipitated and has since been the focal point of the constitutional crisis that Canada is undergoing."[61] But Quebec was not alone in experiencing significant change. In fact, George Grant's famous study of the Canadian destiny, published in 1965, virtually ignored the new nationalism in Quebec and focused almost entirely on the triumph of liberalism. Grant justified his approach by insisting that liberalism was the essence of modernity, and even the strong measures taken by French Canadians to preserve their culture were futile against it.[62] French Canadians have never accepted such a judgment, partly because theirs is a new type of nationalism that attempts to come to terms with modernity. In Canada the complexities of modernity are not captured adequately either by the new liberalism or by the new nationalism. So long as this is the case, federalism remains an open question.

FOUNDATIONS FOR FEDERALISM

Other factors are also relevant to understanding Canada's constitutional malaise. In 1867 the acceptance of Confederation resulted in part from the discovery of a distinctive federalist theory capable of accommodating the divergent aspirations of Canadians. But Canadians increasingly neglect the positive achievements of Confederation. What results is not simply a misunderstanding of the meaning of Confederation. Of greater importance is the impoverishment of Canadian federalist theory that occurs. Contemporary Canada has witnessed the creation of new understandings of federalism, as well as new attempts to reconcile Canadian solitudes. What has not yet emerged is the kind of middle ground that contributed to the achievement of Confederation and formed the original core of Canadian federalist theory. Not only does the absence of such middle ground exacerbate Canada's constitutional difficulties, but it also works against the articulation of a federalist theory capable of responding to contemporary conditions.

Such a suggestion may seem paradoxical: Canadians have available to them new visions of federalism aimed at creating new foundations for Canada. Chief among the new visions are the constitutional theories of Pierre Trudeau. It has been said of Trudeau, by Reginald Whitaker among others, that his motto was reason over passion, yet he developed a passionate commitment to federalism.[63] Not only did he believe that the breakup of Canada would be a crime against humanity, but he regarded the social pluralism implicit in Canadian federalism as superior to the American way of life. According to Kevin J. Christiano, Trudeau claimed "for himself the undisputed role of high priest in a civic cult with an exquisitely wrought theology [of federalism]."[64] His project, Christiano adds, was to transform federalism into a Canadian national ideal or even a civic religion.

As a federalist, Trudeau was also committed to constitutional change. In his *Memoirs* he writes: "I promised Quebec change, and I gave Quebec change. I gave Quebec, and all the rest of Canada, a new made-in-Canada constitution, with a new amending formula and a new charter of rights."[65] Trudeau regarded the Charter as his greatest achievement because it addresses the issue of the Canadian identity and promotes a bilingual Canada. "Writers and poets have always searched for the Canadian identity," he notes. "With the charter in place, we can now say that Canada is a society where all people are equal and where they share some fundamental values based on freedom." Not only did the Charter turn Canada into a country that is more than the sum of its parts, but its adoption was supported by the people of Quebec and Canada. Patriation, Trudeau recalls, was accomplished in conformity with the amending formula established by the Supreme Court. "It was done," he adds, "with the support of almost 60 per cent of all elected members from Quebec. In so far as opinion polls have any value, it was done with the support of the Quebec people."[66]

The *Memoirs* also make explicit the vision of Canada that Trudeau opposed. "All my life, even in my writings long before I entered politics," he insists, "I always fought against special status for Quebec." Not only did his opposition to special status bring him into conflict with Quebec separatists, but he was accused by them of betraying the people of Quebec by failing to transfer special powers to the government of Quebec after the 1980 referendum. The *Memoirs* provide a complex response to the accusation, part of which is Trudeau's insistence that, during the referendum campaign, "I was fighting to have my ideas triumph, not those of my adversaries." It was Quebec nationalists who wanted special powers for Quebec and not Trudeau. Not only does he recall that he was called a traitor for defending Canada, but French Canadians in Quebec were told that they could not expect any sympathy from him because his mother was Scottish. Such attacks demonstrated to him "the kind of intolerance ... the people of Quebec ... were being asked by the separatists to endorse with their votes."[67] Moreover, the *Memoirs* implicitly compare the intolerance of Quebec separatists with the "ethnic cleansing" that has accompanied the breakup of Yugoslavia and other multi-ethnic, pluralistic societies.[68] The implied conclusion is that both examples illustrate what can happen when central governments accede to demands for special status.

Trudeau's uncompromising rejection of special status postulates a fallacious slippery slope; it also neglects a key assumption of Canadian Confederation. In 1867 the Fathers were able to provide a foundation for Canadian federalism because they implicitly rejected foundationalism, the belief that political justification must be grounded on a principle of universal validity (such as reason or human rights) located outside politics itself.[69] What the Fathers provided was a contextual justification; they argued, among other things, that the divergent aspirations of Canadians could be accommodated within the structures of Confederation. Distinctiveness and difference were situated within Confederation rather than opposed to it. But Trudeau's absolute rejection of special status works against a contextual justification of Canadian federalism. When special status is rejected absolutely, significant differences are less easily accommodated within Confederation and federalism becomes less meaningful.

That an absolute rejection of special status can create difficulties for federalism is evident from Trudeau's influential repudiation of the failed 1992 Charlottetown Consensus Report on the Constitution. According to Alan Cairns, the Consensus Report demonstrated the emergence of a multinational Canada as constituted primarily by Quebec, Aboriginals, and the rest of Canada.[70] Others, such as James Tully, have regarded the report as "a new way of seeing Canada ... [which] invited [Canadians] to recognize and affirm the diversity of the federation as a fundamental characteristic itself."[71] Still others believe that the report was a response to the "plethora of irreconcilable voices" that characterize the postmodern condition and that challenge the modern nation state.[72] Trudeau viewed the Consensus Report differently. For him the key issue was rights. The report, he said, gave precedence to group rights over individual rights, thereby establishing "a dictatorship, which arranges citizens in a hierarchy according to their beliefs." Such arrangements, he added, "can lead eventually to civil wars. That's what collective rights are all about."[73] What is striking about Trudeau's discussion is that federal diversity receives almost no recognition in it. Instead, he focuses on the liberal philosophy of the Enlightenment, which he equates with individual dignity and uniform rights. He did not necessarily cease being a federalist even when he rejected the Consensus Report, but his understanding of federalism was such that it failed to recognize the significant diversities that sought accommodation within Canada.

Federalism aside, a significant failure of recognition also increases the potential for political disintegration. A belief of this kind forms the basis of Charles Taylor's influential reflections on contemporary Canada and his prescriptions for reconciling the solitudes. Like Trudeau before him, Taylor celebrates the pluralism of Canada and rejects "ultranationalism," which breeds "a willingness to sacrifice everything else on the altar of the nation."[74] But he also differs from Trudeau. Part of the difference is that Taylor distinguishes ultranationalism from the new nationalism and believes that Quebec's new nationalism can be accommodated within a new Canada. According to him, the old nationalism was defensive and intolerant; its aim was to protect a way of life that was in danger of being destroyed by the more dynamic North American culture. But the new nationalism is creative; it represents "the awakening of underdeveloped societies that were determined to take control of their own history." It also responds to a problem of identity that occurs when the members of a society are denied appropriate recognition.[75] In the case of Quebec, the problem of identity is intimately connected with the French language. The demand for political independence, Taylor suggests, is best understood as a demand that the French language should have adequate scope for its expression, so that native speakers can possess dignity based on the recognized worth of their language. Such a demand can be satisfied within a new Canada. What fuels political disintegration as well as the independence option, according to him, is a failure by the rest of Canada to recognize adequately the legitimate aspirations of Quebec.[76]

Behind Taylor's understanding of Quebec's new nationalism is his still deeper understanding of the malaise of modernity. As he understands it, the new nationalism both springs from the modern malaise and is part of the solution to it. The modern malaise, Taylor writes, is felt most poignantly through the "features of our contemporary culture and society that people experience as a loss." Those features include a disenchantment with the atomistic self-absorption of modern freedom, a disillusionment with the cold efficiency of modern technology, and a sense of political impotence in the face of mounting worldwide catastrophes such as the environmental crisis. What we need, according to Taylor, is a work of retrieval such that the inspiring ideal of modernity, the ethic of authenticity, is restored to its proper place. The retrieval requires recognition of the romantic origins of the ethic of authenticity, as well as acceptance of its dialogical character. "We become fully human agents," Taylor notes, "... through our acquisition of rich human languages ... [and] we define this [agency] always in dialogue with ... the identities our significant others want to recognize in us." When the ethic of authenticity is so understood, it facilitates mutual recognition within cultural communities, works against the destructiveness of self-centred freedom, and enables human beings to see themselves as part of a larger universe "that can make claims on us." The greatest modern danger, according to Taylor, is fragmentation, because a fragmented people is "increasingly less capable of forming a common purpose and carrying it out." The way to overcome fragmentation is by a decentralization of governmental power that brings "successful common action [and] can ... also strengthen identification with the political community."[77]

Although Canadians are not alone in experiencing the modern malaise, Canada is fortunate, Taylor suggests, because its decentralized federalism can provide a starting-point for democratic empowerment. Where Canada is especially deficient, however, is that Canadians have not created a common understanding that can hold the regions together. Moreover, the first failure is rooted in a second: the failure to "understand and accept the real nature of Canadian diversity." The second problem arises because Canadians turn more and more to the American model and to the rights model.[78] They should reject the rights model, which implies for Taylor not a total rejection of the 1982 Charter so much as a restriction of its universalism. When the Charter is restricted, it becomes possible to understand Canada as a country based on deep diversity, so that Canadians are different among themselves and belong to Canada in different ways. French-speaking Quebec might belong through membership in its cultural communities, whereas English-speaking Canadians might identify with procedural liberalism and Charter patriotism.[79] Not only does a Canada based on deep diversity move away from an antagonistic rights model, but French-speaking and English-speaking Canadians become increasingly reconciled. A Canada based on deep diversity, Taylor suggests, is also capable of recognizing the distinctive claims of Aboriginals, feminists, and multiculturalists. Pessimists dismiss deep diversity as too utopian; yet the world, he intimates, is too diverse for the American model.[80]

What Taylor brilliantly recognizes is that a special kind of diversity distinguishes Canada from the United States. As a result, he is able to retrieve federalism from the excessive universalism of Trudeau's understanding of Canada. A further consequence is that Canadian diversities are recognized and Canadian antagonisms are ameliorated. But Taylor's own understanding of Canadian federalism is not without difficulties. When he calls for a radical decentralization of power to provinces and regions, he also implicitly demotes the central government to a service-providing institution. As Alan Cairns has asked of Taylor's proposals, "What will be the source of the federal state's legitimacy if Ottawa is reduced to exclusive control only over defence, external affairs and currency, with a few areas of mixed jurisdiction?" Such a scenario, he adds, may reduce the central government to "just a superstructure with which the deeply diverse Aboriginal and Québécois peoples are only instrumentally linked through membership in their national communities."[81] If Canada is reconstituted as a weak confederacy of three distinct communities, as Taylor's proposals seem to imply, then James Madison's famous objection is also relevant: weak confederacies are inherently unstable because they fail to establish central governments capable of sustaining themselves.[82] Taylor is of course aware of such difficulties, so much so that he rejected René Lévesque's proposals for sovereignty-association; yet his own proposals for reconciling the solitudes appear to reintroduce some of difficulties that he initially avoided.[83]

The questioning of Confederation has produced new images of Canada. One image, powerfully expressed in the writings of Pierre Trudeau, celebrates Canada by drawing attention to the respect for universal human rights implicit in Canadian pluralism. When pluralism is so understood, Canada becomes a country that exalts the equal worth of individuals and denies priority to the particularistic claims of groups and communities. The difficulty with such an understanding is that it can come into conflict with a second tradition of Canadian pluralism and an alternative image of Canada. The second image, subtly expressed in the writings of Charles Taylor, also celebrates pluralism, yet it reminds Canadians that pluralism is about accommodation, the recognition of difference, and the diversity of goods.[84] Both images capture important dimensions of Canada. What each fails to capture adequately, however, is Canadian federalism. Canadian federalism is about divided jurisdiction, divided loyalties, multiple identities, and intersecting communities of belonging.[85] When it is so understood, it becomes capable of mediating the potentially divisive traditions of Canadian pluralism. Images of Canada that kept those traditions apart not only have the effect of exacerbating contemporary constitutional difficulties; they also draw attention away from the moral foundations of Canadian federalism.

FEDERALISM AS A WAY OF LIFE: RETRIEVING THE IMAGE

Not only has contemporary Canadian federalist theory failed to produce the kind of middle ground that provided the original basis for Confederation, but it is also in danger of forgetting the image of federalism that best exemplified the achievement of the Fathers. Part of the difficulty is the enormous influence exercised by American understandings of federalism. That influence is evident, for example, in Pierre Trudeau's politically influential rejection of the Charlottetown Consensus Report and in his recommendations concerning the United States model. "Read above all Essay No. 10 ... in the 'Federalist' Papers by Madison, Jay and Hamilton," Trudeau said. "They found that in a federal system, there was a risk that majorities would abuse the rights of minorities ... And because they wanted to defend individual rights rather than collective rights, they established a Supreme Court." The American model, he added, "has worked out well."[86] Unlike Trudeau, Taylor emphatically rejects both the rights model and the American model, but even he does not fully grasp the significance of Confederation. What concerns him is that the American model works against both the decentralization of power and deep diversity. Similar kinds of concerns were expressed during the Confederation debates of 1865 and were instrumental in securing constitutional autonomy for the provinces. But the debates of 1865 also raised the difficult issue of a common Canadian identity. If Canadians were so different among themselves, what could keep them together? How could a country composed of different nationalities both respect the rights of nationalities and become one nation? Those were questions that troubled the Fathers of Canadian Confederation; they were also questions to which the Framers of the United States Constitution provided no answers.

The contrasts between American and Canadian federalist theory are striking if attention is focused on the middle ground characteristic of each. In the United States the middle ground of federalism was largely the work of James Madison; he constructed a theory that responded not only to the state-sovereignty theories of the anti-federalists but also to ideas of imperial government formulated by Alexander Hamilton. Madison's great discovery was the theory of the compound republic. The essence of the theory is that an extended republic, when combined with a federal system of semi-sovereign political units, provides the best safeguard against the tyranny of faction and the best guarantee of stable republican government. For Madison, as Marvin Meyers has suggested, the theory of the compound republic showed how "liberty can be reconciled with order, democracy with equity, self-interest with patriotism."[87] The middle ground of Canadian federalist theory, as formulated by George-Étienne Cartier, is different. Like Madison before him, Cartier also had to steer between those who favoured an imperial conception of government and those who supported a weak confederacy of the provinces. Unlike Madison's, however, Cartier's middle ground confronted concerns about divergent identities and distinct nationalities, as well as reminders of the war of races. His discovery was a distinctively Canadian theory of federalism that recognized multiple, rather than antagonistic identities and situated them within a common political nationality. For Cartier, the justification of federalism was not that it secured freedom against tyranny, but that it accommodated distinct identities within the political framework of a great nation. The very divisions of federalism, when correctly drawn and coupled with a suitable scheme of minority rights, were for him what sustained the Canadian nation.

Canada, Cartier believed, had to exist as a federal nation if it was to exist at all. Proposals such as Durham's and Macdonald's, which assumed a homogeneous Canadian people and a unitary state, he dismissed as utopian, even as impossible. He also thought that ethnic and racial hatreds could be eliminated if rights and identities were respected. Canadians, he said, could form and sustain a federal nation because the diversity of races was a benefit rather than otherwise, because they shared common sympathies and common objectives as well as commercial interests, because they believed in justice for minorities and opposed ethnic intolerance. He insisted that Canada's greatness as a nation did not depend on the elimination of the smaller nationalities and local identities that formed a part of it. Cartier understood federalism as a condition of nation-building, rather than as a forum for political rivalry. Not only did he regard Canada as more than the sum of its parts, but he also described a Canadian political nationality. It was to be a new nationality that did not seek to eliminate the nationalities that already existed within Canada. Hence it was to be a political nationality with which neither the national origins nor the religion of any individual would interfere.[88]

What is striking about Cartier's image of federalism is that it privileges cooperation over conflict, and mutual understanding over cultural or racial intolerance. In the debates of 1865, his assumptions were repeatedly criticized, as was his advocacy of a federal union. The most common criticism was that federalism would not work because cooperation and mutual understanding could not be taken for granted. That criticism is only partly valid; for although Cartier did regard federalism as presupposing cooperation and mutual accommodation, he also believed that federalism, once adopted, created conditions that facilitated cooperation and mutual understanding. His image of federalism may be more vulnerable to a different kind of criticism: it appears to underestimate the difficulty of creating a Canadian political nationality. A criticism of this kind was stated in the debates of 1865; it is also implicit, for example, in K.C. Wheare's discussion of Canadian federalism. Like Cartier before him, Wheare noted that a federal union implies that those who join it will develop some common nationality. But, he added, "the making and keeping of a Canadian nation is a continuous, delicate and intricate process ... [partly because] French-Canadians are not less a distinct nation in Canada today than they were in 1867."[89]

For Wheare, writing in 1955, the contrast was with the United States. "Americans now, as a result of history," he said, "have one nationality."[90] The contrast between Canada and the United States may be even stronger than Wheare recognized, notwithstanding contemporary warnings about the disuniting of America or the catastrophe of the American Civil War. Contemporary concerns about the disuniting of America spring from the increasing acceptance of multiculturalism and the corresponding fear that such policies invite "the fragmentation of the national community into a quarrelsome spatter of enclaves, ghettos, tribes."[91] But whatever fears some Americans may express about the erosion of the melting-pot, their fears pale into insignificance when compared with contemporary Canadian warnings about the disuniting of Canada, a fact recognized even by those Americans who most oppose multiculturalism. The American Civil War implicitly raises far more important questions for Canadian nationhood. In 1867 the war was a key issue for the Fathers of Confederation; it not only coloured their understanding of federalism, but also affected their proposals for the distribution of power. What gives the American Civil War contemporary relevance is that it raises the issue of state secession, an issue that increasingly concerns Canadians. State secession also reveals hidden dimensions of nationhood – Canadian as well as American.

When state secession is the basis of comparison, Canadian nationhood turns out to be enormously fragile, notwithstanding the fact that the United States had a civil war. A key to the paradox is Abraham Lincoln's message to the United States Congress: the people of the South would never have rebelled had they not believed that to do so was not rebellion at all, but the exercise of a lawful constitutional right.[92] A similar conclusion is supported by a consideration of the writings of John C. Calhoun, the leading exponent of state secession. Not only did he believe that the Constitution presupposed a right of secession, but he also associated that right with doctrines of the double majority, nullification, and interposition. Calhoun believed that such doctrines preserved the Union and prevented civil war because they eliminated majority oppression and ensured a united community no matter how divergent its interests. For him, state secession was an option of last resort, to be exercised when other options had failed and the Union had become oppressive of minority interests.[93] Contemporary Canadian discussions of provincial secession provide a striking contrast because they increasingly regard it as an absolute or unqualified moral right. Such a view is most forcefully stated by Quebec separatists, but it is not confined to them. What separatists are saying, according to David Cameron, is "that Quebec, unilaterally and without regard to the rest of the country, must possess the freedom to organize its affairs as it sees fit, and that the rest of the country has an unlimited obligation to stand aside while Quebec does this."[94] More so than the doctrines that preceded the American Civil War, contemporary Canadian discussions of provincial secession implicitly reveal how precarious nationhood can become.

Canadian nationhood becomes somewhat less fragile if provincial secession ceases to be an absolute right. Even Quebec separatists sometimes recognize that a simple assertion of right is not enough to justify the dissolution of Canada. That is why separatists also appeal to other considerations, such as the collective dignity of French-speaking Québécois or the danger of cultural extinction. According to Allen Buchanan, "the need to preserve a group's culture ... can justify state secession ... under certain highly circumscribed and extreme conditions."[95] But the situation in Canada is problematic, he adds, because "political debate ... on the issue of Quebec's secession is somewhat lacking in sustained discussion of data indicating where current arrangements are in fact adequately protecting French-Canadian culture or whether it is imperiled."[96] The absence of sustained discussion is itself significant. What it may indicate is that the preservation of culture is, for many French-speaking Quebeckers, a secondary consideration when set beside the absolute right of self-determination. With respect to English-speaking Canadians, the absence of such discussion appears to suggest that they have different concerns. For many of them, the equality of rights, when understood as a fundamental principle of democracy, takes precedence over the preservation of local particularisms.[97] Frank Underhill once suggested that "the root of our current difficulties is that French-Canadians and English-Canadians have different pictures in their minds of ... the meaning of Confederation."[98] Much the same idea can be expressed by saying that Confederation has created a fragile political nationality and a tenuous common identity, a result that exacerbates the secession issue.

Not only is the Canadian political nationality fragile, but Canadians have also witnessed the failure of two constitutional initiatives, each with the stated objective of creating a more harmonious country. The declared objective of the 1987 Meech Lake Constitutional Accord was the reconciliation of Quebec to changes introduced by the 1982 Constitution Act without the consent of its government. The failed 1992 Charlottetown Consensus Report on the Constitution was the Canada round; its declared objective was to accommodate Quebec, Aboriginals, and other groups within a more pluralistic and decentralized Canada.[99] Coupled with the fragility of the Canadian political nationality, these constitutional failures are sometimes regarded as evidence of the imminent disintegration of Canada or as foreshadowings of the emergence of a Canada without Quebec and a Quebec without Canada. But the failures are not universally so interpreted. A collection of essays on the failed Charlottetown Consensus Report concludes that there are many Canadians who believe "that Canada has a predicament or impasse, but not a crisis."[100]

Much the same premise forms the basis of *Reimagining Canada*, a book that studies the failure of the Meech Lake and Charlottetown accords yet reminds Canadians of their shared commitment to Canada. The recent constitutional failures, Jeremy Webber writes, initially led to the conclusion that "many were giving up on Canada altogether. And yet, as time passed, it became increasingly clear that many Canadians longed for a solution." Not only was this true outside

Quebec, but even within Quebec confirmed secessionists were a decided minority. "Indeed, many advocates of sovereignty, especially at the grass roots," Webber adds, "retained significant residual loyalty to Canada."[101] This was so partly because Canadians shared a subtle common identity and an almost unconscious common life together. "Almost without knowing it," he observes, "our societies have grown up together, contributing to our political life at the level of the country as a whole, but also intersecting at the popular level more than we realize." However, Webber does not believe that the Canadian Constitution should remain unmodified. Canada needs to accommodate its own diversity by acknowledging the distinctive aspirations of people of English, French, and Aboriginal backgrounds. Part of the solution is to adopt an asymmetrical constitution. Such a constitution would recognize that "federalism is a much more flexible device than is often supposed," and it would come to terms with the fact that Canadian practice is far better than Canadian theory.[102] "In our constitutional practice," Webber writes, "we have often fashioned workable structures for accommodating difference, but in our constitutional theory we have failed to see how those structures were good or how they could ... make a country." For him, the failure creates a tragic situation that Canadians must remedy if Canada is to survive as a nation.[103]

But Canadians already have available to them, in the constitutional vision of George-Étienne Cartier, the outlines of a theory that recognizes their diversity and acknowledges the good of their country. Not only was his vision the inspiring moral ideal of Confederation, but it also articulated values to which Canadians continue to appeal in their effort to come to terms with diversity. Because Cartier accepted diversity, he defended tolerance, mutual accommodation, justice for minorities, and the aspirations of local communities. He also believed that Canadians could create a great nation, a belief that led him to defend the cooperative virtues, the Canadian political nationality, and the nascent Canadian community. In the years after Confederation, Cartier's vision was increasingly displaced by Macdonald's. Yet it was never completely forgotten, not even in the 1960s, the period that witnessed the emergence of new challenges to Canadian federalism. Donald Smiley, for example, attempted to remind Canadians of Cartier's vision and to focus attention on his idea of a Canadian political nationality.[104] But even Smiley left many of Cartier's ideas unexplored, and he eventually diverted attention away from Cartier and towards intrastate federalism.[105] It was in the 1960s that many Canadians came to believe not only that Canada needed a new constitution, but also that Confederation contained no enduring principles.[106] Partly as a result of the Trudeau-Lévesque conflict, many Canadians are attempting to reimagine Canada and to discover a theory of federalism that better accommodates their diversity and more adequately expresses their practices. In some cases, the search has led to an examination of foreign jurisdictions such as Switzerland or the United States, in the belief that they can provide the theoretical framework required. In other cases, Canadian federalism has been supplied with foundations borrowed from Rawlsian political theory or from liberal communitarianism.[107] The study of Canadian federalism is more sophisticated and intellectually richer than ever before, yet a dimension that continues to be neglected is Cartier's vision of Confederation. The irony is that the discovery of an adequate theory of Canadian federalism may turn out to be more a matter of retrieval than invention.

CONCLUSION

Not only do Canadians disagree about their country, but, as Peter Russell has written, "Canada's seemingly endless constitutional odyssey goes on and on."[108] The contemporary odyssey began in the 1960s; it has included a conflict between Quebec nationalism and the pan-Canadian nationalism of Pierre Trudeau, a vote within Quebec on sovereignty, a failed constitutional initiative primarily designed to recognize Quebec's status as a distinct society, and a failed round of constitutional negotiations that attempted to accommodate Quebec and Aboriginal nationalism within a more pluralistic and more decentralized Canada. The contemporary odyssey, Russell warns, is itself destructive of Canadian unity, partly because it undermines Canada's ability to deal with pressing practical problems and partly because it frustrates, demoralizes, and even bores the people.[109] The essence of such a position, which many Canadians share, is that Canada cannot endlessly endure constitutional initiatives that question its right to exist as a single country or dispute the ability of its people to live under a common constitution. Such wrenching initiatives, as Edmund Burke wrote in his famous study of the French Revolution, not only make constitutions "a subject rather of altercation than enjoyment," but they can also break "the whole chain and continuity of the commonwealth."[110]

No constitutional system can endure an endless questioning of its legitimacy, yet the Canadian Constitution continues to be the subject of intense disagreement. At one level, there is no solution to such a difficulty, other than to warn Canadians of the dangers of constitutional instability. But Canadians also share a history, and their history contains a reminder, if not a solution. What it suggests is that the very existence of Canada has depended on the ability to compromise, the recognition of difference, and the willingness to create a community of belonging that seeks to include all Canadians. Much the same idea is expressed by saying that if Canada is to exist at all, it must exist as a federal and pluralistic nation. According to Lenihan, Robertson, and Tassé, the continued viability of Canada depends of the ability of Canadians "to reform the way they think and talk" and adopt as their "meta-vision" a form of pluralistic federalism.[111] In the contemporary context, a federal and pluralistic Canada means the accommodation of the new nationalism in Quebec and the acceptance of a measure of self-government for Aboriginal communities.[112] The existence of Canada requires Canadians, in other words, to come to terms with asymmetrical federalism.[113]

But Canadian federalism is an enormously difficult system of government to operate, and it is made more so by the complex problems that confront Canadians. Canada may eventually dissolve if Canadians refuse to accept the presuppositions of its existence. If new associations or healthy nations emerged,[114] the dissolution of Canada would not necessarily represent the kind of catastrophe envisaged by some Canadians; yet its disappearance might still be regretted. When George Grant reflected on the disappearance of Canada, he acknowledged that his "lament [was] based not on philosophy but on tradition." Canadians, he said, had tried, but had failed to sustain a more ordered and stable society than the liberal experiment in the United States.[115] A different kind of lament would be that Canadians had tried, but had failed to sustain a country that enabled people with different ways of life to live, in addition, a common life. This lament would be based on history as well as philosophy, and its ultimate appeal would be to Cartier's vision of Confederation.

Notes

1 A.R.M. Lower, as reported in R. Cook, *The Craft of History*, 37.
2 Siegfried, *The Race Question in Canada*, 14, 85.
3 Cardinal, *The Unjust Society*, 76. Significantly, the subtitle of the book is "The Tragedy of Canada's Indians."
4 *Preliminary Report of the Royal Commission on Bilingualism and Biculturalism*, 37.
5 Cairns, *Disruptions*, 125–32.
6 Taylor, *Reconciling the Solitudes*, 165–6.
7 Bercuson and Cooper, *Deconfederation*, 159. Compare Jenson, "Naming Nations," 337, and Young, *The Secession of Quebec and the Future of Canada*, 9–13.
8 Dufour, *A Canadian Challenge*, 149–52.
9 Bradley, "Hegel's Theory of Tragedy," 71–2, 86. See also Aristotle, *On Poetry and Style*, 24–7, and Calabresi and Bobbitt, *Tragic Choices*, 17–28.
10 Government of Canada, *Statement on Indian Policy*. See also Weaver, *Making Canadian Indian Policy*, 185–99.
11 *Parliamentary Debates on the Subject of the Confederation of the British North American Provinces*, 60. Subsequently cited as *Confederation Debates*.
12 Berlin, *The Crooked Timber of Humanity*, 13, 18, 17.
13 Rawls, "The Idea of an Overlapping Consensus," 17.
14 Bradley, "Hegel's Theory of Tragedy," 72–3.
15 Morton, "Clio in Canada," 49.
16 Trudeau, *Conversation with Canadians*, 33.
17 Smiley, *The Canadian Political Nationality*, 30.
18 Coyne, "The Meech Lake Accord and the Spending Power Proposals," 246.

19 Cited in R. Cook, *Canada, Quebec, and the Uses of Nationalism*, 190.

20 Connor, "A nation is a nation," 379.

21 Cameron, *Nationalism, Self-Determination and the Quebec Question*, 107.

22 Cairns, *Constitution, Government and Society in Canada*, 190.

23 Creighton, *The Road to Confederation*, 145.

24 Lower, *Evolving Canadian Federalism*, 16.

25 Russell, "Can Canadians Be a Sovereign People?" 691–3.

26 Tocqueville, *Democracy in America*, 2: 337, 340.

27 Boldt, *Surviving as Indians*, 265–8.

28 Turpel, "Aboriginal Peoples and the Canadian Charter," 9, 28, 44–5.

29 Barry, "The Consociational Model and Its Dangers," 136.

30 Bibby, *Mosaic Madness*, 5–15.

31 Taylor, *Multiculturalism and "the Politics of Recognition"*, 64.

32 Craig, *Lord Durham's Report*, 23.

33 Russell, *Constitutional Odyssey*, 190–3.

34 Johnston, *Pierre Trudeau Speaks Out on Meech Lake*, 105.

35 Grant, *Lament for a Nation*, 86.

36 Taylor, *The Malaise of Modernity*, 60, 112–3.

37 Ignatieff, *Blood and Belonging*, 147.

38 Webber, *Reimagining Canada*, 23.

39 Laforest, *Trudeau and the End of a Canadian Dream*, 186, 190.

40 Tamir, *Liberal Nationalism*, 78, 145.

41 Tully, "The Crisis of Identification," 81.

42 Ibid., 95.

43 Kymlicka, *Liberalism, Community and Culture*, 135–205.

44 Mercredi and Turpel, *In the Rapids*, 107, 229.

45 Norman, "Towards a Philosophy of Federalism," 86.

46 Lenihan et al., *Canada*, 7, 53, 149.

47 Whitaker, *A Sovereign Idea*, 184; Laponce, *Languages and Their Territories*,
    163–4.

48 Cairns, *Reconfigurations*.

CHAPTER ONE

1 Trudeau, *Federalism and the French Canadians*, 179.

2 Acton, *Essays on Freedom and Power*, 160.

3 McRae, "The Plural Society and the Western Political Tradition," 676.

4 See, for example, Livingston, *Federalism and Constitutional Change*, 1–15.

5 Cairns, *Disruptions*, 108.

6 See Swinton and Rogerson, *Competing Constitutional Visions*.

7 Hovius and Martin, "The Canadian Charter of Rights and Freedoms in the Supreme Court of Canada," 354.

8 Taylor, "Alternative Futures," 225.

9 Cairns, *Disruptions*, 43.

10 Smiley, "A Dangerous Deed," 78–81.

11 Cairns, *Disruptions*, 108, 136–8.

12 Noel, "Consociational Democracy and Canadian Federalism," 267. See also Laponce, *Languages and Their Territories*.

13 Cairns, *Charter versus Federalism*, 3–10.

14 The Charter raises complex issues for Canadian federalism, which are analysed more fully in chapter 5.

15 It is also true that many Canadians support federalism, as I acknowledge below in my discussion of "Federalism and Fraternity." Both facts are important politically as well as philosophically.

16 See, for example, Walsh, "Open and Closed Morality," 17.

17 Dicey, *Introduction to the Study of the Law of the Constitution*, 142–3. See also Vernon, "The Federal Citizen," 4.

18 C. Berger, *The Writing of Canadian History*, 232–3.

19 For a compelling critique of Macdonald's views, see Vipond, *Liberty and Community*.

20 Rogers, "The Genesis of Provincial Rights," 15–7.

21 Lower, *Evolving Canadian Federalism*, 25–6.

22 F.R. Scott, *Essays on the Constitution*, 5.

23 For a discussion of the tensions between commercial empire and cultural particularisms, see Grant, *Lament for A Nation*, 40–1, 54–5, 76.

24 Silver, *The French-Canadian Idea of Confederation*.

25 Brunet, "The French Canadians' Search for a Fatherland," 56–60.

26 Lévesque, *An Option for Quebec*, 26.

27 Handler, *Nationalism and the Politics of Culture in Quebec*, 49.

28 P.J. Smith, "The Ideological Origins of Canadian Confederation," 3. Macdonald is of course a complex figure. For a discussion that emphasizes the conservative and particularistic dimensions of his thought, see Creighton, *Towards the Discovery of Canada*, 211–28.

29 Lovejoy, *The Great Chain of Being*, 292.

30 Elkins and Simeon, *Small Worlds*, 286–7.

31 Sweeny, *George-Etienne Cartier*, 11, 104, 327.

32 "Business, church and ethnic leaders used Cartier," Brian Young has written, "as their agent and intermediary in imposing their largely harmonious class interests." See B. Young, *George-Etienne Cartier*, 135, xi.

33 Cooper, "The Political Ideas of George Etienne Cartier," 286.

34 *Confederation Debates*, 53–62.

35 Smiley, *The Federal Condition in Canada*, 143.

36 Smiley, *The Canadian Political Nationality*, 128.

37 Smiley, "Reflections on Cultural Nationhood and Political Community in Canada," 28.

38 Careless, "'Limited Identities' in Canada," 1. See also Morton, *The Canadian Identity*, 85, 111.

39 Trudeau, *Federalism and the French Canadians*, 194–7.

40 Lower, "Two Ways of Life," 28.

41 *Confederation Debates*, 56, 55, 59.

42 Ibid., 57.

43 Ibid., 60.

44 Ibid., 60. By joining in the larger union, wrote A.R.M. Lower, "the two races surely tacitly agreed to bury the hatchet and to try to live amicably together." Lower, *Evolving Canadian Federalism*, 16.

45 Cooper, "The Political Ideas of George Etienne Cartier," 291.

46 *Confederation Debates*, 59.

47 Ibid., 60.

48 Cited in R. Cook, *Canada, Quebec, and the Uses of Nationalism*, 190.

49 My discussion of fraternity relies implicitly on Ludwig Wittgenstein's discussion of the meaning of words. Wittgenstein wrote as follows: "... always ask yourself: How did we *learn* the meaning of this word ('good' for instance)? From what sort of examples? in what language-games? Then it will be easier to see that the word must have a family of meanings." See Wittgenstein, *Philosophical Investigations*, s.77. Fraternity, in other words, has a family of meanings; understanding them helps us to obtain a better understanding of Canadian federalism.

50 Anderson, *Imagined Communities*, 7. See also A. Smith, *National Identity*, 76. Terms such as "fraternity" and "the government of men" are used in accordance with historical practice. Whenever possible, their meaning should be understood as gender neutral.

51 Hobsbawn, "Fraternity," 472.

52 See Tarn, "Alexander the Great and the Unity of Mankind," 137, 146. Tarn discusses a type of fraternity that rejects assimilation and takes account of diversity. See also Bergson, *The Two Sources of Morality and Religion*, 77–8; Stephen, *Liberty, Equality, Fraternity*, 221; Glazer, *Ethnic Dilemmas*, 228–9.

53 McCulloch, "The Problem of Fellowship in Communitarian Theory," 447.

54 Bourassa, "French-Canadian Patriotism," 119.

55 Norman, "Towards a Philosophy of Federalism," 86.

56 Trudeau, *Federalism and the French Canadians,* 177. See also Smiley, *The Canadian Political Nationality,* 132–4.

57 King, "Against Federalism," 152.

58 For a discussion of the complexities of American federalism and its connection with civic humanism, see Kramnick, "The 'Great National Discussion,' " 15–23. See also Pangle, *The Spirit of Modern Republicanism,* 28–39.

59 Vernon, "Freedom and Corruption," 775.

60 Vernon, "The Federal Citizen," 11.

61 Whitaker, *Federalism and Democratic Theory,* 45, 32.

62 The complex relationships between moral community and federalism are discussed in more detail in chapters 6, 8, and 10.

63 Johnston, *Pierre Trudeau Speaks Out on Meech Lake,* 30–1.

64 Coyne, "The Meech Lake Accord and the Spending Power Proposals," 246.

65 The difficulties created by the Charter of Rights are discussed in chapters 5 and 6.

66 Horowitz, "Tories, Socialists and the Demise of Canada," 353–9.

67 Taylor, "Why Do Nations Have to Become States?" 22–3.

68 Riker, "Six Books in Search of a Subject," 135, 145.

69 Compare Glazer, *Ethnic Dilemmas,* 228–9.

70 Lijphart, "Consociational Democracy," 83.

71 Trudeau, *Conversation with Canadians,* 207–8. However, Trudeau's understanding of federalism is enormously complex, and some of its elements are antithetical to the Canadian experiment, as chapters 5, 6, and 10 attempt to demonstrate.

72 Wheare, "Federalism and the Making of Nations," 35.

CHAPTER TWO

1 Creighton, *Canada's First Century,* 10. See also Creighton, *The Road to Confederation,* 141–6.

2 Cited in Rogers, "The Genesis of Provincial Rights," 18.

3 *Confederation Debates,* 347.

4 Ibid., 589, 350.

5 Upton, "The Idea of Confederation," 184.

6 P.J. Smith, "The Ideological Origins of Canadian Confederation," 3.

7 *Confederation Debates,* 32–3.

8 Waite, *The Life and Times of Confederation,* 115.

9 *Confederation Debates,* 501, 493.

10 Such was Henri Joly's protest. See *Confederation Debates,* 250.

11 Vipond, *Liberty and Community,* 27–8, 35–6.

12 See, for example, Adair, *Fame and the Founding Fathers*, 93–106.

13 For a discussion of the difficulties raised by the word "federalism," see Diamond, "What the Framers Meant By Federalism," 25–42.

14 Hamilton, *The Federalist*, 129–36. See also Epstein, *The Political Theory of the Federalist*, 147.

15 Kramnick, "The 'Great National Discussion,'" 4. See also Pocock, *The Machiavellian Moment*, 506–9, 521–35.

16 Storing, *The Complete Anti-Federalist*, 1: 24. See also Mason, *The States Rights Debate*, 15.

17 Craig, *Lord Durham's Report*, 23.

18 *Confederation Debates*, 350.

19 Ibid., 599, 607.

20 Ibid., 509.

21 Friedrich, *The Impact of American Constitutionalism Abroad*, 60–1.

22 Munro, *American Influences on Canadian Government*, 11.

23 Waite, *Confederation, 1854–1867*, 28.

24 P.J. Smith, "The Ideological Origins of Canadian Confederation," 28.

25 *Confederation Debates*, 27.

26 Creighton, *Towards the Discovery of Canada*, 217.

27 "A federation," wrote W.L. Morton, "so like a legislative union Macdonald could accept." See Morton, "Confederation," 208. Macdonald's views are of course complex, as is federalism. His strongest objections were to intergovernmental relations; he was more accepting of binationality. Still, he desired such a high degree of centralization that his position is widely and perhaps correctly regarded as inimical both to intergovernmental relations and to binationality.

28 Morton, "Confederation," 224–5.

29 P.J. Smith, "The Ideological Origins of Canadian Confederation," 12–9.

30 DeCelles, "Sir Georges Etienne Cartier," 102.

31 Munro, *American Influences on Canadian Government*, 20.

32 F.R. Scott, "French-Canada and Canadian Federalism," 61.

33 Recent biographical studies of Cartier include Sweeny, *George-Etienne Cartier*, and B. Young, *George-Etienne Cartier*.

34 Storing, *The Complete Anti-Federalist*, 1: 5. See also Pangle, *The Spirit of Modern Republicanism*, 124–7.

35 See, for example, Careless, "'Limited Identities' in Canada," 1.

36 Cited in Waite, *The Life and Times of Confederation*, 322.

37 *Confederation Debates*, 511.

38 Rogers, "The Genesis of Provincial Rights," 20–1. See also Vipond, *Liberty and Community*, 89.

39 See Smiley, *The Canadian Political Nationality*, 8–9, 128–35.

40 *Confederation Debates*, 60.

41 Ibid., 60.

42 Ibid., 60.

43 Ibid., 57. See also Tassé, *Discours de Sir Georges Cartier*, 399–447.

44 *Confederation Debates*, 57. Cartier's understanding of federalism is also discussed in R. Cook, *Canada and the French-Canadian Question*, 44–7; and R. *Cook, The Maple Leaf Forever*, 72–5.

45 *Confederation Debates*, 55, 60.

46 Ibid., 60. See also Cooper, "The Political Ideas of George Etienne Cartier," 291.

47 Dicey, *An Introduction to the Study of the Law of the Constitution*, 142–3.

48 *Confederation Debates*, 54.

49 Ibid., 60.

50 Ibid., 59.

51 Ibid., 59.

52 Morton, *The Canadian Identity*, 105.

53 F.R. Scott, *Essays on the Constitution*, 176–7.

54 Cairns, *Constitution, Government and Society in Canada*, 183, 190.

55 R. Cook, *Provincial Autonomy, Minority Rights, and the Compact Theory*, 2. See also Vipond, *Liberty and Community*, 47–82.

56 R. Cook, *Provincial Autonomy, Minority Rights, and the Compact Theory*, 51, 57.

57 Vipond, *Liberty and Community*, 152.

58 Ibid., 190.

59 Cited in Rogers, "The Genesis of Provincial Rights," 17.

60 F.R. Scott, "The Privy Council and Minority Rights," 677.

61 Morton, "Confederation, 1870–1896," 213–5.

62 *Confederation Debates*, 10.

63 Ibid., 238.

64 Calhoun, *A Disquisition on Government*, 22, 29.

65 Ibid., 102.

66 Kennedy, "Nationalism and Self-Determination," 11.

67 Cameron, "Lord Durham Then and Now," 11. See also Cameron, *Nationalism, Self-Determination and the Quebec Question*, 76–80.

68 Acton, *Essays on Freedom and Power*, 160.

69 Ibid., 199.

70 Ibid., 224.

71 Ibid., 174.

72 Ibid., 168.

73 Cameron, *Nationalism, Self-Determination and the Quebec Question*, 107. See also Wheare, "Federalism and the Making of Nations," 35.

74 J. Smith, "Intrastate Federalism and Confederation," 271. See also J.

Smith, "Canadian Confederation and the Influence of American Federalism," 443.

75 Rogers, "The Genesis of Provincial Rights," 14.

76 *Confederation Debates*, 514.

77 Waite, *The Life and Times of Confederation*, 323. See also Martin, *The Causes of Canadian Confederation*, 19.

CHAPTER THREE

1 See, for example, Marshall, *Constitutional Conventions*, 181–209; Russell, *The Court and the Constitution*. See also Hogg, "Comments on Legislation and Judicial Decisions," 307; Knopff, "Legal Theory and the 'Patriation' Debate," 41.

2 See, for example, the essays in Banting and Simeon, *And No One Cheered*.

3 Trudeau, "Convocation Speech," 295.

4 Russell, *Constitutional Odyssey*, 125–6.

5 Trudeau, "Convocation Speech," 296.

6 Marshall, *Constitutional Conventions*, 197.

7 There is a detailed discussion of section 94 in McConnell, *Commentary on the British North America Act*. But McConnell does not address the issues raised in this chapter.

8 Lyon, "Constitutional Theory and the Martland-Ritchie Dissent," 59. See also Lyon, "The Central Fallacy of Canadian Constitutional Law," 40.

9 C.L. Black, *Structure and Relationship in Constitutional Law*, 7. See also Bobbitt, *Constitutional Fate*, 74–92.

10 *Reference re Amendment of the Constitution of Canada*, 58.

11 Wheare, *Federal Government*, 18–20.

12 F.R. Scott, "Section 94 of the British North America Act," 112.

13 Ibid., 112.

14 F.R. Scott, "The Special Nature of Canadian Federalism," 175.

15 Ibid., 115.

16 Ibid., 114.

17 Newfoundland presents no special difficulties for this claim.

18 F.R. Scott, *Essays on the Constitution*, 122.

19 Ibid.

20 *Confederation Debates*, 41.

21 Ibid.

22 Justice Fauteux's opinion (*Attorney-General of Nova Scotia v. Attorney-General of Canada*, 59), that "the presence of [section 94] ... in the [BNA] Act clearly indicates that the right of one of the legislative bodies to

delegate to the other, cannot be implied under the Act; otherwise the section would be useless," appears to conflate the delegation of powers and the transfer of constitutional jurisdiction. A conflation of this kind has led some writers (such as Cheffins and Tucker, *The Constitutional Process in Canada*, 27) to misinterpret section 94 as a delegation of powers provision.

23 *Citizens Insurance Company v. Parsons*, 96.
24 F.R. Scott, *Essays on the Constitution*, 122.
25 Ibid., 186.
26 *Reference re Amendment of the Constitution of Canada*, 125.
27 F.R. Scott, *Essays on the Constitution*, 117. For a similar view, see McConnell, *Commentary on the British North America Act*, 299; also *Citizens Insurance Company v. Parsons*, 110, where it is suggested that "the province of Quebec is omitted ... for the obvious reason that the law which governs property and civil rights in Quebec is in the main the French law."
28 F.R. Scott, *Essays on the Constitution*, 114.
29 *Reference re Amendment of the Constitution of Canada*, 103.
30 Ibid., 41.
31 See Gérin-Lajoie, *Constitutional Amendment in Canada*, 32–43.
32 *Reference re Authority of Parliament in Relation to the Upper House*, 54.
33 J. Smith, "Origins of the Canadian Amendment Dilemma," 304.
34 Wheare, *The Constitutional Structure of the Commonwealth*, 58–72.
35 Hogg, "Comments on Legislation and Judicial Decisions," 332.
36 See *British North America Acts*, xxxii, lii, liv, lvi, and Marshall, "The United Kingdom Parliament and the British North America Acts," 352.
37 Favreau, *The Amendment of the Constitution of Canada*, 10–6.
38 E.R. Black, *Divided Loyalties*, 188–9.
39 *Report of the Royal Commission of Inquiry on Constitutional Problems*, 2: 173–85. The commissioners' view (at 183) of section 94 as constituting "a clear admission that the Province of Quebec occupies a very special constitutional situation in Canada" is consistent with my argument, as is their suggestion (at 184) that Quebec's jurisdiction over property and civil rights cannot be modified without its consent.
40 Favreau, *The Amendment of the Constitution of Canada*, 10–16.
41 Justices Martland and Ritchie, dissenting.
42 The Chief Justice and Justices Estey and McIntyre, dissenting.
43 *Reference re Attorney-General of Quebec and Attorney-General of Canada*, 402.
44 *Reference re Amendment of the Constitution of Canada*, 61.
45 F.R. Scott, *Essays on the Constitution*, 122.
46 *Reference re Amendment of the Constitution of Canada*, 125.

47 The patriation ruling is also a landmark decision on the question of the relationship between law and convention. For somewhat opposing opinions on the law-convention issue, compare Marshall, *Constitutional Conventions*, 16–8, 210–7, and Heard, *Canadian Constitutional Conventions*, 8–10, 102, 152–6.

48 Smiley, "A Dangerous Deed," 78.

49 Remillard, "Legality, Legitimacy and the Supreme Court," 200–1.

50 Trudeau, "Convocation Speech," 304–5.

51 Ibid., 306.

52 Ibid., 305. See also Laforest, *Trudeau and the End of a Canadian Dream*, 15–37.

53 Trudeau, "Convocation Speech," 299–300. "In this case," writes Trudeau, "because conventions are enforceable through the political process, the courts should not have engaged even in declaring their existence."

CHAPTER FOUR

1 See, for example, Cairns, *Disruptions*, 108–38, 161–80.

2 Smiley, "The Case against the Canadian Charter of Human Rights," 289. See also Trudeau, *A Canadian Charter of Human Rights*.

3 Mandel, *The Charter and the Legalization of Politics in Canada*, 308.

4 Ibid., 311. See also Sigurdson, "Left- and Right-Wing Charterphobia in Canada," 95.

5 Compare Cairns, "The Canadian Constitutional Experiment," 87–114, and Taylor, "Alternative Futures," 183–229. See also Sandel, "The Procedural Republic and the Unencumbered Self," and Gutmann, "Communitarian Critics of Liberalism."

6 See, for example, Harold Laski's influential essay "The Obsolescence of Federalism," 367–9.

7 Trudeau, *Federalism and the French Canadians*, 195.

8 Cited in Milne, *Tug of War*, 25.

9 Trudeau, *Federalism and the French Canadians*, 189.

10 Ibid., 196.

11 Compare Trudeau, "The Values of a Just Society," 363.

12 See Smiley, "The Structural Problem of Canadian Federalism," and his "The Case against the Canadian Charter of Human Rights."

13 Cairns, "The Canadian Constitutional Experiment", 103–14. See also Knopff and Morton, "Nation-Building and the Canadian Charter of Rights and Freedoms."

14 For analytical discussions of Trudeau's political theory, see Mathie,

"Political Community and the Canadian Experience," 3; Whitaker, *A Sovereign Idea*, 132; Christiano, "Federalism as a Canadian National Ideal," 248.

15 Trudeau, *Federalism and the French Canadians*, xxi.

16 Ibid., xxii.

17 Ibid., 189, 192.

18 Acton, *Essays on Freedom and Power*, 160–1. Acton expressed views that Trudeau found congenial and frequently cited.

19 Trudeau, *Federalism and the French Canadians*, 203.

20 See Trudeau, *A Canadian Charter of Human Rights*, 15–27, and the literature cited in note 22.

21 Trudeau, *Conversation with Canadians*, 12; Trudeau, *Approaches to Politics*, 85; Trudeau, "The Values of a Just Society," 357–60.

22 On Trudeau, compare Whitaker, *A Sovereign Idea*, 150–5.

23 See, for example, Riker, *Federalism*, 137–45; Vernon, "Freedom and Corruption," 786–93.

24 Trudeau, *Federalism and the French Canadians*, xxiii. See also Whitaker, *A Sovereign Idea*, 189–99, for a discussion of the relationship between federalism and democratic community.

25 Compare Cairns, "The Government and Societies of Canadian Federalism."

26 Riker, *Federalism*, 139–45.

27 Knopff and Morton, *Charter Politics*, 6.

28 F.R. Scott, *Civil Liberties and Canadian Federalism*, 13.

29 See Lucas, *Democracy and Participation*, 251; Trudeau, *Conversation with Canadians*, 46.

30 Lucas, *On Justice*, 11.

31 T.R. Berger, "Towards the Regime of Tolerance," 96. See also Williams, "The Changing Nature of Citizen Rights," 123–8.

32 See Cairns, *Disruptions*, 133; Taylor, *Reconciling the Solitudes*, 165.

33 Trudeau, "Les Droits de l'homme et la suprématie parlementaire," 12.

34 Unity has as much to do with legitimacy as with cohesion. In the former case, it is a problem of political theory, in the latter of political sociology.

35 Taylor, "Atomism," 39–61; Sandel, *Liberalism and the Limits of Justice*.

36 Pocklington, "Against Inflating Human Rights."

37 Cited in Stillman, "Hegel's Critique of Liberal Theories of Rights," 1087.

38 Tocqueville, *Democracy in America*, 1: 165–171.

39 Taylor, "Alternative Futures," 220–2. See also Taylor, "Cross-Purposes," 171–5, and Mathie, "Political Community and the Canadian Experience," 19–20.

40 Taylor, "Alternative Futures," 213, 225.

41 Ibid., 209.

42 Taylor, "Atomism," 49. See also Taylor, *The Malaise of Modernity*, 109–21.

43 Taylor, "Alternative Futures," 209.

44 Dicey, *An Introduction to the Study of the Law of the Constitution*, 141. See also Smiley, *The Canadian Political Nationality*, 128–35.

45 For a detailed critique of communitarianism, see Kymlicka, *Liberalism, Community, and Culture*.

46 Taylor, "Alternative Futures," 211.

47 Ibid., 211.

48 Ibid., 221. See also Taylor, *Reconciling the Solitudes*, 181–4.

49 Taylor, "Alternative Futures," 222.

50 Locke, *The Second Treatise of Government*, 44.

51 Mill, *Utilitarianism, Liberty, Representative Government*, 131.

52 Ibid., 125.

53 Ibid., 116–17.

54 Elkins, "Facing Our Destiny," 701–5.

55 Kymlicka, *Liberalism, Community, and Culture*, 162.

56 Sandel, *Liberalism and the Limits of Justice*, 147–54.

57 Cited in Williams, "The Changing Nature of Citizen Rights," 128.

58 Russell, "The Effects of a Charter of Rights on the Policy-Making Role of Canadian Courts," 31; Russell, "The Political Purposes of the Canadian Charter of Rights and Freedoms," 51–2.

59 Mandel, *The Charter of Rights and the Legalization of Politics in Canada*, 4.

60 Knopff and Morton, *Charter Politics*, ix, 6, 98. See also Manfredi, *Judicial Power and the Charter*, 214–17.

61 See Unger, *The Critical Legal Studies Movement*; Kairys, *The Politics of Law*, and the January 1984 issue of the *Stanford Law Review*.

62 Gordon, "Critical Legal Histories," 114. See also Kelman, *A Guide to Critical Legal Studies*, 2–3, 12–4. Kelman suggests that the scepticism of the Critical Legal Studies Movement surpasses even that of the American legal realists.

63 See Michelman, "Justification (and Justifiability) of Law in a Contradictory World," 71–99.

64 The ways in which rights presuppose society are discussed in Flathman, *The Practice of Rights*, 183–93, and Finnis, *Natural Law and Natural Rights*, 210–26.

65 Kocis, "An Unresolved Tension in Marx's Critique of Justice and Rights," 414.

66 *Regina v. Oakes*, 200–30. See also Gibson, "Reasonable Limits under the Canadian Charter of Rights and Freedoms," and Manfredi, *Judicial Power and the Charter*, 157–87.

67 Bakan, "Constitutional Argument," 193.

68 Shklar, *Legalism.*

69 See Bobbitt, *Constitutional Fate,* 93–119.

70 For a sophisticated account of the differences between judges and legislators, see Dworkin, *Taking Rights Seriously,* 14–45, 131–49.

71 See Del Vecchio, *Justice.*

72 See C.L. Black, *The People and the Court;* Ely, *Democracy and Distrust.*

73 Barker, *Principles of Social and Political Theory,* 102.

74 Lucas, *On Justice,* 1, 18, 263.

75 See Rawls, *A Theory of Justice,* 5.

76 Monahan, *Politics and the Constitution,* 42–9; Monahan, "The Charter
Then and Now," 117–20; Sigurdson, "Left- and Right-Wing Charterphobia in Canada," 106–14; Knopff and Morton, *Charter Politics,* 256–7.

77 Hand, *The Bill of Rights,* 73.

78 Plato, *The Republic,* 35. Compare Trudeau, *Conversation with Canadians,*
42: "Governments ... should all be prepared to admit that the underlying cause of most disorder is injustice."

79 Waldron, "Theoretical Foundations of Liberalism," 128.

80 For a discussion of the notwithstanding clause, see LaSelva, "Only in
Canada," 383. See also Manfredi, *Judicial Power and the Charter,* 188–211.

81 Smart, *Feminism and the Power of Law,* 2, 145, 138, 163–5.

82 Hosek, "Women and the Constitutional Process," 280.

83 L. Smith, "The Distinct Society Clause in the Meech Lake Accord," 35.

84 See Eberts, "The Use of Litigation under the Canadian Charter of
Rights and Freedoms," 53–69, and Scheingold, *The Politics of Rights.*

85 Compare Rostow, "The Democratic Character of Judicial Review," 88.
According to Rostow, "The discussion of problems and the declaration
of broad principles by the courts is a vital element in the community
experience through which ... policy is made ..., and the Justices are inevitable teachers in a vital national seminar."

CHAPTER FIVE

1 Trudeau, *Federalism and the French Canadians,* 178–9.

2 Trudeau, "The Values of a Just Society," 363–4.

3 Ibid., 363.

4 Russell, "The Political Purposes of the Charter," 42.

5 Smiley, "A Dangerous Deed," 80.

6 Cairns, *Constitution, Government and Society in Canada,* 255.

7 See, for example, Russell, "The Political Purposes of the Canadian
Charter of Rights and Freedoms," 41.

8 Knopff and Morton, "Nation-Building and the Canadian Charter of Rights and Freedoms," 174; Knopff and Morton, *Charter Politics*, 374–84.

9 Trudeau, "The Values of a Just Society," 373–4.

10 Ibid., 383.

11 Ibid., 375.

12 Cited in Cairns, *Constitution, Government and Society in Canada*, 183.

13 See Milne, *The New Canadian Constitution*, 237.

14 Skinner, *Machiavelli*, 55.

15 Ibid., 56

16 Butterfield, *The Statecraft of Machiavelli*, 23–33.

17 Trudeau, *Conversation with Canadians*, 202.

18 Vernon, "The Federal Citizen," 12–3.

19 Trudeau, *Federalism and the French Canadians*, 192; Trudeau, *Conversation with Canadians*, 202.

20 Craig, *Lord Durham's Report*, 23.

21 Trudeau, *Federalism and the French Canadians*, 31, 178–9.

22 Breton, "Multiculturalism and Canadian Nation-Building," 42; Cairns, *Charter versus Federalism*, 8, 15.

23 Trudeau, *Conversation with Canadians*, 32–3.

24 Bellah, "Civil Religion in America," 1–19.

25 A. Smith, *National Identity*, 19–42.

26 Breton, "From Ethnic to Civic Nationalism," 85.

27 McRae, *Consociational Democracy*, 262–8.

28 Horowitz, "Mosaics and Identity," 361.

29 Renan, "What Is a Nation?" 202–3. Compare Trudeau, *Federalism and the French Canadians*, 191–2.

30 Government of Canada, *A National Understanding*, 32.

31 See Cairns, *Disruptions*, 42–7.

32 Trudeau, *Conversation with Canadians*, 91–4.

33 Trudeau, "The Values of a Just Society," 379.

34 Ibid., 384.

35 Ibid., 362; Trudeau, *Conversation with Canadians*, 207.

36 Trudeau, *Federalism and the French Canadians*, 47; Trudeau, "The Values of a Just Society," 361.

37 Trudeau, "The Values of a Just Society," 364.

38 Trudeau, *Conversation with Canadians*, 46.

39 Trudeau, "The Values of a Just Society," 366.

40 Trudeau, *Federalism and the French Canadians*, 57.

41 Trudeau, *A Canadian Charter of Human Rights*, 29.

42 Alan Cairns as cited in Knopff and Morton, "Nation-Building and the

Canadian Charter of Rights and Freedoms," 149. See also Hogg, "Federalism Fights the Charter of Rights," 249, and Knopff and Morton, *Charter Politics*, 374.

43 Cairns, *Charter versus Federalism*, 76–7.
44 Trudeau, "Nationalist Alienation," 333; Trudeau, *Federalism and the French Canadians*, 211.
45 Trudeau, "The Values of a Just Society," 368.
46 See Laponce, *Languages and Their Territories*, 162–4; McRoberts, "Making Canada Bilingual," 141.
47 The language issue raises complex questions, some of which are discussed in chapter 6.
48 Trudeau, *Federalism and the French Canadians*, 55.
49 Cameron, "Lord Durham Then and Now," 19.
50 Dicey, *An Introduction to the Study of the Law of the Constitution*, 140–3. See also Wheare, "Federalism and the Making of Nations," 35.
51 Trudeau, "The Values of a Just Society," 363; Russell, "Can Canadians Be a Sovereign People?" 691.
52 F.R. Scott, *Essays on the Constitution*, 248–9.
53 Trudeau, "The Values of a Just Society," 363.
54 Trudeau, *A Canadian Charter of Human Rights*, 11; Trudeau, *Federalism and the French Canadians*, 57.
55 Johnston, *Pierre Trudeau Speaks Out on Meech Lake*, 94.
56 Resnick, *The Masks of Proteus*, 88–106.
57 Johnston, *Pierre Trudeau Speaks Out on Meech Lake*, 34.
58 Ibid., 8; Trudeau, "The Values of a Just Society," 375.
59 See Massey, "The Locus of Sovereignty," 1229.
60 Trudeau, "The Values of a Just Society," 375.
61 Acton, *Essays on Freedom and Power*, 160. Compare Trudeau, *Federalism and the French Canadians*, 124.
62 Trudeau, *Approaches to Politics*, 61–5.
63 Johnston, *Pierre Trudeau Speaks Out on Meech Lake*, 45.
64 Acton, *Essays on Freedom and Power*, 158–9.
65 Ibid., 170.
66 Trudeau, *A Mess That Deserves a Big No*. Trudeau's criticisms of the Charlottetown accord are discussed in more detail in chapter 10.
67 Cairns, *Disruptions*, 137–8.
68 Cairns, *Charter versus Federalism*, 51. See also Vipond, "Whatever Became of the Compact Theory?" 808.
69 Russell, "Can Canadians Be a Sovereign People?" 692. See also Simeon, "Meech Lake and the Visions of Canada," 306.

70 For an analysis of the dimensions of sovereignty, see Benn, "The Uses of Sovereignty," 67.

71 See, for example, Banting and Simeon, *And No One Cheered,* 348–59.

72 A. Smith, *National Identity,* 72–9.

73 As cited in Russell, "Can Canadians Be a Sovereign People?" 691.

74 Tocqueville, *Democracy in America,* 1: 60.

75 Waite, *The Confederation Debates in the Province of Canada/1865,* 50–1. See also Smiley, *The Canadian Political Nationality,* 9.

76 See F.R. Scott, *The Canadian Constitution and Human Rights,* 1–52.

77 T.R. Berger, "Towards the Regime of Tolerance," 87. See also Mallory, "The Continuing Evolution of Canadian Constitutionalism," 94–5.

78 T.R. Berger, "Towards the Regime of Tolerance," 86–7; Breton, "From Ethnic to Civic Nationalism," 93–100.

79 See Mandel, *The Charter of Rights and the Legalization of Politics in Canada,* 35–64, and Taylor, "Alternative Futures," 225.

80 Turpel, "Aboriginal Peoples and the Canadian Charter," 40.

81 Trudeau, "The Values of a Just Society," 358.

82 Ibid., 359.

83 Turpel, "Aboriginal Peoples and the Canadian Charter," 29.

84 Trudeau, *Conversation with Canadians,* 33.

85 Native Women's Association, *Native Women and Self-Government,* 9–14.

86 Johnston, *Pierre Trudeau Speaks Out on Meech Lake,* 8–22.

87 Ibid., 20; Trudeau, "The Values of a Just Society," 375–6.

88 Laforest, *Trudeau and the End of a Canadian Dream,* 148. Laforest arrives at a similar conclusion, although some of his arguments differ from mine.

89 Government of Canada, *A National Understanding,* 35.

90 Trudeau, *Conversation with Canadians,* 42.

CHAPTER SIX

1 *Confederation Debates,* 59–60.

2 Waite, *The Life and Times of Confederation,* 329.

3 Laponce, *Languages and Their Territories,* and Joy, *Languages in Conflict.*

4 R. Cook, "'I never thought I could be as proud ...,'" 342–56; McRoberts, "Making Canada Bilingual," 141; McRoberts, *English Canada and Quebec.*

5 See Taylor, "Shared and Divergent Values," 53.

6 F.R. Scott, *Essays on the Constitution,* 3; Hobsbawm, *Nations and Nationalism since 1780,* 30–5.

7 Maurice Block as cited in Hobsbawm, *Nations and Nationalism since 1780,* 33.

8 Craig, *Lord Durham's Report*, 28, 150.

9 Ajzenstat, "Liberalism and Assimilation," 240–1.

10 Craig, *Lord Durham's Report*, 23.

11 *Confederation Debates*, 29.

12 Ibid., 60.

13 Morin, *Quebec versus Ottawa*, 133, 148.

14 F.R. Scott, *Essays on the Constitution*, 185.

15 *Confederation Debates*, 31.

16 Silver, *The French-Canadian Idea of Confederation*, 33.

17 Vipond, *Liberty and Community*.

18 Creighton, *The Road to Confederation*, 141–6.

19 Dicey, *Introduction to the Study of the Law of the Constitution*, 142–3.

20 Vernon, "The Federal Citizen," 4.

21 Lower, *Evolving Canadian Federalism*, 16.

22 *Confederation Debates*, 60.

23 Compare Martin, *The Causes of Canadian Confederation*.

24 Jean-Marc Léger's commentary in Lévesque, *An Option for Quebec*, 113.

25 Léger, in Ibid., 112.

26 Lévesque, "National State of the French Canadians," 134.

27 Rioux, *Quebec in Question*, 79.

28 Trudeau, *Federalism and the French Canadians*, 169, 211.

29 See Laforest, "Herder, Kedourie et les errements de l'antinationalisme au Canada," 313.

30 Anderson, *Imagined Communities*, 6.

31 A. Smith, *National Identity*, 75.

32 Anderson, *Imagined Communities*, 7.

33 A. Smith, *National Identity*, 160.

34 Laurin, *Quebec's Policy on the French Language*, 2.

35 Ibid., 28, 43.

36 Lévesque, *An Option for Quebec*, 14.

37 Ibid., 92.

38 Joy, *Languages in Conflict*, 1–17, 131–9.

39 Morin, *Quebec versus Ottawa*, 158.

40 Swiss writers speak of the linguistic sovereignty of the cantons.

41 Laponce, *Languages and Their Territories*, 189. See also McRae, *Conflict and Compromise in Multilingual Societies*, 1: 229–40.

42 Lévesque, *An Option for Quebec*, 27.

43 L. Dion, "The Mystery of Quebec," 288.

44 Chaput, *Why I am a Separatist*, 100. See also Dufour, *A Canadian Challenge*, 55–60.

45 The applicability of perfectionism or purism to Quebec separatists is defended by Handler, *Nationalism and the Politics of Culture in Quebec*, 47–50, 107–8, 166–75. Compare, however, Knopff, "Democracy vs. Liberal Democracy," 638, and Laforest, "Herder, Kedourie et les errements de l'antinationalisme au Canada," 313. See also McRoberts, "Protecting the Rights of Linguistic Minorities", 181–3.

46 Handler, *Nationalism and the Politics of Culture in Quebec*, 170.

47 *Ford v. Quebec*, 625–8.

48 Lévesque, *An Option for Quebec*, 14.

49 Dufour, *A Canadian Challenge*, 17, 59, 98, 150.

50 Trudeau, "The Values of a Just Society," 374–5.

51 Trudeau, *Conversation with Canadians*, 33.

52 Trudeau, *Federalism and the French Canadians*, 53; Trudeau, *Approaches to Politics*, 37.

53 Trudeau, *Conversation with Canadians*, 42.

54 Trudeau, *Federalism and the French Canadians*, 179.

55 Rioux, *Quebec in Question*, 100–1.

56 McRoberts, *English Canada and Quebec*, 16.

57 Trudeau, "The Values of a Just Society," 383.

58 See Trudeau, *A Mess That Deserves a Big No.* Trudeau's criticisms of the Charlottetown accord are discussed in chapter 10.

59 Johnston, *Pierre Trudeau Speaks Out on Meech Lake*, 8.

60 Trudeau, *Federalism and the French Canadians*, 211.

61 Government of Canada, *A National Understanding*, 35.

62 Trudeau, *Federalism and the French Canadians*, 177.

63 Government of Canada, *A National Understanding*, 19; Trudeau, *Federalism and the French Canadians*, 177.

64 Government of Canada, *A National Understanding*, 21.

65 Trudeau, "The Values of a Just Society," 368.

66 Laponce, *Languages and Their Territories*, 155, 164. According to Montefiore, "to be neutral in any conflict is to do one's best to help or hinder the various parties concerned in an equal degree." Montefiore, *Neutrality and Impartiality*, 5.

67 Green, "Are Language Rights Fundamental?" 656–65.

68 Laforest, *Trudeau and the End of a Canadian Dream*, 185.

69 Trudeau, *Conversation with Canadians*, 33.

70 Compare Oliver, "Laurendeau et Trudeau," 339, 357–65.

71 McNeill, *Polyethnicity and National Unity in World History*, 4, 85.

72 Taylor, "Shared and Divergent Values," 61.

73 See Kymlicka, *Liberalism, Community and Culture*, 135–258.

74 Trudeau, "The Values of a Just Society," 359.

75 Johnston, *Pierre Trudeau Speaks Out on Meech Lake*, 81.

76 Government of Canada, *A National Understanding*, 52.

77 Sandel, *Liberalism and the Limits of Justice*.

78 Lévesque, *An Option for Quebec*, 17.

79 Trudeau, *Conversation with Canadians*, 14.

80 Trudeau, *Federalism and the French Canadians*, 170.

81 *Confederation Debates*, 60.

82 See the discussion in chapter 1.

83 Bergson, *The Two Sources of Morality and Religion*, 32, 35, 77, 267.

84 Compare Berlin, *Against the Current*, 45, 54, 67.

85 Compare Cairns, *Charter versus Federalism*, 33–61.

86 Minogue, "Theatricality and Politics," 155.

87 Berlin, "Does Political Theory Still Exist?" 149.

88 McCall et al., "Three Nations," 4.

89 Bercuson and Cooper, *Deconfederation*, vii, 168–9.

90 Oliver, "Laurendeau et Trudeau," 305–8.

91 Cairns, "The Fragmentation of Canadian Citizenship," 210.

92 Creighton, *Towards the Discovery of Canada*, 298. See also Creighton, *The Road to Confederation*, 145.

93 Lower, *Evolving Canadian Federalism*, 4.

94 My analysis is similar to asymmetrical federalism. See Milne, "Equality or Asymmetry," 285; Dufour, *A Canadian Challenge*, 91–100; and McCall et al., "Three Nations," 4–6.

CHAPTER SEVEN

1 Russell, "Can Canadians Be a Sovereign People?" 691–3.

2 See Macpherson, *Democratic Theory*, 3–23.

3 *Preliminary Report of the Royal Commission on Bilingualism and Biculturalism*, 13.

4 Ibid., 137.

5 Tocqueville, *Democracy in America*, 1: 15.

6 Crozier, *The Crisis of Democracy*, 1–9.

7 Taylor, "Alternative Futures," 183.

8 Jefferson as cited in Huntington, "The Founding Fathers and the Division of Powers," 176.

9 Wechsler, "The Political Safeguards of Federalism," 100–1.

10 Morris, *Alexander Hamilton and the Founding of the Nation*, 158.

11 The differences are discussed more fully in chapter 2.

12 Underhill, *In Search of Canadian Liberalism*, 5, 12.

13 Whitaker, "Democracy and the Canadian Constitution," 259.

14 Trudeau, "Some Obstacles to Democracy in Quebec," 103.

15 Ibid., 107, 115, 103.

16 Mill, *Utilitarianism, Liberty, Representative Government*, 361.

17 *Report of the Royal Commission on the Economic Union and Development Prospects for Canada*, 3: 80.

18 See, for example, Smiley, "The Structural Problem of Canadian Federalism," 326.

19 Gibbins, *Senate Reform*, 7.

20 Woodcock, "A Plea for the Anti-Nation," 8.

21 Trudeau, "Constituent Power, Sovereignty and the Constitution," 21.

22 F.R. Scott, *Civil Liberties and Canadian Federalism*, 12–4.

23 McRae, "The Meech Lake Impasse in Theoretical Perspective," 144. Compare Cairns, *Disruptions*, 137–8.

24 R. Cook, "The Canadian Dilemma," 147.

25 Ibid., 146.

26 Taylor, "Shared and Divergent Values," 59.

27 McRae, *Consociational Democracy*, 238–68.

28 Acton, *Essays on Freedom and Power*, 141.

29 See also Barry, "The Consociational Model and Its Dangers," 136.

30 Cairns, *Disruptions*, 108–38.

31 Gallie, *Philosophy and the Historical Understanding*, 158.

32 Ibid., 178.

33 Tocqueville, *Democracy in America*, 1: 6.

34 Mill, *Essays on Politics and Culture*, 183.

35 See, for example, the discussion in Mill, *Essays on Politics and Culture*, 228–9, 255.

36 Tocqueville, *Democracy in America*, 2: 340.

37 Siegfried, *The Race Question in Canada*, 14, 85.

38 Ibid., 85, 87.

39 Underhill's introduction to Siegfried, *The Race Question in Canada*, 1.

40 Siegfried, *The Race Question in Canada*, 117.

41 Lederman, *Continuing Canadian Constitutional Dilemmas*, 57.

42 Knopff, "Liberal Democracy and the Challenge of Nationalism in Canadian Politics," 23.

43 Compare Ryle, *Dilemmas*, 5–14.

44 Lower, *Evolving Canadian Federalism*, 16.

45 Johnston, *Pierre Trudeau Speaks Out on Meech Lake*.

46 Government of Quebec, *Quebec-Canada*, 41.

47 Trudeau, "Federalism, Nationalism, and Reason," 191–2.

48 Government of Quebec, *Quebec-Canada*, 15.

49 Taylor, "Shared and Divergent Values," 54. See also S. Dion, "Le Nation-alisme dans la convergence culturelle," 291.

50 Creighton, *The Road to Confederation*, 145.

51 Johnston, *Pierre Trudeau Speaks Out on Meech Lake*, 8. See also Milne, "Equality or Asymmetry," 285.

52 Kymlicka, *Liberalism, Community and Culture*, 183–205.

53 Taylor, *Multiculturalism and "the Politics of Recognition,"* 64.

54 See Wheare, *Federal Government*, 1–14.

55 Dworkin, "Liberalism," 113.

56 Kymlicka, "Liberalism, Individualism, and Minority Rights," 194–9. See also Laponce, *Languages and Their Territories*, 150–64.

57 Danley, "Liberalism, Aboriginal Rights, and Cultural Minorities," 168.

58 Tocqueville, *Democracy in America*, 1: 176.

59 Ibid., 1: 178.

60 Ibid., 1: 170.

61 See also Ranney, "The Bases of American Federalism," 1–8.

62 Creighton, *Towards the Discovery of Canada*, 298.

63 *Confederation Debates*, 53–62.

64 A. Smith, "The Myth of the 'Modern Nation' and the Myths of Nations," 9–12.

65 Rawls, "The Idea of an Overlapping Consensus," 17. See also Barker, *Principles of Social and Political Theory*, 160–7. Barker included such virtues within "the political principle of fraternity."

66 Cameron, "Lord Durham Then and Now," 10.

67 Taylor, *Multiculturalism and "the Politics of Recognition,"* 49.

68 Gilbert, "Democracy and Individuality," 20, 26.

69 Taylor, *Multiculturalism and "the Politics of Recognition,"* 36.

70 Webber, *Reimagining Canada*, 190–1.

71 Cairns, "Constitution-Making, Government Self-Interest, and the Prob-lem of Legitimacy," 380–1.

72 Cairns, *Charter versus Federalism*, 108.

73 McRae, "The Meech Lake Impasse in Theoretical Perspective," 144–5.

74 Corry, "The Uses of a Constitution," 3.

75 Dufour, *A Canadian Challenge*, 91–100.

76 McCall et al., "Three Nations," 4–6. See also Cairns, "The Fragmentation of Citizenship," 181.

77 For sharply opposed positions on asymmetrical federalism, see Webber, *Reimagining Canada*, 229–59, and Lenihan et al., *Canada*, 127–44.

78 Dufour, *A Canadian Challenge,* 139. See also Robertson, *A House Divided,* 27, 70–1.

79 See, for example, S. Dion, "Le Nationalisme dans la convergence culturelle," 291. Dion's essay also contains a stimulating discussion of Tocqueville.

80 Tocqueville believed that America had avoided the danger; France had not. See Tocqueville, *The Old Regime and the French Revolution,* xi–xiv, 48–51.

CHAPTER EIGHT

1 Boldt, *Surviving as Indians,* 1–64.

2 Compare, for example, *Report of the Royal Commission on the Economic Union and Development Prospects of Canada,* 3: 362–72, and Simeon, "Aboriginal Self-Government and Canadian Political Values," 49–56.

3 Weaver, "Federal Difficulties with Aboriginal Rights," 140–1.

4 Gibbins and Ponting, "An Assessment of the Probable Impact of Aboriginal Self-Government in Canada," 174–5, and *Report of the Royal Commission on the Economic Union and Development Prospects for Canada,* 3: 369.

5 Conceptions of a right that are atomistic or that confer negative freedom are inadequate models for Aboriginal rights. See, for example, Dworkin, *Taking Rights Seriously,* 184.

6 Boldt and Long, "Tribal Traditions and European-Western Political Ideologies," 342.

7 Government of Canada, *Statement on Indian Policy,* 6.

8 Cardinal, *The Unjust Society,* 1. See also Weaver, *Making Canadian Indian Policy,* 55, 101, 132, 166, 196.

9 Turpel, "Aboriginal Peoples and the Canadian *Charter,*" 45, 37.

10 Flanagan, "The Sovereignty and Nationhood of Canadian Indians," 369. However, Trudeau publicly opposed the Charlottetown accord, which contained provisions for Aboriginal self-government.

11 Kymlicka, *Liberalism, Community, and Culture,* 166–9.

12 Ibid., 208.

13 Kymlicka, "Liberalism, Individualism, and Minority Rights," 188–94. Compare Ajzenstat, "Liberalism and Assimilation," 239.

14 Kymlicka, "Liberalism, Individualism, and Minority Rights," 196. Compare T.R. Berger, *Northern Frontier, Northern Homeland,* 4–11.

15 Kymlicka, "Liberalism, Individualism, and Minority Rights," 204.

16 Ibid., 187. See also Schwartz, *First Principles, Second Thoughts,* 36.

17 See, for example, Svensson, "Liberal Democracy and Group Rights," 421, and Van Dyke, "Collective Entities and Moral Rights," 21.

18 Erasmus, "Native Rights," 180.

19 Danley, "Liberalism, Aboriginal Rights, and Cultural Minorities," 182.

20 *Regina v. Sparrow*, 390, 404.

21 Cardinal, *The Unjust Society*, 80–95.

22 Assembly of First Nations, *To the Source*, 2.

23 *Worcester v. Georgia*, 542, 552, 556.

24 *Regina v. Sparrow*, 408, 410, 411, 417.

25 *Sparrow v. Regina* (British Columbia Court of Appeal), 603.

26 Mercredi and Turpel, *In the Rapids*, 35.

27 Simeon, "Aboriginal Self-Government and Canadian Political Values," 51. See also Mercredi and Turpel, *In the Rapids*, 32.

28 Wheare, "Federalism and the Making of Nations," 35.

29 Cairns, "The Charlottetown Accord," 47. See also Arendt, *The Origins of Totalitarianism*, 267–302.

30 Macpherson, *The Real World of Democracy*, 3. See, for example, Cunningham, "Democracy and Three-Nation Asymmetry," 18.

31 A dialogue exists, in that each side attempts to persuade the other, and both sides are responsive to opposing considerations, at least in the long run.

32 Weaver, *Making Canadian Indian Policy*, 188–97.

33 Trudeau, *Conversation with Canadians*, 21.

34 Assembly of First Nations, *To the Source*, 28.

35 Plamenatz, *On Alien Rule and Self-Government*, 48.

36 Boldt and Long, "Tribal Traditions and European-Western Ideologies," 336, 339.

37 Mercredi and Turpel, *In the Rapids*, 115.

38 See, for example, C.H. Scott, "Custom, Tradition, and the Politics of Culture," 326. "Societies which have emphasized consensus-style democracy," Scott writes, "may stress such participatory processes as general assemblies, *ad hoc* leadership review, and referenda, while eschewing such adversarial forms as party politics – as approaches taken by the Dene and Inuit of the Northwest Territories illustrate."

39 Boldt, *Surviving as Indians*, 167–221. See also Fanon, *Black Skin, White Masks*, 83–108.

40 Assembly of First Nations, *To the Source*, vii, 20.

41 Rousseau, *The Social Contract and Discourses*, 54–6. See also Jouvenel, "Rousseau's Theory of the Forms of Government," 490–4.

42 Rousseau, *The Government of Poland*, 25. See also Barber, *The Death of Communal Liberty*, 3–9, 170–203.

43 Popper, *The Open Society and Its Enemies*, 1: 184. See also Sabine, "The Two Democratic Traditions."

44 Bergson, *The Two Sources of Morality and Religion*, 267, 281–3. See also Walsh, "Open and Closed Morality," 17–30.

45 Government of Canada, *Statement on Indian Policy*, 5, 9.

46 Trudeau, *Conversation with Canadians*, 14–5.

47 Cardinal, *The Unjust Society*, 167–8.

48 Assembly of First Nations, *To the Source*, 70.

49 Howard, "Cultural Absolutism and the Nostalgia for Community," 337.

50 Mercredi and Turpel, *In the Rapids*, 217.

51 Fanon, *The Wretched of the Earth*, 41, 198, 211. See also Caute, *Fanon*, 68–90.

52 Assembly of First Nations, *To the Source*, vii, 4, 10, 14. See also Clark, *Native Liberty, Crown Sovereignty*, 3–10.

53 Fanon, *The Wretched of the Earth*, 210.

54 Assembly of First Nations, *To the Source*, 2, 16, 61.

55 Boldt, *Surviving as Indians*, 149.

56 Assembly of First Nations, *To the Source*, 61–4; Turpel, "Aboriginal Peoples and the Canadian *Charter*," 41–4.

57 Mercredi and Turpel, *In the Rapids*, 210.

58 The text of the Charlottetown accord is reprinted in C. Cook, *Constitutional Predicament*, 226–49. The accord also contained other provisions relating to Aboriginals, such as support for Aboriginal representation in the House of Commons.

59 Cairns, "The Charlottetown Accord," 39. The quotation from Sanders is cited by Cairns.

60 Native Women's Association, *Native Women and Self-Government*, 10, 14. See also Medcalf, *Law and Identity*, 103–28; and Jamieson, *Indian Women and the Law in Canada*, 79–92.

61 Fanon, *The Wretched of the Earth*, 43, 45.

62 Dyck, *Indigenous Peoples and the Nation-State*, 15.

63 Tennant, *Aboriginal Peoples and Politics*, 13.

64 McNeil, "Aboriginal Nations and Quebec's Boundaries," 107.

65 Assembly of First Nations, *To the Source*, 25, and Cardinal, *The Unjust Society*, 12–5.

66 See, for example, Wilkinson, *American Indians, Time, and the Law*, 14, 116, 120–2.

67 Tully, "Multirow Federalism and the Charter," 184–7, 194. See also Ryder, "The Demise and Rise of the Classical Paradigm in Canadian Federalism," 314–22.

68 Cameron, *Nationalism, Self-Determination and the Quebec Question*, 107.

69 Gibbins and Ponting, "An Assessment of the Probable Impact of Aboriginal Self-Government in Canada," 178.

70 Slattery, "First Nations and the Constitution," 276.

71 Cairns, "Aboriginal Canadians, Citizenship and the Constitution," 256.

72 Plamenatz, *On Alien Rule and Self-Government*, 146.

73 Richard Gwyn, as cited in Cairns, "The Charlottetown Accord," 51.

74 Sartre, *Anti-Semite and Jew*, 79, 95.

75 Compare Fanon, *Black Skin, White Masks*, 210–32.

76 Dyck, "'Telling it like it is,' " 201, 204.

77 Cairns, *Disruptions*, 214.

CHAPTER NINE

1 *Preliminary Report of the Royal Commission on Bilingualism and Biculturalism*, 13.

2 Cairns, "The Fragmentation of Canadian Citizenship," 181; Breton, "The Production and Allocation of Symbolic Resources," 123; Taylor, "Shared and Divergent Values," 53.

3 For a discussion of expressivism, see, for example, Yael Tamir, "Whose History?" 146.

4 See, for example, Bibby, *Mosaic Madness*.

5 Berlin, *Four Essays on Liberty*, 167; Morton, "Canada: The One and the Many," 285.

6 Cairns, *Charter versus Federalism*, 11–32.

7 Taylor, "Alternative Futures," 224–5; Cairns, *Charter versus Federalism*, 124–5; McCall et al., "Three Nations," 4.

8 Trudeau, *A Time for Action*, 4.

9 Lower, "Two Ways of Life," 15.

10 Ibid., 19. "No one can suggest," wrote Lower, "that the English conquest was cruel, as conquests go, or the English government harsh. If the French in Canada had had a choice of conquerors they could not have selected more happily. But conquerors are conquerors."

11 Dufour, *A Canadian Challenge*, 25–32.

12 Karmis, "Interpréter l'identité québécoise," 309, 321.

13 Lower, "Two Ways of Life," 19.

14 McRae, "The Meech Lake Impasse in Theoretical Perspective," 151.

15 Lower, "Two Ways of Life," 28, 19.

16 Acton, *Essays on Freedom and Power*, 169.

17 See, for example, Trudeau, *Federalism and the French Canadians*, 124.

18 Cameron, *Nationalism, Self-Determination and the Quebec Question*, 79–80.

19 Dicey, *Introduction to the Study of the Law of the Constitution*, 142–3.

20 For Cartier's speech, see *Confederation Debates*, 53–62.

21 *Confederation Debates,* 60.

22 Berlin, *Concepts and Categories,* 143.

23 See, for example, Adair, *Fame and the Founding Fathers,* 93–106.

24 *Confederation Debates,* 60, 59.

25 Smiley, *The Canadian Political Nationality,* 30, 129.

26 Horowitz, "Mosaics and Identity," 361, 363.

27 Holmes, "Nationalism in Canadian Foreign Policy," 204.

28 Grant, *Lament for a Nation,* 21, 22.

29 Trudeau, *Conversation with Canadians,* 32–3.

30 Dufour, *A Canadian Challenge,* 150.

31 Kohn, *American Nationalism,* 3.

32 Bellah, "Civil Religion in America," 5, 12.

33 MacIntyre, "Is Patriotism a Virtue?" 55.

34 Ranney, "The Bases of American Federalism," 2.

35 Glazer, "Individual Rights against Group Rights," 100.

36 Glazer, *Ethnic Dilemmas,* 229.

37 Glazer, "Individual Rights against Group Rights," 99.

38 Schlesinger, *The Disuniting of America.*

39 Holmes, "Nationalism in Canadian Foreign Policy," 217.

40 Cameron, *Nationalism, Self-Determination and the Quebec Question,* 79.

41 McRae, *Conflict and Compromise in Multilingual Societies,* 1: 240. See also Siegfried, *Switzerland,* 199–201.

42 As cited in McRae, *Switzerland,* 12. See also Kohn, *Nationalism and Liberty,* 115–9.

43 See, for example, Castonguay, "Why Hide the Facts?" 13.

44 Trudeau,"The Values of a Just Society," 367–8. See also McRae, "The Principle of Territoriality and the Principle of Personality in Multilingual States," 33.

45 F.R. Scott, *Essays on the Constitution,* 380, 388. Compare McRoberts, "Making Canada Bilingual," 141.

46 Cited in Steinberg, *Why Switzerland?* 181. See also Barber, *The Death of Communal Liberty,* 182–3.

47 Taylor, *The Pattern of Politics,* 130.

48 Meinecke, *Cosmopolitanism and the National State,* 9–22; R. Cook, *Canada, Quebec, and the Uses of Nationalism,* 184.

49 Trudeau, "Statement on Multiculturalism," 349.

50 Breton, "From Ethnic to Civic Nationalism," 87.

51 Berlin, *The Crooked Timber of Humanity,* 5–6, 12–3.

52 Ibid., 15; Berlin, *Four Essays on Liberty,* 167.

53 Berlin, *Four Essays on Liberty,* 171; Berlin, *The Crooked Timber of Humanity,* 18.

54 Bibby, *Mosaic Madness,* 12–14.

55 Horowitz, "Mosaics and Identity," 364; Bibby, *Mosaic Madness,* 178.

56 Berlin, *The Crooked Timber of Humanity,* 11. See also Taylor, "The Diversity of Goods," 129.

57 Kedourie, *Nationalism,* 10; Trudeau, *Federalism and the French Canadians,* 182.

58 Barnard, "National Culture and Political Legitimacy," 251. See also Fichte, *Addresses to the German Nation,* 3, 7, 191.

59 Barnard, "National Culture and Political Legitimacy," 247.

60 Kedourie, *Nationalism,* 139.

61 Holmes, "Nationalism in Canadian Foreign Policy," 216

62 Trudeau, *Federalism and the French Canadians,* 169. Compare, however, Laforest, "Herder, Kedourie et les errements de l'antinationalisme au Canada," 313.

63 R. Cook, *Canada, Quebec, and the Uses of Nationalism,* 194.

64 Berlin, *Four Essays on Liberty,* 167–72.

65 Berlin, *Vico and Herder,* 195, 198, 185.

66 Trudeau, "Federalism, Nationalism, and Reason," 191–6.

67 Johnston, *Pierre Trudeau Speaks Out on Meech Lake,* 31.

68 Steinberg, *Why Switzerland?* 127; Kohn, *Nationalism and Liberty,* 89–95.

69 Assembly of First Nations, *To the Source*; Rémillard, "Quebec's Quest for Survival and Equality via the Meech Lake Accord," 28.

70 Whitaker, *Federalism and Democratic Theory,* 42.

71 Mill, "Coleridge," 138–9. See also Barry, "Self-Government Revisited," 135–42.

72 Breton, "The Production and Allocation of Symbolic Resources," 136. See also Breton, "Multiculturalism and Canadian Nation-Building," 27.

73 Whitaker, *A Sovereign Idea,* 250, 233.

CHAPTER TEN

1 Plato, *Euthyphro, Apology, Crito,* 37.

2 *Confederation Debates,* 33.

3 Ibid., 347, 350.

4 Ibid., 482, 508, 530.

5 R. Cook, *Provincial Autonomy, Minority Rights, and the Compact Theory,* 2, 57–8.

6 Black and Cairns, "A Different Perspective on Canadian Federalism," 83, 95.

7 Vipond, *Liberty and Community,* 47–112.

8 Rogers, "The Genesis of Provincial Rights," 9–10.

9 Vipond, *Liberty and Community*, 10, 40.

10 Morton, "Confederation, 1870–1896," 224–5.

11 Cairns, *Constitution, Government and Society in Canada*, 79.

12 Laski, "The Obsolescence of Federalism," 367.

13 Trudeau, *Federalism and the French Canadians*, 198.

14 James Bryce, *The American Commonwealth*, 1: 353; Adair, *Fame and the Founding Fathers*, 94–103.

15 Smiley, "The Rowell-Sirois Report, Provincial Autonomy and Post-War Canadian Federalism," 81, 79.

16 Pigeon, "The Meaning of Provincial Autonomy," 44, 35, 44. Pigeon's article is concerned mainly with Quebec's place within the Canadian federal system.

17 Neumann, "Federalism and Freedom," 46–9, 51.

18 Riker, *Federalism*, 140–1.

19 Smiley, *Constitutional Adaptation and Canadian Federalism*, 4.

20 Mallory, "The Five Faces of Federalism," 60–1.

21 E.R. Black, *Divided Loyalties*, 106.

22 Simeon, *Federal-Provincial Diplomacy*, 286–92; Smiley, *Constitutional Adaptation and Canadian Federalism*, 122–7.

23 Cairns, *Constitution, Government and Society in Canada*, 169. See also Gagnon, "Canadian Federalism," 147.

24 Black and Cairns, "A Different Perspective on Canadian Federalism," 83.

25 Cairns, *Constitution, Government and Society in Canada*, 169.

26 Ibid., 171, 184, 171, 190. See also Smiley, *Constitutional Adaptation and Canadian Federalism*, 111–28.

27 Lijphart, "Consociational Democracy," 76, 79.

28 Lijphart, "Cultural Diversity and Theories of Political Integration," 11.

29 Ormsby, *The Emergence of the Federal Concept in Canada*, 122–5.

30 Noel, "Consociational Democracy and Canadian Federalism," 268.

31 Simeon, *Federal-Provincial Diplomacy*, 292.

32 Ormsby, *The Emergence of the Federal Concept in Canada*, 125.

33 Stevenson, *Ex Uno Plures*, 15.

34 P.J. Smith, "Ideological Origins of Canadian Confederation," 3.

35 Stevenson, *Ex Uno Plures*, 7.

36 Groulx, *The Iron Wedge*. Compare Oliver, *The Passionate Debate*, 196–225.

37 Groulx, *The Iron Wedge*, 8–9, 38, 40–1.

38 Ibid., 18, 158. See also Handler, *Nationalism and the Politics of Culture in Quebec*, 30–51.

39 L. Dion, *Quebec*, 36.

40 Laforest, "Herder, Kedourie et les errements de l'antinationalisme au Canada," 313.

41 Kwavnick, *The Tremblay Report,* 209.

42 Trudeau, *Federalism and the French Canadians,* 101.

43 Brunet, "The French Canadians' Search for a Fatherland," 60.

44 Lévesque, *An Option for Quebec,* 25.

45 Laforest, "Herder, Kedourie et les errements de l'antinationalisme au Canada," 328–34.

46 Barnard, *Herder's Social and Political Thought,* 63.

47 Ibid., 59.

48 Ignatieff, *Blood and Belonging,* 173.

49 Lenihan et al., *Canada,* 115.

50 I. Young, "Polity and Group Difference," 257. See also Tamir, "Whose History?" 146.

51 Trudeau, *Federalism and the French Canadians,* 189. As Trudeau noted, "nationhood being little more than a state of mind, and every sociologically distinct group within the nation having a contingent right of secession, the will of the people was in constant danger of dividing up."

52 Underhill, "Some Reflections on the Liberal Tradition in Canada," 35–6.

53 Porter, *The Vertical Mosaic,* 366, 369.

54 Ibid., 3, 7.

55 Ibid., 166, 558.

56 Ibid., 383.

57 Ibid., 73, 385.

58 Mill, *The Subjection of Women,* 17–18.

59 Ajzenstat, *The Political Thought of Lord Durham,* 73–100.

60 Hayek, *Law, Legislation and Liberty,* 2: 85.

61 Lalande, *In Defence of Federalism,* 49.

62 Grant, *Lament for a Nation,* 90, 76.

63 Whitaker, "Reason, Passion and Interest," 21–5.

64 Christiano, "Federalism as a Canadian National Ideal," 265.

65 Trudeau, *Memoirs,* 283.

66 Ibid., 323, 327. Compare Laforest, *Trudeau and the End of a Canadian Dream,* 15–37.

67 Trudeau, *Memoirs,* 283, 282.

68 Ibid., 353–4.

69 Herzog, *Without Foundations,* 19–22.

70 Cairns, "The Charlottetown Accord," 26.

71 Tully, "Diversity's Gambit Declined," 196.

72 Emberley, "Globalism and Localism," 217.

73 Trudeau, *A Mess That Deserves a Big No*, 12, 57.

74 Taylor, *Reconciling the Solitudes*, 57.

75 Ibid., 5, 6, 13.

76 Ibid., 195.

77 Taylor, *The Malaise of Modernity*, 1, 22, 33, 89, 112, 118.

78 Ibid., 119.

79 Taylor, *Reconciling the Solitudes*, 183.

80 Ibid., 109–12, 183–4.

81 Cairns, "Book Review," 156.

82 Meyers, *The Mind of the Founder*, 69–98.

83 Taylor, *Reconciling the Solitudes*, 57. See also Smiley, *The Association Dimension of Sovereignty-Association*, 2–21.

84 Taylor, "The Diversity of Goods," 129.

85 Cairns, "Book Review," 156–7.

86 Trudeau, *A Mess That Deserves a Big No*, 47–8.

87 Meyers, *The Mind of the Founder*, xxxi.

88 *Confederation Debates*, 53–62.

89 Wheare, "Federalism and Making of Nations," 36, 35.

90 Ibid., 35.

91 Schlesinger, *The Disuniting of America*, 137–8.

92 Abraham Lincoln as cited by Jaffa, "'Partly Federal, Partly National,' " 110.

93 Calhoun, *A Disquistion on Government*, 28, 36–40.

94 Cameron, *Nationalism, Self-Determination and the Quebec Question*, 155.

95 Buchanan, *Secession*, 153.

96 Ibid., 62.

97 Bercuson and Cooper, *Deconfederation*, 167–72.

98 Underhill, *The Image of Confederation*, 50.

99 Russell, *Constitutional Odyssey*, 154.

100 C. Cook, *Constitutional Predicament*, 23, 24. Cook bases his conclusion on the authority of the contributors. They include Alan C. Cairns, Alain Noel, Barry Cooper, Janet Ajzenstat, F.L. Morton, James Tully, and Peter Emberley.

101 Webber, *Reimagining Canada*, 18.

102 Ibid., 318, 314, 23.

103 Ibid., 23.

104 Smiley, *The Canadian Political Nationality*, 2, 9, 128–35.

105 Smiley, "The Structural Problem of Canadian Federalism," 326.

106 See, for example, the literature discussed in Cairns, "The Living Canadian Constitution," and reprinted in Cairns, *Constitution, Government and Society in Canada*.

107 Some of the more prominent attempts to supply Canadian federalism with theoretical foundations are discussed in the prologue, as well as throughout the book.

108 Russell, *Constitutional Odyssey,* 191. See also Russell, "The End of Mega Constitutional Politics in Canada?" 217–21.

109 Russell, *Constitutional Odyssey,* 193.

110 Burke, *Reflections on the Revolution in France,* 188, 193.

111 Lenihan et al., *Canada,* 155.

112 Quebec nationalism and Aboriginal self-government have already been discussed in chapters 6 and 8.

113 Tarlton, "Symmetry and Asymmetry as Elements of Federalism," 861. Canadian discussions of asymmetrical federalism include Cairns "Constitutional Change and the Three Equalities," Milne, "Equality or Asymmetry," and McRoberts, "Disagreeing on Fundamentals."

114 For sophisticated discussions, see Gibbins, "Speculations on a Canada without Quebec," 264–73, and Young, *The Secession of Quebec and the Future of Canada,* 287–306.

115 Grant, *Lament for a Nation,* 96, 4.

Bibliography

Acton, Lord. *Essays on Freedom and Power.* Ed. Gertrude Himmelfarb. Cleveland: Meridian, 1962.

Adair, Douglass. *Fame and the Founding Fathers.* New York: Norton, 1974.

Ajzenstat, Janet. "Liberalism and Assimilation: Lord Durham Reconsidered." In *Political Thought in Canada.* Ed. Stephen Brooks. Toronto: Irwin Publishing, 1984.

– *The Political Thought of Lord Durham.* Kingston and Montreal: McGill-Queen's University Press, 1988.

Anderson, Benedict. *Imagined Communities.* London: Verso, 1991.

Arendt, Hannah. *The Origins of Totalitarianism.* New York: Meridian, 1971.

Aristotle. *On Poetry and Style.* Trans. G.M.A. Grube. Indianapolis: Bobbs-Merrill, 1958.

Assembly of First Nations. *To the Source.* Ottawa: Commissioners' Report published by the Assembly of First Nations, 1992.

Attorney-General of Nova Scotia v. Attorney-General of Canada. Supreme Court Reports (1951): 31.

Bakan, Joel C. "Constitutional Argument: Interpretation and Legitimacy in Canadian Constitutional Thought." *Osgoode Hall Law Journal* 27 (1989): 123–93.

Banting, Keith, and Simeon, Richard, eds. *And No One Cheered.* Toronto: Methuen, 1983.

Barber, Benjamin. *The Death of Communal Liberty.* Princeton: Princeton University Press, 1974.

Barker, Ernest. *Principles of Social and Political Theory.* Oxford: Oxford University Press, 1967.

Barnard, F.M. *Herder's Social and Political Thought.* Oxford: Clarendon Press, 1965.

– "National Culture and Political Legitimacy: Herder and Rousseau." *Journal of the History of Ideas* 44 (1983): 231–53.

Barry, Brian. "The Consociational Model and Its Dangers." In B. Barry, *Democracy, Power and Justice*. Oxford: Oxford University Press, 1989.

– "Self-Government Revisited." In *The Nature of Political Theory*. Ed. David Miller and Larry Siedentop. Oxford: Clarendon Press, 1983.

Bellah, Robert. "Civil Religion in America." *Daedalus* 96 (1967): 1–21.

Benn, Stanley. "The Uses of Sovereignty." In *In Defense of Sovereignty*. Ed. W.J. Stankiewicz. London: Oxford University Press, 1969.

Bercuson, David J., and Cooper, Barry. *Deconfederation: Canada without Quebec*. Toronto: Key Porter, 1991.

Berger, Carl. *The Writing of Canadian History*. Toronto: Oxford University Press, 1976.

Berger, Thomas R. *Northern Frontier, Northern Homeland*. Vancouver: Douglas & MacIntrye, 1988.

– "Towards the Regime of Tolerance." In *Political Thought in Canada*. Ed. Stephen Brooks. Toronto: Irwin, 1984.

Bergson, Henri. *The Two Sources of Morality and Religion*. Trans. R. Ashley Audra and Cloudesley Brereton. New York: Anchor Books, 1935.

Berlin, Isaiah. *Against the Current*. London: Hogarth Press, 1979.

– *Concepts and Categories*. New York: Viking Press, 1979.

– *The Crooked Timber of Humanity*. New York: Knopf, 1991.

– "Does Political Theory Still Exist?" In Isaiah Berlin, *Concepts and Categories*. New York: Viking Press, 1979.

– *Four Essays on Liberty*. London: Oxford University Press, 1967.

– *Vico and Herder*. London: Chatto & Windus, 1980.

Bibby, Reginald. *Mosaic Madness*. Toronto: Stoddart, 1990.

Black, Charles L. *The People and the Court*. Englewood Cliffs: Prentice-Hall, 1960.

– *Structure and Relationship in Constitutional Law*. Baton Rouge: Louisiana State University Press, 1969.

Black, Edwin R. *Divided Loyalties: Canadian Concepts of Federalism*. Montreal: McGill-Queen's University Press, 1975.

– and Cairns, Alan C. "A Different Perspective on Canadian Federalism." In *Canadian Federalism: Myth or Reality*. Ed. J. Peter Meekison. Toronto: Methuen, 1971.

Bobbitt, Philip. *Constitutional Fate*. New York: Oxford University Press, 1982.

Boldt, Menno. *Surviving as Indians*. Toronto: University of Toronto Press, 1993.

– and Long, J. Anthony. "Tribal Traditions and European-Western Political Ideologies: The Dilemma of Canada's Native Indians." In *The Quest for Justice*. Ed. Menno Boldt and J. Anthony Long. Toronto: University of Toronto Press, 1985.

Bourassa, Henri. "French-Canadian Patriotism." In *French-Canadian Nationalism*. Ed. R. Cook. Toronto: MacMillan, 1969.

Bradley, A.C. "Hegel's Theory of Tragedy." In A.C. Bradley, *Oxford Lectures on Poetry*. London: Macmillan, 1950.

Breton, Raymond. "From Ethnic to Civic Nationalism: English Canada and Quebec." *Ethnic and Racial Studies* 11 (1988): 85–102.

– "Multiculturalism and Canadian Nation-Building." In *The Politics of Gender, Ethnicity and Language in Canada*. Ed. Alan Cairns and Cynthia Williams. Toronto: University of Toronto Press, 1986.

– "The Production and Allocation of Symbolic Resources." *Canadian Journal of Sociology and Anthropology* 21 (1984): 123–44.

British North America Acts: The Role of Parliament. First Report of the Foreign Affairs Committee of the UK Parliament. London: Her Majesty's Stationery Office, 1981.

Brunet, Michel. "The French Canadians' Search for a Fatherland." In *Nationalism in Canada*. Ed. Peter Russell. Toronto: McGraw-Hill, 1966.

Bryce, James. *The American Commonwealth.* 2 vols. New York: Macmillan, 1928.

Buchanan, Allen. *Secession.* Boulder: Westview Press, 1991.

Burke, Edmund. *Reflections on the Revolution in France.* Ed. Conor Cruise O'Brien. Harmondsworth: Penguin, 1969.

Butterfield, Herbert. *The Statecraft of Machiavelli.* New York: Collier Books, 1967.

Cairns, Alan C. "Aboriginal Canadians, Citizenship and the Constitution." In Alan C. Cairns, *Reconfigurations: Canadian Citizenship and Constitutional Change*. Toronto: McClelland and Stewart, 1995.

– "Book Review: Reconciling the Solitudes." *Canadian Journal of Political Science* 27 (1994): 155–7.

– "The Canadian Constitutional Experiment." *Dalhousie Law Journal* 9 (1984–85): 87–114.

– "The Charlottetown Accord: Multinational Canada v. Federalism." In *Constitutional Predicament*. Ed. Curtis Cook. Montreal & Kingston: McGill-Queen's University Press, 1994.

– *Charter versus Federalism.* Montreal: McGill-Queen's University Press, 1992.

– *Constitution, Government and Society in Canada.* Toronto: McClelland and Stewart, 1988. Contains the essays "The Government and Societies of Canadian Federalism" and "The Other Crisis of Canadian Federalism," originally published earlier.

– "Constitution-Making, Government Self-Interest, and the Problem of Legitimacy." In *Political Support in Canada*. Ed. Allan Kornberg and Harold Clarke. Durham: Duke University Press, 1983.

– "Constitutional Change and the Three Equalities." In *Options for a New*

Canada. Ed. Ronald L. Watts and Douglas M. Brown. Toronto: University of Toronto Press, 1991.

– *Disruptions: Constitutional Struggles, from the Charter to Meech Lake.* Toronto: McClelland and Stewart, 1991.

– "The Fragmentation of Canadian Citizenship." In *Belonging.* Ed. William Kaplan. Montreal: McGill-Queen's University Press, 1993.

– "The Government and Societies of Canadian Federalism." *Canadian Journal of Political Science* 10 (1977): 695–725.

– *Reconfigurations: Canadian Citizenship and Constitutional Change.* Toronto: McClelland and Stewart, 1995.

Calabresi, Guido, and Bobbitt, Philip. *Tragic Choices.* New York: Norton, 1978.

Calhoun, John C. *A Disquistion on Government.* Ed. C. Gordon Post. Indianapolis: Bobbs-Merrill, 1953.

Cameron, David R. "Lord Durham Then and Now." *Journal of Canadian Studies* 25 (1990): 5–23.

– *Nationalism, Self-Determination and the Quebec Question.* Toronto: Macmillan, 1974.

Cardinal, Harold. *The Unjust Society: The Tragedy of Canada's Indians.* Edmonton: Hurtig, 1969.

Careless, J.M.S. "'Limited Identities' in Canada." *Canadian Historical Review* 50 (1969): 1–10.

Castonguay, Charles. "Why Hide the Facts? The Federalist Approach to the Language Crisis in Canada." *Canadian Public Policy* 5 (1979): 4–15.

Caute, David. *Fanon.* London: Collins, 1970.

Chaput, Marcel. *Why I am a Separatist.* Trans. Robert A. Taylor. Toronto: Ryerson Press, 1962.

Cheffins, R.I., and Tucker, R.N. *The Constitutional Process in Canada.* Toronto: McGraw-Hill Ryerson, 1976.

Christiano, Kevin J. "Federalism as a Canadian National Ideal: The Civic Rationalism of Pierre Elliott Trudeau." *Dalhousie Review* 69 (1989–90): 248–69.

Citizens Insurance Company v. Parsons. Appeal Cases 7 (1881): 96.

Clark, Bruce. *Native Liberty, Crown Sovereignty.* Montreal & Kingston: McGill-Queen's University Press, 1990.

Connor, Walker. "A nation is a nation, is a state, is an ethnic group is a ...." *Ethnic and Racial Studies* 1 (1978): 377–400.

Cook, Curtis, ed. *Constitutional Predicament.* Montreal & Kingston: McGill-Queen's University Press, 1994.

Cook, Ramsay. *Canada and the French-Canadian Question.* Toronto: Macmillan, 1966.

– *Canada, Quebec, and the Uses of Nationalism.* Toronto: McClelland and Stewart, 1986.

– "The Canadian Dilemma: Locke, Rousseau, or Acton?" In R. Cook, *Canada and the French-Canadian Question.* Toronto: Macmillan, 1966.

– *The Craft of History.* Toronto: Canadian Broadcasting Corporation, 1973.

– "'I never thought I could be as proud ...': The Trudeau-Lévesque Debate." In *Towards a Just Society.* Ed. Thomas Axworthy and Pierre Trudeau. Markham, Ontario: Viking, 1990.

– *The Maple Leaf Forever.* Toronto: Macmillan, 1971.

– *Provincial Autonomy, Minority Rights, and the Compact Theory, 1867–1921.* Ottawa: Information Canada, 1969.

Cooper, John. "The Political Ideas of George Etienne Cartier." *Canadian Historical Review* 23 (1942): 286–94.

Corry, J.A. "The Uses of a Constitution." In *The Constitution and the Future of Canada.* Toronto: Richard De Boo, 1978.

Coyne, Deborah. "The Meech Lake Accord and the Spending Power Proposals: Fundamentally Flawed." In *The Meech Lake Primer.* Ed. Michael Behiels. Ottawa: University of Ottawa Press, 1989.

Craig, G., ed. *Lord Durham's Report.* Toronto: McClelland and Stewart, 1963.

Creighton, Donald. *Canada's First Century.* Toronto: Macmillan, 1970.

– *The Road to Confederation.* Toronto: Macmillan, 1964.

– *Towards the Discovery of Canada.* Toronto: Macmillan, 1972.

Crozier, Michel, et al. *The Crisis of Democracy.* New York: New York University Press, 1975.

Cunningham, Frank. "Democracy and Three-Nation Asymmetry." *Canadian Forum,* December 1992, 18–9.

Danley, John R. "Liberalism, Aboriginal Rights, and Cultural Minorities." *Philosophy and Public Affairs* 20 (1991): 168–85.

DeCelles, Alfred. "Sir Georges Etienne Cartier." In Stephen Leacock et al., *Mackenzie, Baldwin, Lafontaine, Hincks, Papineau, Cartier.* New York: Oxford University Press, 1926.

Del Vecchio, Giorgio. *Justice.* Edinburgh: Edinburgh University Press, 1952.

Diamond, Martin. "What the Framers Meant by Federalism." In *A Nation of States.* Ed. Robert Goldwin. Chicago: Rand McNally, 1974.

Dicey, A.V. *An Introduction to the Study of the Law of the Constitution.* 10th ed. London: Macmillan, 1959.

Dion, Léon. "The Mystery of Quebec." *Daedalus* 117 (1988): 283–317.

– *Quebec, the Unfinished Revolution.* Trans. Thérèse Romer. Montreal: McGill-Queen's University Press, 1976.

Dion, Stéphane. "Le Nationalisme dans la convergence culturelle." In

L'Engagement intellectuel. Ed. Raymond Hudon and Réjean Pelletier. Sainte-Foy: Les Presses de l'Université Laval, 1991.

Dufour, Christian. *A Canadian Challenge.* Halifax: Institute for Research on Public Policy, 1990.

Dworkin, Ronald. "Liberalism." In *Private and Public Morality.* Ed. Stuart Hampshire. Cambridge: Cambridge University Press, 1978.

– *Taking Rights Seriously.* Cambridge: Harvard University Press, 1977.

Dyck, Noel, ed. *Indigenous Peoples and the Nation-State.* St John's: Institute of Social and Economic Research, 1985.

– "'Telling it like it is': Some Dilemmas of Fourth World Ethnography and Advocacy." In *Anthropology, Public Policy and Native Peoples in Canada.* Ed. Noel Dyck and James B. Waldram. Montreal & Kingston: McGill-Queen's University Press, 1993.

Eberts, Mary. "The Use of Litigation under the Canadian Charter of Rights and Freedoms as a Strategy for Achieving Change." In *Minorities and the Canadian State.* Ed. Neil Nevitte and Allan Kornberg. Oakville: Mosaic Press, 1985.

Elkins, David J. "Facing Our Destiny: Rights and Canadian Distinctiveness." *Canadian Journal of Political Science* 22 (1989): 699–716.

– and Simeon, Richard. *Small Worlds* Toronto: Methuen, 1980.

Ely, John Hart. *Democracy and Distrust.* Cambridge: Harvard University Press, 1980.

Emberley, Peter. "Globalism and Localism: Constitutionalism in a New World Order." In *Constitutional Predicament.* Ed. Curtis Cook. Montreal & Kingston: McGill-Queen's University Press, 1994.

Epstein, David. *The Political Theory of the Federalist.* Chicago: University of Chicago Press, 1984.

Erasmus, Georges. "Native Rights." In *Meech Lake and Canada.* Ed. Roger Gibbins. Edmonton: Academic, 1988.

Fanon, Frantz. *Black Skin, White Masks.* Trans. Charles Lam Markmann. New York: Grove, 1968.

– *The Wretched of the Earth.* Trans. Constance Farrington. New York: Grove, 1968.

Favreau, Guy. *The Amendment of the Constitution of Canada.* Ottawa: Queen's Printer, 1965.

Fichte, Johann Gottlieb. *Addresses to the German Nation.* Ed. George Armstrong Kelly. New York: Harper Torchbooks, 1968.

Finnis, John. *Natural Law and Natural Rights.* Oxford: Clarendon Press, 1980.

Flanagan, Thomas. "The Sovereignty and Nationhood of Canadian Indians." *Canadian Journal of Political Science* 28 (1985): 367–74.

Flathman, Richard. *The Practice of Rights.* Cambridge: Cambridge University Press, 1976.

Ford v. Quebec. Dominion Law Reports (4th) 54 (1989): 577.

Friedrich, Carl J. *The Impact of American Constitutionalism Abroad.* Boston: Boston University Press, 1967.

Gagnon, Alain. "Canadian Federalism: A Working Balance." In *Federalism and Nationalism.* Ed. Murray Forsyth. New York: St. Martin's, 1989.

Gallie, W.B. *Philosophy and the Historical Understanding.* New York: Schocken Books, 1968.

Gérin-Lajoie, Paul. *Constitutional Amendment in Canada.* Toronto: University of Toronto Press, 1950.

Gibbins, Roger. *Senate Reform: Moving towards the Slippery Slope.* Kingston: Institute of Intergovernmental Relations, 1983.

– "Speculations on a Canada without Quebec." In *The Charlottetown Accord, the Referendum, and the Future of Canada.* Ed. Kenneth McRoberts and Patrick Monahan. Toronto: University of Toronto Press, 1993.

– and Ponting, J. Rick. "An Assessment of the Probable Impact of Aboriginal Self-Government in Canada." In *The Politics of Gender, Ethnicity and Language in Canada.* Ed. Alan Cairns and Cynthia Williams. Toronto: University of Toronto Press, 1986.

Gibson, Dale. "Reasonable Limits under the Canadian Charter of Rights and Freedoms." *Manitoba Law Journal* 15 (1985): 27–52.

Gilbert, Alan. "Democracy and Individuality." *Social Philosophy and Policy* 3 (1986): 19–58.

Glazer, Nathan. *Ethnic Dilemmas 1964–1982.* Cambridge: Harvard University Press, 1983.

– "Individual Rights against Group Rights." In *Human Rights.* Ed. Eugene Kamenka and Alice Erh-Soon Tay. London: Edward Arnold, 1978.

Gordon, Robert. "Critical Legal Histories." *Stanford Law Review* 36 (1984): 57–125.

Government of Canada. *A National Understanding: The Official Languages of Canada.* Canada: Minister of Supply and Services, 1977.

– *Statement on Indian Policy, 1969.* Ottawa: Queen's Printer, 1969.

Government of Quebec. *Quebec-Canada: A New Deal.* Quebec: Éditeur Officiel, 1979.

Grant, George. *Lament for a Nation.* Toronto: McClelland and Stewart, 1970.

Green, L. "Are Language Rights Fundamental?" *Osgoode Hall Law Review* 25 (1987): 639–69.

Groulx, Lionel. *The Iron Wedge.* Trans. J.S. Wood. Ottawa: Carleton University Press, 1986.

Gutmann, Amy. "Communitarian Critics of Liberalism." *Philosophy and Public Affairs* 14 (1985): 308–22.

Hamilton, Alexander. *The Federalist.* Co-authored with John Jay and James Madison. Ed. B.F. Wright. Cambridge: Harvard University Press, 1961.

Hand, Learned. *The Bill of Rights.* New York: Atheneum, 1977.

Handler, Richard. *Nationalism and the Politics of Culture in Quebec.* Madison: University of Wisconsin Press, 1988.

Hayek, Friedrich A. *Law, Legislation and Liberty.* Vol. 2., *The Mirage of Social Justice.* Chicago: University of Chicago Press, 1976.

Heard, Andrew. *Canadian Constitutional Conventions.* Toronto: Oxford University Press, 1991.

Herzog, Don. *Without Foundations.* Ithaca: Cornell University Press, 1985.

Hobsbawm, E.J. "Fraternity." *New Society* 3 (1975): 471–3.

– *Nations and Nationalism since 1780.* Cambridge: Cambridge University Press, 1990.

Hogg, Peter. "Comments on Legislation and Judicial Decisions." *Canadian Bar Review* 60 (1982): 307–34.

– "Federalism Fights the Charter of Rights." In *Federalism and the Political Community.* Ed. D. Shugarman and R. Whitaker. Peterborough: Broadview Press, 1989.

Holmes, John. "Nationalism in Canadian Foreign Policy." In *Nationalism in Canada.* Ed. Peter Russell. Toronto: McGraw-Hill, 1966.

Horowitz, Gad. "Mosaics and Identity." In *Canadian Political Thought.* Ed. H.D. Forbes. Toronto: Oxford University Press, 1985.

– "Tories, Socialists and the Demise of Canada." In *Canadian Political Thought.* Ed. H.D. Forbes. Toronto: Oxford University Press, 1985.

Hosek, Chaviva. "Women and the Constitutional Process." In *And No One Cheered.* Ed. Keith Banting and Richard Simeon. Toronto: Methuen, 1983.

Hovius, Berend, and Martin, Robert. "The Canadian Charter of Rights and Freedoms in the Supreme Court of Canada." *Canadian Bar Review* 61 (1983): 354–76.

Howard, Rhoda E. "Cultural Absolutism and the Nostalgia for Community." *Human Rights Quarterly* 15 (1993): 315–38.

Huntington, Samuel. "The Founding Fathers and the Division of Powers." In *Area and Power.* Ed. Arthur Maass. Glencoe: The Free Press, 1959.

Ignatieff, Michael. *Blood and Belonging.* Toronto: Penguin, 1993.

Jaffa, Harry V. "'Partly Federal, Partly National': The Political Theory of the Civil War." In *A Nation of States.* Ed. Robert A. Goldwin. Chicago: Rand McNally, 1974.

Jamieson, Kathleen. *Indian Women and the Law in Canada: Citizens Minus.* Ottawa: Minister of Supply and Services, 1978.

Jenson, Jane. "Naming Nations: Making Nationalist Claims in Canadian Public Discourse." *Canadian Review of Sociology and Anthropology* 30 (1993): 337–58.

Johnston, Donald, ed. *Pierre Trudeau Speaks Out on Meech Lake.* Toronto: General Paperbacks, 1990.

Jouvenel, Bertrand de. "Rousseau's Theory of the Forms of Government." In *Hobbes and Rousseau.* Ed. Maurice Cranston and Richard S. Peters. Garden City: Doubleday, 1972.

Joy, Richard J. *Languages in Conflict.* Toronto: McClelland and Stewart, 1972.

Kairys, David, ed. *The Politics of Law.* New York: Pantheon, 1982.

Karmis, Dimitrios. "Interpréter l'identité québécoise." In *Québec: État et société.* Ed. Alain-G. Gagnon. Montréal: Éditions Québec/Amérique, 1994.

Kedourie, Elie. *Nationalism.* London: Hutchinson, 1969.

Kelman, Mark. *A Guide to Critical Legal Studies.* Cambridge: Harvard University Press, 1987.

Kennedy, W.P.M. "Nationalism and Self-Determination." *Canadian Historical Review* 2 (1921): 6–18.

King, Preston. "Against Federalism." In *Knowledge and Belief in Politics.* Ed. R. Benewick. London: George Allen, 1973.

Knopff, Rainer. "Democracy vs. Liberal Democracy: The Nationalist Conundrum." *Dalhousie Review* 58 (1978–79): 638–46.

– "Legal Theory and the 'Patriation' Debate." *Queen's Law Journal* 7 (1981): 41–67.

– "Liberal Democracy and the Challenge of Nationalism in Canadian Politics." *Canadian Review of Studies in Nationalism* 9/10 (1982–83): 23–42.

– and Morton, F.L. *Charter Politics.* Scarborough: Nelson, 1992.

– "Nation-Building and the Canadian Charter of Rights and Freedoms." In *Constitutionalism, Citizenship and Society in Canada.* Ed. Alan Cairns and Cynthia Williams. Toronto: University of Toronto Press, 1985.

Kocis, Robert. "An Unresolved Tension in Marx's Critique of Justice and Rights." *Political Studies* 34 (1986): 406–22.

Kohn, Hans. *American Nationalism.* New York: Macmillan, 1957.

– *Nationalism and Liberty: The Swiss Example.* London: George Allen and Unwin, 1956.

Kramnick, Isaac. "The 'Great National Discussion': The Discourse of Politics in 1787." *William and Mary Quarterly* 45 (1988): 3–32.

Kwavnick, David, ed. *The Tremblay Report.* Toronto: McClelland and Stewart, 1973.

Kymlicka, Will. *Liberalism, Community, and Culture.* Oxford: Clarendon Press, 1989.

– "Liberalism, Individualism, and Minority Rights." In *Law and the Community.* Ed. Allan Hutchinson and Leslie Green. Toronto: Carswell, 1989.

Laforest, Guy. "Herder, Kedourie et les errements de l' antinationalisme au
   Canada." In *L'Engagement intellectuel*. Ed. Raymond Hudon and Réjean Pelle-
   tier. Sainte-Foy: Les Presses de l'Université Laval, 1991.
– *Trudeau and the End of a Canadian Dream*. Trans. P. Leduc Browne and M.
   Weinroth. Montreal & Kingston: McGill-Queen's University Press, 1995.
Lalande, Gilles. *In Defence of Federalism*. Toronto: McClelland and Stewart, 1978.
Laponce, J.A. *Languages and Their Territories*. Toronto: University of Toronto
   Press, 1987.
LaSelva, Samuel. "Only in Canada: Reflections on the Charter's Notwith-
   standing Clause." *Dalhousie Review* 63 (1983–84): 383–98.
Laski, Harold. "The Obsolescence of Federalism." *The New Republic* 98 (1939):
   367–9.
Laurin, Camille. *Quebec's Policy on the French Language*. Québec: Ministre de
   Communications, 1977.
Lederman, W.R. *Continuing Canadian Constitutional Dilemmas*. Toronto: Butter-
   worths, 1981.
Lenihan, Donald G., Robertson, Gordon, and Tassé, Roger. *Canada: Reclaiming
   the Middle Ground*. Montreal: Institute for Research on Public Policy, 1994.
Lévesque, René. "National State of the French Canadians." In *Quebec States
   Her Case*. Ed. F. Scott and M. Oliver. Toronto: Macmillan, 1964.
– *An Option for Quebec*. Toronto: McClelland and Stewart, 1968.
Lijphart, Arend. "Consociational Democracy." In *Consociational Democracy*. Ed.
   Kenneth McRae. Toronto: McClelland and Stewart, 1974.
– "Cultural Diversity and Theories of Political Integration." *Canadian Journal
   of Political Science* 4 (1971): 1–14.
Livingston, William. *Federalism and Constitutional Change*. Oxford: Clarendon
   Press, 1956.
Locke, John. *The Second Treatise of Government*. Ed. Thomas P. Peardon. Indian-
   apolis: Bobbs-Merrill, 1952.
Lovejoy, A. *The Great Chain of Being*. Cambridge: Harvard University Press, 1964.
Lower, A.R.M. *Evolving Canadian Federalism*. Durham: Duke University Press,
   1958.
– "Two Ways of Life: The Primary Antithesis of Canadian History." In *Ap-
   proaches to Canadian History*. Ed. Carl Berger. Toronto: University of Toronto
   Press, 1967.
Lucas, J.R. *Democracy and Participation*. Harmondsworth: Penguin, 1976.
– *On Justice*. Oxford: Clarendon Press, 1980.
Lyon, Noel. "The Central Fallacy of Canadian Constitutional Law." *McGill
   Law Journal* 22 (1976): 40–61.
– "Constitutional Theory and the Martland-Ritchie Dissent." In *The Court and*

the Constitution. Ed. Peter Russell. Kingston: Institute of Intergovernmental Relations, 1982.

McCall, Christina, et al. "Three Nations." *Canadian Forum,* March 1992, 4–6.

McConnell, W.H. *Commentary on the British North America Act.* Toronto: Macmillan, 1977.

McCulloch, Caroline. "The Problem of Fellowship in Communitarian Theory." *Political Studies* 32 (1984): 437–50.

MacIntyre, Alasdair. "Is Patriotism a Virtue?" In *Social and Political Philosophy.* Ed. John Arthur and William H. Shaw. Englewood Cliff, N.J.: Prentice Hall, 1992.

McNeil, Kent. "Aboriginal Nations and Quebec's Boundaries." In *Negotiating with a Sovereign Quebec.* Ed. Daniel Drache and Roberto Perin. Toronto: Lorimer, 1992.

McNeill, W.H. *Polyethnicity and National Unity in World History.* Toronto: University of Toronto Press, 1986.

Macpherson, C.B. *Democratic Theory.* Oxford: Clarendon Press, 1973.

– *The Real World of Democracy.* Toronto: CBC Publications, 1965.

McRae, Kenneth. *Conflict and Compromise in Multilingual Societies.* Vol. 1, *Switzerland.* Waterloo: Wilfrid Laurier University Press, 1983.

– *Consociational Democracy.* Toronto: McClelland and Stewart, 1974.

– "The Meech Lake Impasse in Theoretical Perspective." In *Democracy With Justice.* Ed. Alain Gagnon and Brian Tanguay. Ottawa: Carleton University Press, 1992.

– "The Plural Society and the Western Political Tradition." *Canadian Journal of Political Science* 12 (1979): 673–88.

– "The Principle of Territoriality and the Principle of Personality in Multilingual States." *Linguistics* 154–160 (August 1975): 33–54.

– *Switzerland: Example of Cultural Coexistence.* Toronto: Canadian Institute of International Affairs, 1964.

McRoberts, Kenneth. "Disagreeing on Fundamentals: English Canada and Quebec." In *The Charlottetown Accord, the Referendum, and the Future of Canada.* Ed. Kenneth McRoberts and Patrick J. Monahan. Toronto: University of Toronto Press, 1993.

– *English Canada and Quebec: Avoiding the Issue.* North York: Robarts Centre for Canadian Studies at York University, 1991.

– "Making Canada Bilingual: Illusions and Delusions of Federal Language Policy." In *Federalism and Political Community.* Ed. D. Shugarman and R. Whitaker. Peterborough: Broadview Press, 1989.

– "Protecting the Rights of Linguistic Minorities." In *Negotiating with a Sovereign Quebec.* Ed. Daniel Drache and Roberto Perin. Toronto: James Lorimer, 1992.

Mallory, J.R. "The Continuing Evolution of Canadian Constitutionalism." In *Constitutionalism, Citizenship, and Society in Canada*. Ed. Alan Cairns and Cynthia Williams. Toronto: University of Toronto Press, 1985.

– "The Five Faces of Federalism." In *Canadian Federalism: Myth or Reality*. Ed. J. Peter Meekison. Toronto: Methuen, 1971.

Mandel, Michael. *The Charter of Rights and the Legalization of Politics in Canada*. Toronto: Wall and Thompson, 1989.

Manfredi, Christopher P. *Judicial Power and the Charter*. Toronto: McClelland and Stewart, 1993.

Marshall, Geoffrey. *Constitutional Conventions*. Oxford: Clarendon Press, 1986.

– "The United Kingdom Parliament and the British North America Acts." *Alberta Law Review* 19 (1981): 352–68.

Martin, Ged, ed. *The Causes of Canadian Confederation*. Fredericton: Acadiensis Press, 1990.

Mason, Alpheus. *The States Rights Debate*. Englewood Cliffs: Prentice-Hall, 1964.

Massey, Calvin. "The Locus of Sovereignty: Judicial Review, Legislative Supremacy, and Federalism in the Constitutional Traditions of Canada and the United States." *Duke Law Journal* 6 (1990): 1129–310.

Mathie, William. "Political Community and the Canadian Experience." *Canadian Journal of Political Science* 12 (1979): 3–20.

Medcalf, Linda. *Law and Identity*. Beverly Hills: Sage, 1978.

Meinecke, Friedrich. *Cosmopolitanism and the National State*. Princeton: Princeton University Press, 1970.

Mercredi, Ovide, and Turpel, Mary Ellen. *In the Rapids: Navigating the Future of First Nations*. Toronto: Viking, 1993.

Meyers, Marvin, ed. *The Mind of the Founder: Sources of the Political Thought of James Madison*. Indianapolis: Bobbs-Merrill, 1973.

Michelman, Frank I. "Justification (and Justifiability) of Law in a Contradictory World." In *Justification*. Ed. J.R. Pennock and J.W. Chapman. New York: New York University Press, 1986.

Mill, John Stuart. "Coleridge." In J.S. Mill, *Essays on Politics and Culture*. Ed. Gertrude Himmelfarb. New York: Anchor Books, 1963.

– *Essays on Politics and Culture*. Ed. Gertrude Himmelfarb. New York: Anchor Books, 1963.

– *The Subjection of Women*. Ed. Wendell Robert Carr. Cambridge: M.I.T. Press, 1970.

– *Utilitarianism, Liberty, Representative Government*. Ed. A.D. Lindsay. London: Dent, 1962.

Milne, David. "Equality or Asymmetry: Why Choose?" In *Options for a New Canada*. Ed. R. Watts and D. Brown. Toronto: University of Toronto Press, 1991.

– *The New Canadian Constitution.* Toronto: James Lorimer, 1982.

– *Tug of War.* Toronto: James Lorimer, 1986.

Minogue, K.R. "Theatricality and Politics: Machiavelli's Concept of Fantasia." In *The Morality of Politics.* Ed. B. Parekh and R.N. Berki. London: George Allen & Unwin, 1972.

Monahan, Patrick. "The Charter Then and Now." In *Protecting Rights and Freedoms.* Ed. Philip Bryden et al. Toronto: University of Toronto Press, 1994.

– *Politics and the Constitution.* Toronto: Methuen, 1987.

Montefiore, Alan, ed. *Neutrality and Impartiality.* Cambridge: Cambridge University Press, 1975.

Morin, Claude. *Quebec versus Ottawa.* Trans. Richard Howard. Toronto: University of Toronto Press, 1976.

Morris, Richard, ed. *Alexander Hamilton and the Founding of the Nation.* New York: Harper and Row, 1957.

Morton, W.L. "Canada: The One and the Many." In *Contexts of Canada's Past.* Ed. A.B. McKillop. Toronto: Macmillan, 1980.

– *The Canadian Identity.* Toronto: University of Toronto Press, 1972.

– "Clio in Canada: The Interpretation of Canadian History." In *Approaches to Canadian History.* Ed. Carl Berger. Toronto: University of Toronto Press, 1967.

– "Confederation, 1870–1896." In *Contexts of Canada's Past.* Ed. A.B. McKillop. Toronto: Macmillan, 1980.

Munro, William B. *American Influences on Canadian Government.* Toronto: Macmillan, 1929.

Native Women's Association. *Native Women and Self-Government.* Ottawa: Native Women's Association of Canada, 1992.

Neumann, Franz L. "Federalism and Freedom: A Critique." In *Federalism Mature and Emergent.* Ed. Arthur W. Macmahon. New York: Russell & Russell, 1962.

Noel, S.J.R. "Consociational Democracy and Canadian Federalism." In *Consociational Democracy.* Ed. Kenneth McRae. Toronto: McClelland and Stewart, 1974.

Norman, Wayne J. "Towards a Philosophy of Federalism." In *Group Rights.* Ed. Judith Baker. Toronto: University of Toronto Press, 1994.

Oliver, Michael. "Laurendau et Trudeau: leurs opinions sur le Canada." In *L'Engagement intellectuel.* Ed. Raymond Hudon and Réjean Pelletier. Sainte-Foy: Les Presses de l' Université Laval, 1991.

– *The Passionate Debate.* Montreal: Vehicule Press, 1991.

Ormsby, William. *The Emergence of the Federal Concept in Canada, 1839–1845.* Toronto: University of Toronto Press, 1969.

Pangle, Thomas. *The Spirit of Modern Republicanism.* Chicago: University of Chicago Press, 1988.

Parliamentary Debates on the Subject of the Confederation of the British North American Provinces. Quebec: Hunter, Rose, 1865.

Pigeon, L.-P. "The Meaning of Provincial Autonomy." In *The Courts and the Canadian Constitution.* Ed. W.R. Lederman. Toronto: McClelland and Stewart, 1964.

Plamenatz, John. *On Alien Rule and Self-Government.* London: Longmans, 1960.

Plato. *Euthypro, Apology, Crito.* Trans. F.J. Church. Indianapolis: Bobbs-Merrill, 1956.

– *The Republic.* Trans. Francis Macdonald Cornford. New York: Oxford University Press, 1968.

Pocklington, Thomas C. "Against Inflating Human Rights." *Windsor Yearbook of Access to Justice* 2 (1982): 77–86.

Pocock, J.G.A. *The Machiavellian Moment.* Princeton: Princeton University Press, 1975.

Popper, K.R. *The Open Society and Its Enemies.* 2 vols. London: Routledge, 1969.

Porter, John. *The Vertical Mosaic.* Toronto: University of Toronto Press, 1965.

Preliminary Report of the Royal Commission on Bilingualism and Biculturalism. Ottawa: Queen's Printer, 1965.

Ranney, John C. "The Bases of American Federalism." *William and Mary Quarterly* 3 (1946): 1–35.

Rawls, John. "The Idea of an Overlapping Consensus." *Oxford Journal of Legal Studies* 7 (1987): 1–25.

– *A Theory of Justice.* Cambridge: Harvard University Press, 1971.

Reference re Amendment of the Constitution of Canada. Dominion Law Reports (3d) 125 (1982): 1.

Reference re Attorney-General of Quebec and Attorney-General of Canada. Dominion Law Report (3d) 140 (1983): 385.

Reference re Authority of Parliament in Relation to the Upper House. Supreme Court Reports 1 (1980): 54.

Regina v. Oakes. Dominion Law Reports (4th) 26 (1986): 200.

Regina v. Sparrow. Dominion Law Reports (4th) 70 (1990): 385.

Rémillard, Gil. "Legality, Legitimacy and the Supreme Court." In *And No One Cheered.* Ed. Keith Banting and Richard Simeon. Toronto: Methuen, 1983.

– "Quebec's Quest for Survival and Equality via the Meech Lake Accord." In *The Meech Lake Primer.* Ed. Michael D. Behiels. Ottawa: University of Ottawa Press, 1989.

Renan, Ernest. "What Is a Nation?" In *Modern Political Doctrines.* Ed. Alfred Zimmerman. London: Oxford University Press, 1939.

Report of the Royal Commission of Inquiry on Constitutional Problems. Vol. 2. Quebec City: Queen's Printer, 1956.

Report of the Royal Commission on the Economic Union and Development Prospects for Canada. Vol. 3. Ottawa: Minister of Supply and Services, 1985.

Resnick, Philip. *The Masks of Proteus.* Montreal & Kingston: McGill-Queen's University Press, 1990.

– *Toward a Canada-Quebec Union.* Montreal & Kingston: McGill-Queen's University Press, 1991.

Riker, William H. *Federalism.* Boston: Little, Brown, 1964.

– "Six Books in Search of a Subject or Does Federalism Exist and Does It Matter?" *Comparative Politics* 2 (1969–70): 135–46.

Rioux, Marcel. *Quebec in Question.* Trans. James Boake. Toronto: James Lewis & Samuel, 1971.

Robertson, Gordon. *A House Divided: Meech Lake, Senate Reform and the Canadian Union.* Halifax: Institute for Research on Public Policy, 1989.

Rogers, Norman McL. "The Genesis of Provincial Rights," *Canadian Historical Review* 14 (1933): 9–23.

Rostow, Eugene V. "The Democratic Character of Judicial Review." In *Judicial Review and the Supreme Court.* Ed. Leonard W. Levy. New York: Harper and Row, 1967.

Rousseau, Jean-Jacques. *The Government of Poland.* Trans. Willmore Kendall. Indianapolis: Bobbs-Merrill, 1972.

– *The Social Contract and Discourses.* Trans. G.D.H. Cole. London, Dent, 1968.

Russell, Peter. "Can Canadians Be a Sovereign People?" *Canadian Journal of Political Science* 24 (1991): 691–709.

– *Constitutional Odyssey.* Toronto: University of Toronto Press, 1992.

– *The Court and the Constitution.* Kingston: Institute of Intergovernmental Relations, 1982.

– "The Effects of a Charter of Rights on the Policy-Making Role of Canadian Courts." *Canadian Public Administration* 25 (1982): 1–33.

– "The End of Mega Constitutional Politics in Canada?" In *The Charlottetown Accord, the Referendum, and the Future of Canada.* Ed. Kenneth McRoberts and Patrick J. Monahan. Toronto: University of Toronto Press, 1993.

– "The Political Purposes of the Canadian Charter of Rights and Freedoms." *Canadian Bar Review* 61 (1983): 30–54.

– "The Political Purposes of the Charter: Have They Been Fulfilled?" In *Protecting Rights and Freedoms.* Ed. Philip Bryden et al. Toronto: University of Toronto Press, 1994.

Ryder, Bruce. "The Demise and Rise of the Classical Paradigm in Canadian Federalism: Promoting Autonomy for Provinces and First Nations." *McGill Law Journal* 36 (1991): 308–81.

Ryle, Gilbert. *Dilemmas*. Cambridge: Cambridge University Press, 1960.

Sabine, George H. "The Two Democratic Traditions." *Philosophical Review* 61 (1952): 451–74.

Sandel, Michael J. *Liberalism and the Limits of Justice*. Cambridge: Cambridge University Press, 1982.

– "The Procedural Republic and the Unencumbered Self." *Political Theory* 12 (1984): 81–96.

Sartre, Jean-Paul. *Anti-Semite and Jew*. Trans. George J. Becker. New York: Schocken, 1965.

Scheingold, Stuart A. *The Politics of Rights*. New Haven: Yale University Press, 1974.

Schlesinger, Arthur M., Jr. *The Disuniting of America*. New York: W.W. Norton, 1992.

Schwartz, Bryan. *First Principles, Second Thoughts: Aboriginal Peoples, Constitutional Reform and Canadian Statecraft*. Montreal: Institute for Research on Public Policy, 1986.

Scott, Colin H. "Custom, Tradition, and the Politics of Culture: Aboriginal Self-Government in Canada." In *Anthropology, Public Policy and Native Peoples in Canada*. Ed. Noel Dyck and James B. Waldron. Montreal & Kingston: McGill-Queen's University Press, 1993.

Scott, F.R. *The Canadian Constitution and Human Rights*. Toronto: Canadian Broadcasting Corporation, 1959.

– *Civil Liberties and Canadian Federalism*. Toronto: University of Toronto Press, 1959.

– *Essays on the Constitution*. Toronto: University of Toronto Press, 1977.

– "French-Canada and Canadian Federalism." In *Evolving Canadian Federalism*. Ed. A.R.M. Lower. Durham: Duke University Press, 1958.

– "The Privy Council and Minority Rights." *Queen's Quarterly* 37 (1930): 669–78.

– "Section 94 of the British North America Act." In F.R. Scott, *Essays on the Constitution*. Toronto: University of Toronto Press, 1977.

– "The Special Nature of Canadian Federalism." In F.R. Scott, *Essays on the Constitution*. Toronto: University of Toronto Press, 1977.

Shklar, Judith. *Legalism*. Cambridge: Harvard University Press, 1964.

Siegfried, André. *The Race Question in Canada*. Ed. Frank H. Underhill. Toronto: McClelland and Stewart, 1966.

– *Switzerland: A Democratic Way of Life*. Trans. Edward Fitzgerald. London: Jonathan Cape, 1950.

Sigurdson, Richard. "Left- and Right-Wing Charterphobia in Canada: A Critique of the Critics." *International Journal of Canadian Studies* 7–8 (1993): 95–115.

Silver, A.I. *The French-Canadian Idea of Confederation, 1864–1900.* Toronto: University of Toronto Press, 1982.

Simeon, Richard. "Aboriginal Self-Government and Canadian Political Values." In *Aboriginal Peoples and Constitutional Reform.* Ed. David C. Hawkes and Evelyn J. Peters. Kingston: Institute of Intergovernmental Relations, 1987.

– *Federal-Provincial Diplomacy.* Toronto: University of Toronto Press, 1972.

– "Meech Lake and the Visions of Canada." In *Competing Constitutional Visions.* Ed. K.E. Swinton and C.J. Rogerson. Toronto: Carswell, 1988.

Skinner, Quentin. *Machiavelli.* Oxford: Oxford University Press, 1981.

Slattery, Brian. "First Nations and the Constitution: A Question of Trust." *Canadian Bar Review* 71 (1992): 261–93.

Smart, Carol. *Feminism and the Power of Law.* London: Routledge, 1989.

Smiley, Donald V. *The Association Dimension of Sovereignty-Association: A Response to the Quebec White Paper.* Kingston: Institute of Intergovernmental Affairs, 1980.

– *The Canadian Political Nationality.* Toronto: Methuen, 1967.

– "The Case against the Canadian Charter of Human Rights." *Canadian Journal of Political Science* 2 (1969): 277–91.

– *Constitutional Adaptation and Canadian Federalism since 1945.* Ottawa: Information Canada, 1970.

– "A Dangerous Deed: The Constitution Act, 1982." In *And No One Cheered.* Ed. Keith Banting and Richard Simeon. Toronto: Methuen, 1983.

– *The Federal Condition in Canada.* Toronto: McGraw-Hill Ryerson, 1987.

– "Reflections on Cultural Nationhood and Political Community in Canada." In *Entering the Eighties: Canada in Crisis.* Ed. K. Carty and P. Ward. Toronto: Oxford University Press, 1980.

– "The Rowell-Sirois Report, Provincial Autonomy and Post-War Canadian Federalism." In *Canadian Federalism: Myth or Reality.* Ed. J. Peter Meekison. Toronto: Methuen, 1971.

– "The Structural Problem of Canadian Federalism." *Canadian Public Administration* 14 (1971): 326–43.

Smith, Anthony. "The Myth of the 'Modern Nation' and the Myths of Nations." *Ethnic and Racial Studies* 11 (1988): 1–26.

– *National Identity.* Harmondsworth: Penguin Books, 1991.

Smith, Jennifer. "Canadian Confederation and the Influence of American Federalism." *Canadian Journal of Political Science* 21 (1988): 443–63.

– "Intrastate Federalism and Confederation." In *Political Thought in Canada.* Ed. Stephen Brooks. Toronto: Irwin, 1984.

– "Origins of the Canadian Amendment Dilemma." *Dalhousie Review* 61 (1981–82): 291–306.

Smith, Lynn. "The Distinct Society Clause in the Meech Lake Accord: Could

It Affect Equality Rights for Women?" In *Competing Constitutional Visions.* Ed. Katherine E. Swinton and Carol J. Rogerson. Toronto: Carswell, 1988.

Smith, Peter J. "The Ideological Origins of Canadian Confederation." *Canadian Journal of Political Science* 20 (1987): 3–29.

Sparrow v. Regina. Western Weekly Reports 2 (1987): 577.

Steinberg, Jonathan. *Why Switzerland?* Cambridge: Cambridge University Press, 1976.

Stephen, James Fitzjames. *Liberty, Equality, Fraternity.* Ed. R.J. White. Cambridge: Cambridge University Press, 1967.

Stevenson, Garth. *Ex Uno Plures.* Montreal & Kingston: McGill-Queen's University Press, 1993.

Stillman, Peter G. "Hegel's Critique of Liberal Theories of Rights." *American Political Science Review* 68 (1974): 1086–92.

Storing, Herbert J. *The Complete Anti-Federalist.* Vol. 1. Chicago: University of Chicago Press, 1981.

Svensson, Frances. "Liberal Democracy and Group Rights: The Legacy of Individualism and Its Impact on American Indian Tribes." *Political Studies* 27 (1979): 421–39.

Sweeny, Alastair. *George-Etienne Cartier.* Toronto: McClelland and Stewart, 1976.

Swinton, Katherine E., and Rogerson, Carol J., ed. *Competing Constitutional Visions.* Toronto: Carswell, 1988.

Tamir, Yael. *Liberal Nationalism.* Princeton: Princeton University Press, 1993.

– "Whose History? What Ideas?" In *Isaiah Berlin: A Celebration.* Ed. Edna and Avishai Margalit. London: Hogarth Press, 1991.

Tarlton, Charles D. "Symmetry and Asymmetry as Elements of Federalism." *Journal of Politics* 27 (1965): 861–74.

Tarn, W.W. "Alexander the Great and the Unity of Mankind." *Proceedings of the British Academy* 19 (1933): 123–63.

Tassé, Joseph, ed. *Discours de Sir Georges Cartier.* Montréal: Eusèbe Senécal, 1893.

Taylor, Charles. "Alternative Futures: Legitimacy, Identity and Alienation in Late Twentieth Century Canada." In *Constitutionalism, Citizenship and Society in Canada.* Ed. Alan Cairns and Cynthia Williams. Toronto: University of Toronto Press, 1985.

– "Atomism." In *Powers, Possessions and Freedoms.* Ed. Alkis Kontos. Toronto: University of Toronto Press, 1979.

– "Cross-Purposes: The Liberal-Communitarian Debate." In *Liberalism and the Moral Life.* Ed. Nancy L. Rosenblum. Cambridge: Harvard University Press, 1989.

– "The Diversity of Goods." In *Utilitarianism and Beyond.* Ed. Amartya Sen and Bernard Williams. Cambridge: Cambridge University Press, 1982.

– *The Malaise of Modernity.* Concord: Anansi, 1991.
– *Multiculturalism and "The Politics of Recognition."* Princeton: Princeton University Press, 1992.
– *The Pattern of Politics.* Toronto: McClelland and Stewart, 1970.
– *Reconciling the Solitudes.* Montreal & Kingston: McGill-Queen's University Press, 1993.
– "Shared and Divergent Values." In *Options for a New Canada.* Ed. R. Watts and D. Brown. Toronto: University of Toronto Press, 1991.
– "Why Do Nations Have to Become States?" In *Philosophers Look at Confederation.* Ed. S. French. Montreal: Canadian Philosophical Association, 1979.
Tennant, Paul. *Aboriginal Peoples and Politics.* Vancouver: University of British Columbia Press, 1990.
Tocqueville, Alexis de. *Democracy in America.* Trans. Phillips Bradley. 2 vols. New York: Vintage Books, 1945.
– *The Old Regime and the French Revolution.* Trans. Stuart Gilbert. Garden City: Anchor Books, 1955.
Trudeau, Pierre Elliott. *Approaches to Politics.* Toronto: Oxford University Press, 1970.
– *A Canadian Charter of Human Rights.* Ottawa: Queen's Printer, 1968.
– "Constituent Power, Sovereignty and the Constitution." In *Federalism in Peril.* Ed. A.R. Riggs and Tom Velk. Vancouver: Fraser Institute, 1992.
– *Conversation with Canadians.* Toronto: University of Toronto Press, 1972.
– "Convocation Speech at the Opening of the Bora Laskin Law Library." *University of Toronto Law Journal* 41 (1991): 295–306.
– "Les Droits de l'homme et la suprématie parlementaire," In *Human Rights, Federalism and Minorities.* Ed. Allan Gotlieb. Toronto: Canadian Institute of International Affairs, 1970.
– *Federalism and the French Canadians.* Toronto: Macmillan, 1968.
– "Federalism, Nationalism, and Reason." In P.E. Trudeau, *Federalism and the French Canadians.* Toronto: Macmillan, 1968.
– *Memoirs.* Toronto: McClelland and Stewart, 1993.
– *A Mess That Deserves a Big No.* Toronto: Robert Davies Publishing, 1992.
– "Nationalist Alienation." In *Canadian Political Thought.* Ed. H.D. Forbes. Toronto: Oxford University Press, 1985.
– "Some Obstacles to Democracy in Quebec." In P.E. Trudeau, *Federalism and the French Canadians.* Toronto: Macmillan, 1968.
– "Statement on Multiculturalism." In *Canadian Political Thought.* Ed. H.D. Forbes. Toronto: Oxford University Press, 1985.
– *A Time for Action: Toward the Renewal of the Canadian Federation.* Canada: Minister of Supply and Services, 1978.

- "The Values of a Just Society." In *Towards a Just Society*. Ed. Thomas S. Axworthy and Pierre Elliott Trudeau. Markham: Viking, 1990.

Tully, James. "The Crisis of Identification: The Case of Canada." *Political Studies* (Special Issue) 42 (1994): 77–96.

- "Diversity's Gambit Declined." In *Constitutional Predicament*. Ed. Curtis Cook. Montreal & Kingston: McGill-Queen's University Press, 1994.

- "Multirow Federalism and the Charter." In *Protecting Rights and Freedoms*. Ed. Philip Bryden et al. Toronto: University of Toronto Press, 1994.

Turpel, Mary Ellen. "Aboriginal Peoples and the Canadian *Charter*: Interpretive Monopolies, Cultural Differences." *Canadian Human Rights Yearbook* 6 (1989–90): 3–45.

Underhill, Frank. *The Image of Confederation*. Toronto: Canadian Broadcasting Corporation, 1964.

- *In Search of Canadian Liberalism*. Toronto: Macmillan, 1960.

- "Some Reflections on the Liberal Tradition in Canada." In *Approaches to Canadian History*. Ed. Carl Berger. Toronto: University of Toronto Press, 1967.

Unger, Roberto. *The Critical Legal Studies Movement*. Cambridge: Harvard University Press, 1986.

Upton, L.F.S. "The Idea of Confederation: 1754–1858." In *The Shield of Achilles*. Ed. W.L. Morton. Toronto: McClelland and Stewart, 1968.

Van Dyke, Vernon. "Collective Entities and Moral Rights: Problems in Liberal-Democratic Thought." *Journal of Politics* 44 (1982): 21–40.

Vernon, Richard. "The Federal Citizen." In *Perspectives on Canadian Federalism*. Ed. R. Olling and M. Westmacott. Scarborough: Prentice-Hall, 1988.

- "Freedom and Corruption: Proudhon's Federal Principle." *Canadian Journal of Political Science* 14 (1981): 775–95.

Vipond, Robert. *Liberty and Community: Canadian Federalism and the Failure of the Constitution*. Albany: State University of New York Press, 1991.

- "Whatever Became of the Compact Theory? Meech Lake and the New Politics of Constitutional Amendment in Canada." *Queen's Quarterly* 96 (1989): 793–811.

Waite, Peter. *Confederation, 1854–1867*. Toronto: Holt, Rinehart, and Winston, 1972.

- *The Confederation Debates in the Province of Canada/1865*. Toronto: McClelland and Stewart, 1969.

- *The Life and Times of Confederation*. Toronto: University of Toronto Press, 1962.

Waldron, Jeremy. "Theoretical Foundations of Liberalism." *Philosophical Quarterly* 37 (1987): 127–50.

Walsh, W.H. "Open and Closed Morality." In *The Morality of Politics*. Ed. B. Parekh and R.N. Berki. London: George Allen, 1972.

Weaver, Sally. "Federal Difficulties with Aboriginal Rights." In *The Quest for Justice*. Ed. Menno Boldt and J. Anthony Long. Toronto: University of Toronto Press, 1985.

– *Making Canadian Indian Policy*. Toronto: University of Toronto Press, 1981.

Webber, Jeremy. *Reimagining Canada*. Kingston & Montreal: McGill-Queen's University Press, 1994.

Wechsler, Herbert. "The Political Safeguards of Federalism." In *Federalism Mature and Emergent*. Ed. Arthur Macmahon. New York: Russell & Russell, 1962.

Wheare, K.C. *The Constitutional Structure of the Commonwealth*. Oxford: Clarendon Press, 1960.

– *Federal Government*. 4th ed. London: Oxford University Press, 1967.

– "Federalism and the Making of Nations." In *Federalism Mature and Emergent*. Ed. Arthur Macmahon. New York: Russell & Russell, 1962.

Whitaker, Reginald. "Democracy and the Canadian Constitution." In *And No One Cheered*. Ed. Keith Banting and Richard Simeon. Toronto: Methuen, 1983.

– *Federalism and Democratic Theory*. Kingston: Institute of Intergovernmental Relations, 1983.

– "Reason, Passion and Interest: Pierre Trudeau's Eternal Liberal Triangle." *Canadian Journal of Political and Social Theory* 4 (1980): 5–31.

– *A Sovereign Idea*. Montreal & Kingston: McGill-Queen's University Press, 1992.

Wilkinson, Charles F. *American Indians, Time, and the Law*. New Haven: Yale University Press, 1987.

Williams, Cynthia. "The Changing Nature of Citizen Rights." In *Constitutionalism, Citizenship and Society in Canada*. Ed. Alan Cairns and Cynthia Williams. Toronto: University of Toronto Press, 1985.

Wittgenstein, Ludwig. *Philosophical Investigations*. Trans. G.E.M. Anscombe. Oxford: Basil Blackwell, 1972.

Woodcock, George. "A Plea for the Anti-Nation." In *Nationalism or Local Control*. Ed. Viv Nelles and Abraham Rotstein. Toronto: New Press, 1973.

Worcester v. Georgia. Peters 6 (1832): 515.

Young, Brian. *George-Etienne Cartier: Montreal Bourgeois*. Montreal: McGill-Queen's University Press, 1981.

Young, Iris. "Polity and Group Difference: A Critique of the Ideal of Universal Citizenship." *Ethics* 99 (1989): 250–74.

Young, Robert A. *The Secession of Quebec and the Future of Canada*. Montreal & Kingston: McGill-Queen's University Press, 1995.

Index

Aboriginal peoples, ix, 94, 95–6, 117, 131, 147; and the Canadian Charter, 7, 94, 95–6, 138–9, 148–50; and the Canadian community, 150, 151–2; and cultural membership, 139–40; a cultural solitude, 142, 153; and equal partnership, 151–2; a founding nation, 140; and history, 141–2, 148; and liberalism, 138–43; and the Meech Lake Constitutional Accord, 143; and the Métis, 151–2; the Native Women's Association, 149–50; and the politics of embarrassment, 150; and poverty, 137; and Quebec, 150; *Regina v. Sparrow*, 141; Statement on Indian Policy, 6, 138, 143, 146, 147; and the Supreme Court of Canada, 140–1; the tragedy of, 4; *Worcester v. Georgia*, 141

Aboriginal self-government, 10–11, 14, 29; and the Canadian Charter, 138, 148–50; and Canadian democracy, 144–7; and Canadian federalism, 142–3, 146, 151–2, 171; and the Canadian political morality, 140, 152; and the Charlottetown accord, 137, 143, 149; and decolonization, 147–51, 152–3; a democratic challenge, 138, 144, 153–4; as a dialogue of democracy, 138, 143–7, 153–4; and the face-to-face society, 144–5, 219n38; and the ideals of democracy, 145–7; and the incommensurability thesis, 138–9, 142, 146–7; a liberal conception of, 139–41; and multiple identities, 146, 152; paradoxical character, 137–8, 150; as a strategy for emancipation, 147–52; and treaty federalism, 147, 151–2

Acton, Lord: and absolutist politics, 28, 46, 166; and Calhoun, 45–6; critique of nationalism, 46, 125, 166–7; liberal assumptions of, 46, 124–5; on the multinational state and federalism, 47, 158–9, 160, 162–3, 167; and Rousseau, 91; Trudeau's use of, 45, 91

American Civil War, 34, 41, 190–1

American federalism: the anti-federalists and, 34–5; Calhoun on,

164–70; and Switzerland, 163–4;
and the United States, 160–3
Canadian mosaic, xiv, 84, 166, 180
Canadian nationhood: and the
Canadian Charter, 7, 66, 70,
81–96; as a community of belonging, 107–18, 164–70, 194–5; and
Confederation, 35–7, 39–42; crisis of, 119, 130, 155–6, 160,
161–3, 165, 169–70, 192–5; and
deconfederation, 5, 117; demise
of, 12–13, 136, 194–5; as a democratic experiment, 119–37, 143–7;
distinctiveness of, 85, 132, 160–4,
186–8; federal foundations of,
xiii, 8–9, 22–7, 37–42, 189–90,
195; fragility of, 38–9, 84, 85,
123, 128–9, 130, 155–6, 160,
190–4; and justice, 7–8; and patriation, 49; pluralism of, 111–12,
164–6, 169–70, 186–8; and Quebec, 107, 157; and solitudes, 11,
142, 153; Three Nations idea,
117, 140
Canadian political nationality, 8, 23,
25–7, 39–42, 92–7, 114–16, 132,
140, 152, 155–60, 164, 167–70,
171–2, 190–4
Canadian unity, 19, 66–70, 81–2,
97–8, 113, 123, 163–4, 186–8
Cardinal, Harold, 4, 146
Cartier, George-Étienne: and Acton,
159; on the American Civil War,
41; and Canadian nationhood, 25,
37–42, 99, 189; conflicting assessments of, 23, 199n32; founder of
Canadian federalist theory, xi–xii,
16, 18, 23–7, 30, 32, 37–42, 47–8,
115, 159–60, 177, 188–90, 194,
195; and fraternity, 23, 25–7, 115;

and Grant, 195; and Jefferson, 38;
and Macdonald, xi, 37, 177; and
Madison, 32, 38, 47–8, 188–9;
and Mill, 169; on minority rights,
44; on monarchy, 42; and the
moral foundations of Canadian
federalism, 11–12, 16, 24, 159–60,
189–90; neglect of, xi, 15, 193–4;
on political nationality, 23, 39–41,
93–4, 115, 155–6, 159–60,
168–70, 189–94; and provincial
autonomy, 37, 177; on racial diversity, 25; vision of Confederation, 6, 23–6, 41, 93, 128
Chaput, Marcel, 106
Charlottetown accord, x, 18, 91,
109, 116, 134–5, 137, 143, 149,
157–8, 184–5, 188, 192–3
Charter sceptics, 64, 70
Christiano, Kevin J., 183
Citizens Insurance Company v. Parsons,
53
civil religion, 161, 183
closed society, 114–16, 145–6
colonialism: and Aboriginal peoples,
147–54; Fanon on racism and,
147–8, 150, 153
common values, 88, 96, 118, 129,
134–5, 150, 151–2, 155–6, 159–60,
168–70
communitarians: criticism of the
Canadian Charter, 70–5, 76; and
Lévesque, 113, 114
community, 126; and Aboriginal
peoples, 150, 151–2; and Canadian federalism, 8–9, 23, 28–9,
39–42, 70–5, 112–18, 156,
168–70, 187–8; Québécois nation
as, 103–7,
compact theory, 43, 90, 102, 151, 173

dialogue, 143, 219n31
Dicey, A.V., 20, 41
Diefenbaker, John, 161
Dion, Léon, 105, 178
dualism: Canadian, 13, 21–2, 43, 90,
   102, 128–31, 140, 173
Dufour, Christian, 135, 157
Dunkin, Christopher, 33, 35, 38–9,
   47–8, 172
Durham, Lord, 6, 116; and Aboriginal peoples, 147; on assimilation,
   12, 133; on French-Canadian culture, 101; liberal assumptions of,
   101, 181; on nationhood and nationality, 101; on the war of races,
   12, 35
Dyck, Noel, 150, 153

Elkins, David J., 23
equality: and Aboriginal peoples,
   131, 138, 151; aspiration of,
   125–8; and asymmetrical federalism, 132–6; and Canadian democracy, 126; and citizenship, 81,
   86–7, 184; and the "colour-blind"
   constitution, 131; as equal opportunity, 138, 180–2; as equal partnership, 151; and liberalism, 126,
   180–2; provincial, 108, 130,
   161–2; and Quebec's specificity,
   130, 181–2; Tocqueville on democracy and, 10, 126
Erasmus, Georges, 140
essentially contested concepts, 125–6
Estey, Justice, 54, 56, 61
expressivism, 155–6, 166, 167–8,
   179–80

Fanon, Frantz: and Aboriginal peoples, 148; on racism and colonial-

ism, 147–8; and Sartre, 153; on
   violence and decolonization,
   147–8, 150
Fathers of Confederation, 137; and
   Canadian nationhood, 99, 100–3,
   114–15; and constitutional
   amendment, 9–10, 49, 53–4, 57,
   63; and democracy, 10, 121, 127;
   as machiavellian figures, 116
federal citizen, 23, 41, 102, 146,
   152, 155–6, 168–9, 187–8
federalism: Actonian, 45–7, 91,
   157–60; asymmetrical, 135, 193,
   195; and citizenship, 23, 41, 102,
   146, 152, 155–6, 168–9, 187–8;
   classical, 173–4; and community,
   25–7, 112–16, 168–70; compact
   theory of, 43, 90, 102, 151, 173;
   and the compound republic, 34,
   121, 174, 188–9; consociational,
   18, 20, 30, 171, 176–7; cooperative, 175, 176–7; and democracy,
   119–20, 128, 131–2, 144–6,
   151–2; federal-provincial diplomacy, 171, 175, 176–7; *fédéralisme
   rentable*, 115; formal, 27; and freedom, 27–8, 34, 174–5; and the
   imagination, 99–100, 114–18; instrumental, 22, 68, 129, 172; intrastate, 70, 123, 193; and justice,
   7–9, 44–5, 68–70, 96–8; justifications of, 27–8, 34, 174–5; majoritarian, 61; and multinationalism,
   45–7, 157–60; and nationalism,
   25–7, 45–7, 114–16, 159, 178–80,
   185–8; obsolescence of, 174;
   open soul and closed soul, 115;
   and patriotism, 27, 131–2; political, 175; and political nationality,
   23, 40–1, 115, 190–1; political